כְּשֶׁרָאוּ אוֹתוֹ הִשְׁתַּחֲווּ לוֹ, אֲבָל הָיוּ כַּמָּה שֶׁהַסָּפֵק קִנֵּן בְּלִבָּם
keshera'u oto hishtachavu lo, aval hayu kammah shehassafek kinnen belibbam
And when they saw him, they worshipped him; but some doubted.

נִגַּשׁ יֵשׁוּעַ לְדַבֵּר אִתָּם וְאָמַר: נִתְּנָה לִי כָּל סַמְכוּת בַּשָּׁמַיִם וּבָאָרֶץ
niggash yeshua ledabber ittam ve'amar: nittnah li kol samchut bashamayim uva'aretz
And Jesus came to them and spake unto them, saying, All authority hath been given unto me in heaven and on earth.

עַל כֵּן לְכוּ וַעֲשׂוּ אֶת כָּל הַגּוֹיִים לְתַלְמִידִים
al ken lechu va'asu et kol haggoyim letalmidim
Go ye therefore, and make disciples of all the nations,

הַטְבִּילוּ אוֹתָם לְשֵׁם הָאָב וְהַבֵּן וְרוּחַ הַקֹּדֶשׁ
hatbilu otam leshem ha'av vehabben veruach hakkodesh
baptizing them into the name of the Father and of the Son and of the Holy Spirit:

וְלַמְּדוּ אוֹתָם לִשְׁמֹר אֶת כָּל מַה שֶּׁצִּוִּיתִי אֶתְכֶם
velammdu otam lishmor et kol mah shetzivviti etchem
teaching them to observe all things whatsoever I commanded you:

הִנֵּה אִתְּכֶם אֲנִי כָּל הַיָּמִים עַד קֵץ הָעוֹלָם
hinneh ittechem ani kol hayamim ad ketz ha'olam
and lo, I am with you always, even unto the end of the world.

וְהִנֵּה הוּא הוֹלֵךְ לִפְנֵיכֶם לַגָּלִיל. שָׁם תִּרְאוּ אוֹתוֹ. הִנֵּה אָמַרְתִּי לָכֵן
vehinneh hu holech lifneichem laggalil. sham tir'u oto. hinneh amarti lachen
and lo, he goeth before you into Galilee; there shall ye see him: lo, I have told you.

הֵן עָזְבוּ מַהֵר אֶת הַקֶּבֶר בְּיִרְאָה וּבְשִׂמְחָה גְדוֹלָה, וְרָצוּ לְהוֹדִיעַ לְתַלְמִידָיו
hen azevu maher et hakkever beyir'ah uvesimchah gedolah, veratzu lehodia letalmidav
And they departed quickly from the tomb with fear and great joy, and ran to bring his disciples word.

פִּתְאוֹם פָּגַשׁ אוֹתָן יֵשׁוּעַ וְאָמַר: שָׁלוֹם לָכֶן. הֵן נִגְּשׁוּ אֵלָיו, אָחֲזוּ בְּרַגְלָיו וְהִשְׁתַּחֲווּ לוֹ
pit'om pagash otan yeshua ve'amar: shalom lachen. hen niggeshu elav, achazu beraglav vehishtachavu lo
And behold, Jesus met them, saying, All hail. And they came and took hold of his feet, and worshipped him.

אָמַר לָהֶן יֵשׁוּעַ: אַל תִּפְחַדְנָה, לֵכְנָה וְהַגֵּדְנָה לְאַחַי שֶׁיֵּלְכוּ לַגָּלִיל וְשָׁם יִרְאוּנִי
amar lahen yeshua: al tifchadnah, lechenah vehaggedenah le'achai sheyelechu laggalil vesham yir'uni
Then saith Jesus unto them, Fear not: go tell my brethren that they depart into Galilee, and there shall they see me.

בְּשָׁעָה שֶׁהָלְכוּ בָּאוּ הָעִירָה כַּמָּה מִן הַשּׁוֹמְרִים
besha'ah shehalechu ba'u ha'irah kammah min hashomerim
Now while they were going, behold, some of the guard came into the city,

וְהוֹדִיעוּ לְרָאשֵׁי הַכֹּהֲנִים אֵת כָּל אֲשֶׁר קָרָה
vehodi'u lerashei hakkohanim et kol asher karah
and told unto the chief priests all the things that were come to pass.

רָאשֵׁי הַכֹּהֲנִים הִתְכַּנְּסוּ עִם הַזְּקֵנִים וּלְאַחַר הִתְיָעֲצוּת נָתְנוּ לַחַיָּלִים סְכוּם כֶּסֶף נִכָּר
rashei hakkohanim hitkannesu im hazzekenim ule'achar hitya'atzut natenu lachayalim sehum kesef nikkar
And when they were assembled with the elders, and had taken counsel, they gave much money unto the soldiers,

בְּאָמְרָם: הַגִּידוּ כָּךְ: בָּאוּ תַּלְמִידָיו בַּלַּיְלָה וְגָנְבוּ אוֹתוֹ כַּאֲשֶׁר יָשַׁנּוּ
be'ameram: haggidu kach: ba'u talmidav ballaylah veganevu oto ka'asher yashannu
saying, Say ye, His disciples came by night, and stole him away while we slept.

וְאִם זֶה יִוָּדַע לַנָּצִיב, אֲנַחְנוּ נְשַׁכְנֵעַ אוֹתוֹ וְנִפְטֹר אֶתְכֶם מִדְּאָגָה
ve'im zeh yivvada lannatziv, anachnu neshachnea oto veniftor etchem midde'agah
And if this come to the governor's ears, we will persuade him, and rid you of care.

הֵם לָקְחוּ אֶת הַכֶּסֶף וְעָשׂוּ כְּמוֹ שֶׁהוֹרוּ לָהֶם
hem lakechu et hakkesef ve'asu kemo shehoru lahem
So they took the money, and did as they were taught:

וְאָמְנָם שֵׁמַע הַדָּבָר הַזֶּה נָפוֹץ בְּקֶרֶב הָעָם עַד הַיּוֹם הַזֶּה
ve'amenam shema haddavar hazzeh nafotz bekerev ha'am ad hayom hazzeh
and this saying was spread abroad among the Jews, and continueth until this day.

בֵּינְתַיִם הָלְכוּ אַחַד־עָשָׂר הַתַּלְמִידִים לַגָּלִיל, אֶל הָהָר אֲשֶׁר אָמַר לָהֶם יֵשׁוּעַ
beinetayim halechu achad-'asar hattalmidim laggalil, el hahar'asher amar lahem yeshua
But the eleven disciples went into Galilee, unto the mountain where Jesus had appointed them.

אָמַר לָהֶם פִּילָטוֹס: הִנֵּה לָכֶם מִשְׁמָר, לְכוּ וְשִׁמְרוּ כְּמוֹ שֶׁאַתֶּם יוֹדְעִים
amar lahem pilatos. Hinneh lachem mishmar, lechu veshimru kemo she'attem yode'im
Pilate said unto them, Ye have a guard: go, make it as sure as ye can.

הֵם הָלְכוּ וְהִבְטִיחוּ אֶת הַקֶּבֶר בְּכָךְ שֶׁשָּׂמוּ חוֹתָם עַל הָאֶבֶן וְהִצִּיבוּ מִשְׁמָר
hem halechu vehivtichu et hakkever bechach shasamu chotam al ha'even vehitzivu mishmar
So they went, and made the sepulchre sure, sealing the stone, the guard being with them.

כח

אַחֲרֵי הַשַּׁבָּת, עִם עֲלוֹת הַשַּׁחַר שֶׁל יוֹם רִאשׁוֹן
acharei hashabbat, im alot hashachar shel yom rishon
Now late on the sabbath day, as it began to dawn toward the first day of the week,

בָּאוּ מִרְיָם הַמַּגְדָּלִית וּמִרְיָם הָאַחֶרֶת לִרְאוֹת אֶת הַקֶּבֶר
ba'u miryam hammagdalit umiryam ha'acheret lir'ot et hakkever
came Mary Magdalene and the other Mary to see the sepulchre.

לְפֶתַע הָיְתָה רְעִידַת אֲדָמָה חֲזָקָה
lefeta hayetah re'idat adamah chazakah
And behold, there was a great earthquake;

כִּי מַלְאַךְ יהוה יָרַד מִן הַשָּׁמַיִם, נִגַּשׁ וְגָלַל אֶת הָאֶבֶן מִן הַפֶּתַח וְיָשַׁב עָלֶיהָ
ki mal'ach hashem yarad min hashamayim, niggash vegalal et ha'even min happetach veyashav aleiha
for an angel of the Lord descended from heaven, and came and rolled away the stone, and sat upon it.

מַרְאֵהוּ הָיָה כְּבָרָק וּלְבוּשׁוֹ לָבָן כַּשֶּׁלֶג
mar'ehu hayah kevarak ulevusho lavan kasheleg
His appearance was as lightning, and his raiment white as snow:

וּמִפַּחְדּוֹ נִבְהֲלוּ הַשּׁוֹמְרִים וְהָיוּ כְּמֵתִים
umippachdo nivhalu hashomerim vehav kemetim
and for fear of him the watchers did quake, and became as dead men.

אָמַר הַמַּלְאָךְ אֶל הַנָּשִׁים: אַל תִּפְחַדְנָה אַתֶּן. אֲנִי יוֹדֵעַ כִּי אֶת יֵשׁוּעַ שֶׁנִּצְלַב אַתֶּן מְחַפְּשׂוֹת
amar hammal'ach el hannashim: al tifchadnah atten. ani yodea ki et yeshua shennitzlav atten mechappsot
And the angel answered and said unto the women, Fear not ye; for I know that ye seek Jesus, who hath been crucified.

הוּא אֵינֶנּוּ כָּאן, שֶׁהֲרֵי קָם לִתְחִיָּה כְּפִי שֶׁאָמַר. בּוֹאנָה וּרְאֶינָה אֶת הַמָּקוֹם שֶׁשָּׁכַב בּוֹ
hu einennu kan, sheharei kam litchiyah kefi she'amar. bonah ure'einah et hammakom sheshachav bo
He is not here; for he is risen, even as he said. Come, see the place where the Lord lay.

לֵכְנָה מַהֵר וְהַגֵּדְנָה לְתַלְמִידָיו: הוּא קָם מִן הַמֵּתִים
lechnah maher vehaggedenah letalmidav: hu kam min hammetim
And go quickly, and tell his disciples, He is risen from the dead;

לְעֵת עֶרֶב
le'et erev
And when even was come,

בָּא אִישׁ עָשִׁיר תּוֹשַׁב רָמָתַיִם, יוֹסֵף שְׁמוֹ, שֶׁגַּם הוּא נַעֲשָׂה לְתַלְמִיד שֶׁל יֵשׁוּעַ
ba ish ashir toshav ramatayim, yosef shemo, sheggam hu na'asah letalmid shel yeshua
there came a rich man from Arimathæa, named Joseph, who also himself was Jesus' disciple:

הוּא בָּא אֶל פִּילָטוֹס וּבִקֵּשׁ אֶת גּוּפַת יֵשׁוּעַ. אָז צִוָּה פִּילָטוֹס לִמְסֹר אוֹתָהּ
hu ba el pilatos uvikkesh et gufat yeshua. Az tzivvah pilatos limsor otah
this man went to Pilate, and asked for the body of Jesus. Then Pilate commanded it to be given up.

יוֹסֵף לָקַח אֶת הַגּוּפָה, עָטַף אוֹתָהּ בְּסָדִין נָקִי
yosef lakach et haggufah, ataf otah besadin naki
And Joseph took the body, and wrapped it in a clean linen cloth,

וְהִנִּיחַ אוֹתָהּ בְּקִבְרוֹ הֶחָדָשׁ שֶׁלּוֹ אֲשֶׁר חָצַב בַּסֶּלַע
vehinniach otah bekivro hechadash shello asher chatzav bassela
and laid it in his own new tomb, which he had hewn out in the rock:

לְאַחַר שֶׁגָּלַל אֶבֶן גְּדוֹלָה עַל פֶּתַח הַקֶּבֶר הָלַךְ לְדַרְכּוֹ
le'achar sheggalal even gedolah al petach hakkever halach ledarko
and he rolled a great stone to the door of the tomb, and departed.

וּמִרְיָם הַמַּגְדָּלִית וּמִרְיָם הָאַחֶרֶת הָיוּ שָׁם, יוֹשְׁבוֹת מוּל הַקֶּבֶר
umiryam hammagdalit umiryam ha'acheret hayu sham, yoshevot mul hakkever
And Mary Magdalene was there, and the other Mary, sitting over against the sepulchre.

לְמָחֳרַת עֶרֶב הַשַׁבָּת
lemochorat erev hashabbat
Now on the morrow, which is the day after the Preparation,

נִקְהֲלוּ רָאשֵׁי הַכֹּהֲנִים וְהַפְּרוּשִׁים אֶל פִּילָטוֹס
nik'halu rashei hakkohanim vehapperushim el pilatos
the chief priests and the Pharisees were gathered together unto Pilate,

אָמְרוּ לוֹ: אֲדוֹנֵנוּ, נִזְכַּרְנוּ כִּי בְּעֵת שֶׁהָיָה חַי אָמַר הַמַּתְעֶה הַהוּא, 'אַחֲרֵי שְׁלוֹשָׁה יָמִים קוֹם אָקוּם
ameru lo: adonenu, nizkarnu ki be'et shehayah chai amar hammat'eh hahu, acharei sheloshah yamim kom akum
saying, Sir, we remember that that deceiver said while he was yet alive, After three days I rise again.

לָכֵן צַוֵּה נָא שֶׁיִּשָּׁמֵר הַקֶּבֶר עַד הַיּוֹם הַשְּׁלִישִׁי, שֶׁמָּא יָבוֹאוּ תַּלְמִידָיו וְיִגְנְבוּ אוֹתוֹ
lachen tzavveh na sheyishamer hakkever ad hayom hashelishi, shemma yavo'u talmidav veyignevu oto
Command therefore that the sepulchre be made sure until the third day, lest haply his disciples come and steal him away,

לְאַחַר מִכֵּן יֹאמְרוּ לָעָם הוּא קָם מִן הַמֵּתִים, וְתִהְיֶה הַתַּרְמִית הָאַחֲרוֹנָה גְּרוּעָה מִן הָרִאשׁוֹנָה
le'achar mikken yomeru la'am hu kam min hammetim, vetihyeh hattarmit ha'acharonah geru'ah min harishonah
and say unto the people, He is risen from the dead: and the last error will be worse than the first.

מִיָּד רָץ אֶחָד מֵהֶם, לָקַח סְפוֹג
miyad ratz echad mehem, lakach sefog
And straightway one of them ran, and took a sponge,

וּמִלֵּא אוֹתוֹ חֹמֶץ, הִצְמִיד אוֹתוֹ אֶל קָנֶה וְהִגִּישׁ לוֹ לִשְׁתּוֹת
umillei oto chometz, hitzmid oto el kaneh vehiggish lo lishtot
and filled it with vinegar, and put it on a reed, and gave him to drink.

אַךְ יֶתֶר הָאֲנָשִׁים אָמְרוּ: הָבָה נִרְאֶה אִם יָבוֹא אֵלִיָּהוּ לְהַצִּיל אוֹתוֹ
ach yeter ha'anashim ameru: havah nir'eh im yavo eliyahu lehatzil oto
And the rest said, Let be; let us see whether Elijah cometh to save him.

יֵשׁוּעַ צָעַק שׁוּב בְּקוֹל גָּדוֹל וְנָפַח אֶת רוּחוֹ
yeshua tza'ak shuv bekol gadol venafach et rucho
And Jesus cried again with a loud voice, and yielded up his spirit.

וְהִנֵּה נִקְרְעָה פָּרֹכֶת הַמִּקְדָּשׁ לִשְׁתַּיִם, מִלְמַעְלָה עַד לְמַטָּה
vehinneh nikre'ah parochet hammikdash lishtayim, milma'lah ad lemattah
And behold, the veil of the temple was rent in two from the top to the bottom;

הָאָרֶץ רָעֲדָה, הַסְּלָעִים נִבְקְעוּ
ha'aretz ra'adah, hassela'im nivke'u
and the earth did quake; and the rocks were rent;

הַקְּבָרִים נִפְתְּחוּ וְגוּפוֹת רַבּוֹת שֶׁל קְדוֹשִׁים יְשֵׁנֵי עָפָר נֵעוֹרוּ
hakkevarim niftechu vegufot rabbot shel kedoshim yeshenei afar ne'oru
and the tombs were opened; and many bodies of the saints that had fallen asleep were raised;

הֵם יָצְאוּ מִן הַקְּבָרִים אַחֲרֵי שֶׁהוּא קָם, נִכְנְסוּ לְעִיר הַקֹּדֶשׁ וְנִרְאוּ לְרַבִּים
hem yatze'u min hakkevarim acharei shehu kam, nichnesu le'ir hakkodesh venir'u lerabbim
and coming forth out of the tombs after his resurrection they entered into the holy city and appeared unto many.

שַׂר הַמֵּאָה וְהָאֲנָשִׁים אֲשֶׁר אִתּוֹ, הַשּׁוֹמְרִים אֶת יֵשׁוּעַ, כִּרְאוֹתָם אֶת רְעִידַת הָאֲדָמָה
sar hamme'ah veha'anashim asher itto, hashomerim et yeshua', kir'otam et re'idat ha'adamah
Now the centurion, and they that were with him watching Jesus, when they saw the earthquake,

וְאֶת כָּל הַנַּעֲשָׂה, נִתְמַלְּאוּ פַּחַד רַב וְאָמְרוּ: בֶּאֱמֶת בֶּן־אֱלֹהִים הָיָה זֶה
ve'et kol hanna'aseh, nitmalle'u pachad rav ve'ameru. Emet ben-'elohim hayah zeh
and the things that were done, feared exceedingly, saying, Truly this was the Son of God.

גַּם נָשִׁים רַבּוֹת שֶׁהָלְכוּ אַחֲרֵי יֵשׁוּעַ מִן הַגָּלִיל וְשֵׁרְתוּ אוֹתוֹ הָיוּ שָׁם וְהִתְבּוֹנְנוּ מֵרָחוֹק
gam nashim rabbot shehalechu acharei yeshua min haggalil vesheretu oto hayu sham vehitbonenu merachok
And many women were there beholding from afar, who had followed Jesus from Galilee, ministering unto him:

בֵּינֵיהֶן הָיוּ מִרְיָם הַמַּגְדָּלִית, מִרְיָם אֵם יַעֲקֹב וְיוֹסֵף, וְאִמָּם שֶׁל בְּנֵי זַבְדַּי
beineihen hayu miryam hammagdalit, miryam em ya'akov veyosef, ve'immam shel benei zavdai
among whom was Mary Magdalene, and Mary the mother of James and Joses, and the mother of the sons of Zebedee.

וְהָעוֹבְרִים שָׁם גִּדְּפוּ אוֹתוֹ, הֵנִיעוּ רֹאשָׁם
veha'overim sham gidfu oto, heni'u rosham
And they that passed by railed on him, wagging their heads,

וְאָמְרוּ: הַהוֹרֵס אֶת בֵּית הַמִּקְדָּשׁ וּבוֹנֶה אוֹתוֹ בִּשְׁלוֹשָׁה יָמִים! הוֹשַׁע אֶת עַצְמְךָ
ve'ameru: hahores et beit hammikdash uvoneh oto bishloshah yamim! hosha et atzmecha
and saying, Thou that destroyest the temple, and buildest it in three days, save thyself:

אִם בֶּן־הָאֱלֹהִים אַתָּה, וְרֵד מִן הַצְּלָב
im ben-ha'elohim attah, vered min hatzelav
if thou art the Son of God, come down from the cross.

כָּךְ גַּם הִתְלוֹצְצוּ רָאשֵׁי הַכֹּהֲנִים עִם הַסּוֹפְרִים וְהַזְּקֵנִים בְּאָמְרָם
kach gam hitlotzetzu rashei hakkohanim im hassoferim vehazzekenim be'omram
In like manner also the chief priests mocking him, with the scribes and elders, said,

אֲחֵרִים הוֹשִׁיעַ; אֶת עַצְמוֹ אֵינֶנּוּ יָכוֹל לְהוֹשִׁיעַ
acherim hoshia'; et atzmo einennu yachol lehoshia'
He saved others; himself he cannot save.

מֶלֶךְ יִשְׂרָאֵל הוּא! שֶׁיֵּרֵד עַכְשָׁו מִן הַצְּלָב וְנַאֲמִין בּוֹ
melech yisra'el hu! sheyered achshav min hatzelav vena'amin bo
He is the King of Israel; let him now come down from the cross, and we will believe on him.

בָּטַח בֵּאלֹהִים, עַתָּה יְפַלְּטֵהוּ אִם חָפֵץ בּוֹ, כִּי אָמַר בֶּן אֱלֹהִים אָנִי
batach belohim, attah yefalletehu im chafetz bo, ki amar ben elohim ani
He trusteth on God; let him deliver him now, if he desireth him: for he said, I am the Son of God.

כָּךְ חֵרְפוּהוּ גַּם הַשּׁוֹדְדִים שֶׁנִּצְלְבוּ אִתּוֹ
kach cherefuhu gam hashodedim shennitzlevu itto
And the robbers also that were crucified with him cast upon him the same reproach.

מִשָּׁעָה שְׁתֵּים־עֶשְׂרֵה בַּצָּהֳרַיִם הִשְׂתָּרֵר חֹשֶׁךְ עַל כָּל הָאָרֶץ עַד הַשָּׁעָה שָׁלוֹשׁ
misha'ah sheteim-'esreh batzohorayim histarer choshech al kol ha'aretz ad hasha'ah shalosh
Now from the sixth hour there was darkness over all the land until the ninth hour.

וּבְעֶרֶךְ בְּשָׁעָה שָׁלוֹשׁ צָעַק יֵשׁוּעַ בְּקוֹל גָּדוֹל
uve'erech besha'ah shalosh tza'ak yeshua bekol gadol
And about the ninth hour Jesus cried with a loud voice, saying,

אֵלִי, אֵלִי, לְמָה שְׁבַקְתַּנִי כְּלוֹמַר, אֵלִי, אֵלִי, לָמָה עֲזַבְתָּנִי
eli, eli, lemah shevaktani kelomar, eli, eli, lamah azavtani
Eli, Eli, lama sabachthani? that is, My God, my God, why hast thou forsaken me?

כַּמָּה מִן הָעוֹמְדִים שָׁם שָׁמְעוּ זֹאת וְאָמְרוּ: לְאֵלִיָּהוּ הוּא קוֹרֵא
kammah min ha'omedim sham shame'u zot ve'ameru: le'eliyahu hu korei
And some of them that stood there, when they heard it, said, This man calleth Elijah.

וְכָרְעוּ לְפָנָיו כְּשֶׁהֵם מִתְלוֹצְצִים בּוֹ וְאוֹמְרִים: שָׁלוֹם לְךָ, מֶלֶךְ הַיְהוּדִים
vechare'u lefanayu keshehem mitlotzetzim bo ve'omerim. Shalom lecha, melech hayehudim
and they kneeled down before him, and mocked him, saying, Hail, King of the Jews!

הֵם יָרְקוּ בוֹ, לָקְחוּ אֶת הַקָּנֶה וְהִכּוּהוּ עַל רֹאשׁוֹ
hem yareku bo, lakechu et hakkaneh vehikkuhu al rosho
And they spat upon him, and took the reed and smote him on the head.

לְאַחַר שֶׁהִתְלוֹצְצוּ בּוֹ הֵסִירוּ מֵעָלָיו אֶת הַמְּעִיל
le'achar shehitlotzetzu bo hesiru me'alav et hamme'il
And when they had mocked him, they took off from him the robe,

הִלְבִּישֻׁהוּ אֶת בְּגָדָיו וְהוֹבִילוּהוּ לְהִצָּלֵב
hilbishuhu et begadav vehoviluhu lehitzalev
and put on him his garments, and led him away to crucify him.

בְּצֵאתָם מָצְאוּ אִישׁ מֵאֶרֶץ קִירֶנְיָה, שִׁמְעוֹן שְׁמוֹ
betzetam matz'u ish me'eretz kirenyah, shim'on shemo
And as they came out, they found a man of Cyrene, Simon by name:

וְהִכְרִיחוּ אוֹתוֹ לָשֵׂאת אֶת צְלָבוֹ
vehichrichu oto laset et tzelavo
him they compelled to go with them, that he might bear his cross.

הֵם בָּאוּ אֶל מָקוֹם הַנִּקְרָא גָּלְגָּתָא, כְּלוֹמַר מְקוֹם הַגֻּלְגֹּלֶת
hem ba'u el makom hannikra galegotta, klomar mekom haggulgolet
And when they were come unto a place called Golgotha, that is to say, The place of a skull,

וְנָתְנוּ לוֹ לִשְׁתּוֹת יַיִן מָהוּל בִּמְרֹרַת צֶמַח הָרֹאשׁ. הוּא טָעַם, אַךְ לֹא רָצָה לִשְׁתּוֹת
venatenu lo lishtot yayin mahul bimrorat tzemach harosh. hu ta'am, ach lo ratzah lishtot
they gave him wine to drink mingled with gall: and when he had tasted it, he would not drink.

אַחֲרֵי שֶׁצְּלָבוּ אוֹתוֹ חִלְּקוּ אֶת בְּגָדָיו בְּהַפִּילָם גּוֹרָל
acharei shetzalevu oto chilleku et begadav behappilam goral
And when they had crucified him, they parted his garments among them, casting lots;

וַיֵּשְׁבוּ לִשְׁמֹר עָלָיו שָׁם
veyashevu lishmor alav sham
and they sat and watched him there.

מֵעַל לְרֹאשׁוֹ שָׂמוּ אֶת כְּתַב אַשְׁמָתוֹ: זֶה הוּא יֵשׁוּעַ מֶלֶךְ הַיְהוּדִים
me'al lerosho samu et ketav ashmato: zeh hu yeshua melech hayehudim
And they set up over his head his accusation written, THIS IS JESUS THE KING OF THE JEWS.

אוֹתָהּ שָׁעָה נִצְלְבוּ אִתּוֹ שְׁנֵי שׁוֹדְדִים, אֶחָד מִימִינוֹ וְאֶחָד מִשְּׂמֹאלוֹ
otah sha'ah nitzlevu itto shenei shodedim, echad miymino ve'echad mismolo
Then are there crucified with him two robbers, one on the right hand and one on the left.

וְאוּלָם רָאשֵׁי הַכֹּהֲנִים וְהַזְּקֵנִים שִׁכְנְעוּ אֶת הֲמוֹן הָעָם לְבַקֵּשׁ אֶת בַּר־אַבָּא וּלְהַכְחִיד אֶת יֵשׁוּעַ
ve'ulam rashei hakkohanim vehazzekenim shichne'u et hamon ha'am levakkesh et bar-'abba ulehachchid et yeshua
Now the chief priests and the elders persuaded the multitudes that they should ask for Barabbas, and destroy Jesus.

פָּנָה אֲלֵיהֶם הַנָּצִיב וְשָׁאַל: אֶת מִי מִשְּׁנֵיהֶם תִּרְצוּ שֶׁאֲשַׁחְרֵר לָכֶם
panah aleihem hannatziv vesha'al: et mi misheneihem tirtzu she'ashachrer lachem
But the governor answered and said unto them, Which of the two will ye that I release unto you?

אָמְרוּ: אֶת בַּר־אַבָּא
amru: et bar-'abba
And they said, Barabbas.

שָׁאַל אוֹתָם פִּילָטוֹס: אִם כֵּן, מָה אֶעֱשֶׂה לְיֵשׁוּעַ הַנִּקְרָא מָשִׁיחַ אָמְרוּ כֻּלָּם: שֶׁיִּצָּלֵב
sha'al otam pilatos. Im ken, mah e'eseh leyeshua hannikra mashiach. ameru kullam: sheyitzalev
Pilate saith unto them, What then shall I do unto Jesus who is called Christ? They all say, Let him be crucified.

שָׁאַל: אֲבָל מָה רָעָה עָשָׂה? אַךְ הֵם צָעֲקוּ בְּיֶתֶר שְׂאֵת: שֶׁיִּצָּלֵב
sha'al: aval mah ra'ah asah? ach hem tza'aku beyeter se'et: sheyitzalev
And he said, Why, what evil hath he done? But they cried out exceedingly, saying, Let him be crucified.

כְּשֶׁרָאָה פִּילָטוֹס כִּי אֵינוֹ מוֹעִיל דָּבָר וּמָה גַּם שֶׁמִּתְרַגֶּשֶׁת מְהוּמָה, לָקַח מַיִם
keshera'ah pilatos ki eino mo'il davar umah gam shemmitraggeshet mehumah, lakach mayim
So when Pilate saw that he prevailed nothing, but rather that a tumult was arising, he took water,

וְרָחַץ אֶת יָדָיו לִפְנֵי הֶהָמוֹן בְּאָמְרוֹ: נָקִי אָנֹכִי מִדָּמוֹ שֶׁל זֶה. זֶהוּ עִנְיַנְכֶם
verachatz et yadav lifnei hehamon be'amero. Naki anochi middamo shel zeh. Zehu inyanchem
and washed his hands before the multitude, saying, I am innocent of the blood of this righteous man; see ye to it.

עָנוּ וְאָמְרוּ כָּל הָעָם: דָּמוֹ עָלֵינוּ וְעַל בָּנֵינוּ
anu ve'ameru kol ha'am: damo aleinu ve'al baneinu
And all the people answered and said, His blood be on us, and on our children.

אָז שִׁחְרֵר לָהֶם אֶת בַּר־אַבָּא, וְאֶת יֵשׁוּעַ הִלְקָה וּמָסַר לִצְלִיבָה
az shichrer lahem et bar-'abba, ve'et yeshua hilkah umasar litzlivah
Then released he unto them Barabbas; but Jesus he scourged and delivered to be crucified.

לָקְחוּ חַיָּלֵי הַנָּצִיב אֶת יֵשׁוּעַ לְבֵית הַמִּמְשָׁל וְהִקְהִילוּ אֵלָיו אֶת כָּל הַגְּדוּד
lakechu chayalei hannatziv et yeshua leveit hammimshal vehik'hilu elav et kol haggdud
Then the soldiers of the governor took Jesus into the Prætorium, and gathered unto him the whole band.

הִפְשִׁיטוּהוּ וְהֶעֱטוּ עָלָיו מְעִיל שָׁנִי
hifshituhu vehe'etu alav me'il shani
And they stripped him, and put on him a scarlet robe.

וּלְאַחַר שֶׁשָּׂרְגוּ עֲטֶרֶת קוֹצִים שָׂמוּ אוֹתָהּ עַל רֹאשׁוֹ, נָתְנוּ קָנֶה בְּיַד יְמִינוֹ
ule'achar shesaregu ateret kotzim samu otah al rosho, natenu kaneh beyad yemino
And they platted a crown of thorns and put it upon his head, and a reed in his right hand;

יֵשׁוּעַ עָמַד לִפְנֵי הַנָּצִיב. שָׁאַל אוֹתוֹ הַנָּצִיב:
yeshua amad lifnei hannatziv. sha'al oto hannatziv
Now Jesus stood before the governor: and the governor asked him, saying,

אַתָּה מֶלֶךְ הַיְּהוּדִים הֵשִׁיב יֵשׁוּעַ: אַתָּה אוֹמֵר
attah melech hayehudim? heshiv yeshua. Attah omer
Art thou the King of the Jews? And Jesus said unto him, Thou sayest.

וְלֹא עָנָה דָבָר כַּאֲשֶׁר הֶאֱשִׁימוּהוּ רָאשֵׁי הַכֹּהֲנִים וְהַזְּקֵנִים
velo anah davar ka'asher he'eshimuhu rashei hakkohanim vehazzekenim
And when he was accused by the chief priests and elders, he answered nothing.

אָמַר אֵלָיו פִּילָטוֹס: אֵינְךָ שׁוֹמֵעַ כַּמָּה הֵם מְעִידִים נֶגְדְּךָ
amar elav pilatos einecha shomea kammah hem me'idim negdecha
Then saith Pilate unto him, Hearest thou not how many things they witness against thee?

אַךְ הוּא לֹא הֵשִׁיב לוֹ גַּם לֹא עַל טַעֲנָה אַחַת, לְתִמְהוֹנוֹ הָרַב שֶׁל הַנָּצִיב
ach hu lo heshiv lo gam lo al ta'anah achat, letimhono harav shel hannatziv
And he gave him no answer, not even to one word: insomuch that the governor marvelled greatly.

בֶּחָג הָיָה הַנָּצִיב נוֹהֵג לְשַׁחְרֵר לָעָם אָסִיר אֶחָד עַל־פִּי בְּחִירָתָם
bechag hayah hannatziv noheg leshachrer la'am asir echad al-pi bechiratam
Now at the feast the governor was wont to release unto the multitude one prisoner, whom they would.

אוֹתָהּ עֵת הָיָה לָהֶם אָסִיר מְפֻרְסָם, יֵשׁוּעַ בַּר־אַבָּא שְׁמוֹ
otah et hayah lahem asir mefursam, yeshua bar-'abba shemo
And they had then a notable prisoner, called Barabbas.

לָכֵן כַּאֲשֶׁר נִקְהֲלוּ שָׁאַל אוֹתָם פִּילָטוֹס
lachen ka'asher nik'halu sha'al otam pilatos
When therefore they were gathered together, Pilate said unto them,

אֶת מִי אַתֶּם רוֹצִים שֶׁאֲשַׁחְרֵר לָכֶם, אֶת יֵשׁוּעַ בַּר־אַבָּא אוֹ אֶת יֵשׁוּעַ הַנִּקְרָא מָשִׁיחַ
et mi attem rotzim she'ashachrer lachem, et yeshua bar-'abba o et yeshua hannikra mashiach
Whom will ye that I release unto you? Barabbas, or Jesus who is called Christ?

כִּי יָדַע שֶׁמִּקִּנְאָה מָסְרוּ אוֹתוֹ
ki yada shemmikkin'ah masru oto
For he knew that for envy they had delivered him up.

כַּאֲשֶׁר יָשַׁב עַל כֵּס הַמִּשְׁפָּט שָׁלְחָה אֵלָיו אִשְׁתּוֹ לֵאמֹר:
ka'asher yashav al kes hammishpat shalchah elav ishto lemor
And while he was sitting on the judgment-seat, his wife sent unto him, saying,

אַל יִהְיֶה לְךָ דָּבָר עִם אוֹתוֹ צַדִּיק, כִּי רַבּוֹת סָבַלְתִּי הַיּוֹם בַּחֲלוֹם בִּגְלָלוֹ
al yihyeh lecha davar im oto tzaddik, ki rabbot savalti hayom bachalom biglalo
Have thou nothing to do with that righteous man; for I have suffered many things this day in a dream because of him.

יְהוּדָה שֶׁהִסְגִּירוֹ, כְּשֶׁרָאָה שֶׁהִרְשִׁיעוּ אוֹתוֹ, הִתְחָרֵט
yehudah shehisgiro, kshera'ah shehirshi'u oto, hitcharet
Then Judas, who betrayed him, when he saw that he was condemned, repented himself,

וְהֶחֱזִיר לְרָאשֵׁי הַכֹּהֲנִים וְלַזְּקֵנִים אֶת שְׁלוֹשִׁים שִׁקְלֵי הַכֶּסֶף
vehechezir lerashei hakkohanim velazzekenim et sheloshim shiklei hakkesef
and brought back the thirty pieces of silver to the chief priests and elders,

בְּאָמְרוֹ חָטָאתִי, כִּי דָּם נָקִי הִסְגַּרְתִּי אַךְ הֵם אָמְרוּ: מָה אִכְפַּת לָנוּ? זֶה עִנְיָנְךָ שֶׁלְּךָ
be'omro chatati, ki dam naki hisgarti. ach hem ameru. Mah ichpat lanu? zeh inyancha shellcha
saying, I have sinned in that I betrayed innocent blood. But they said, What is that to us? see thou to it.

הוּא הִשְׁלִיךְ אֶת הַכֶּסֶף לְתוֹךְ בֵּית אוֹצַר הַמִּקְדָּשׁ, הָלַךְ מִשָּׁם וְתָלָה אֶת עַצְמוֹ
hu hishlich et hakkesef letoch beit otzar hammikdash, halach misham vetalah et atzmo
And he cast down the pieces of silver into the sanctuary, and departed; and he went away and hanged himself.

לָקְחוּ רָאשֵׁי הַכֹּהֲנִים אֶת הַכֶּסֶף וְאָמְרוּ
lakechu rashei hakkohanim et hakkesef ve'ameru
And the chief priests took the pieces of silver, and said,

אָסוּר לְהַכְנִיס אֶת הַכֶּסֶף לְאוֹצַר הַמִּקְדָּשׁ, כִּי מְחִיר דָּמִים הוּא
asur lehachnis et hakkesef le'otzar hammikdash, ki mechir damim hu
It is not lawful to put them into the treasury, since it is the price of blood.

הִתְיָעֲצוּ וְקָנוּ בּוֹ אֶת שְׂדֵה הַיּוֹצֵר לִקְבוּרַת הַזָּרִים
hitya'atzu vekanu bo et sedeh hayotzer lkvurat hazzarim
And they took counsel, and bought with them the potter's field, to bury strangers in.

עַל כֵּן נִקְרָא הַשָּׂדֶה הַהוּא שְׂדֵה הַדָּם עַד הַיּוֹם הַזֶּה
al ken nikra hassadeh hahu sedeh haddam ad hayom hazzeh
Wherefore that field was called, The field of blood, unto this day.

אָז נִתְקַיֵּם מַה שֶּׁנֶּאֱמַר בְּיַד יִרְמְיָהוּ הַנָּבִיא
az nitkayem mah shenne'emar beyad yirmeyahu hannavi
Then was fulfilled that which was spoken through Jeremiah the prophet, saying,

וַיִּקְחוּ שְׁלוֹשִׁים הַכֶּסֶף, אֶדֶר הַיְקָר
vayikchu sheloshim hakkesef, eder hayekar
And they took the thirty pieces of silver, the price of him that was priced,

אֲשֶׁר יָקַר מֵעַל בְּנֵי יִשְׂרָאֵל
asher yakar me'al benei yisra'el
whom certain of the children of Israel did price;

וַיִּתְּנוּ אוֹתָם בְּעַד שְׂדֵה הַיּוֹצֵר כַּאֲשֶׁר צִוַּנִי יהוה
vayittenu otam be'ad sedeh hayotzer ka'asher tzivvani hashem
and they gave them for the potter's field, as the Lord appointed me.

כְּשֶׁיָּצָא אֶל מְבוֹא הֶחָצֵר רָאֲתָה אוֹתוֹ אַחֶרֶת וְאָמְרָה לַנִּמְצָאִים שָׁם
kesheyatza el mevo hechatzer ra'atah oto acheret ve'amerah lannimtza'im sham
And when he was gone out into the porch, another maid saw him, and saith unto them that were there,

זֶה הָיָה עִם יֵשׁוּעַ מִנַּצְרֶת
zeh hayah im yeshua minnatzeret
This man also was with Jesus of Nazareth.

שׁוּב הִכְחִישׁ בִּשְׁבוּעָה וְאָמַר: אֵינֶנִּי מַכִּיר אֶת הָאִישׁ
shuv hichchish bishvu'ah ve'amar: eineni makkir et ha'ish
And again he denied with an oath, I know not the man.

לְאַחַר שָׁעָה קַלָּה נִגְּשׁוּ הָעוֹמְדִים שָׁם וְאָמְרוּ אֶל כֵּיפָא
le'achar sha'ah kallah niggeshu ha'omedim sham ve'ameru el keifa
And after a little while they that stood by came and said to Peter,

בֶּאֱמֶת גַּם אַתָּה מֵהֶם, כִּי הַמִּבְטָא שֶׁלְּךָ מְגַלֶּה אוֹתְךָ
be'emet gam attah mehem, ki hammivta shellcha megalleh otecha
Of a truth thou also art one of them; for thy speech maketh thee known.

אָז הֵחֵל לְקַלֵּל וּלְהִשָּׁבַע שֶׁאֵינֶנּוּ מַכִּיר אֶת הָאִישׁ וּמִיָּד קָרָא הַתַּרְנְגוֹל
az hechel lekallel ulehishava she'einennu makkir et ha'ish. umiyad kara hattarnegol
Then began he to curse and to swear, I know not the man. And straightway the cock crew.

נִזְכַּר כֵּיפָא בַּדָּבָר שֶׁאָמַר לוֹ יֵשׁוּעַ
nizkar keifa baddavar she'amar lo yeshua
And Peter remembered the word which Jesus had said,

בְּטֶרֶם יִקְרָא הַתַּרְנְגוֹל, שָׁלוֹשׁ פְּעָמִים תִּתְכַּחֵשׁ לִי, יָצָא הַחוּצָה וּבָכָה בְּכִי מַר
beterem yikra hattarnegol, shalosh pe'amim titkachesh li, yatza hachutzah uvachah bechi mar
Before the cock crow, thou shalt deny me thrice. And he went out, and wept bitterly.

כז

עִם בֹּקֶר
im boker
Now when morning was come,

נוֹעֲצוּ כָּל רָאשֵׁי הַכֹּהֲנִים וְזִקְנֵי הָעָם עַל יֵשׁוּעַ כְּדֵי לַהֲמִית אוֹתוֹ
no'atzu kol rashei hakkohanim veziknei ha'am al yeshua kedei lehamit oto
all the chief priests and the elders of the people took counsel against Jesus to put him to death:

הֵם קָשְׁרוּ אוֹתוֹ, הוֹלִיכוּהוּ מִשָּׁם וּמְסָרוּהוּ לְפִילָטוֹס הַנָּצִיב
hem kasheru oto, holichuhu misham umesaruhu lepilatos hannatziv
and they bound him, and led him away, and delivered him up to Pilate the governor.

אוּלָם יֵשׁוּעַ שָׁתַק
ulam yeshua shatak
But Jesus held his peace.

אָמַר אֵלָיו הַכֹּהֵן הַגָּדוֹל: אֲנִי מַשְׁבִּיעַ אוֹתְךָ בֵּאלֹהִים חַיִּים שֶׁתֹּאמַר לָנוּ אִם אַתָּה הַמָּשִׁיחַ בֶּן־הָאֱלֹהִים
amar elav hakkohen hagadol: ani mashbia otecha belohim chayim shettomar lanu im attah hammashiach ben-ha'elohim
And the high priest said unto him, I adjure thee by the living God, that thou tell us whether thou art the Christ, the Son of God.

הֵשִׁיב לוֹ יֵשׁוּעַ: אַתָּה אָמַרְתָּ, אַךְ אוֹמֵר אֲנִי לָכֶם
heshiv lo yeshua. attah amarta, ach omer ani lachem
Jesus saith unto him, Thou hast said: nevertheless I say unto you,

מֵעַתָּה תִּרְאוּ אֶת בֶּן־הָאָדָם יוֹשֵׁב לִימִין הַגְּבוּרָה וּבָא עִם עַנְנֵי הַשָּׁמַיִם
me'attah tir'u et ben-ha'adam yoshev limin haggvurah uva im anenei hashamayim
Henceforth ye shall see the Son of man sitting at the right hand of Power, and coming on the clouds of heaven.

הֵשִׁיבוּ: בֶּן־מָוֶת הוּא. מִיָּד קָרַע הַכֹּהֵן הַגָּדוֹל אֶת בְּגָדָיו וְאָמַר: מְגַדֵּף הוּא
Miyad kara hakkohen haggadol et begadav ve'amar: megaddef hu
Then the high priest rent his garments, saying, He hath spoken blasphemy:

מַה לָּנוּ עוֹד צֹרֶךְ בְּעֵדִים? הִנֵּה כָּעֵת שְׁמַעְתֶּם אֶת הַגִּדּוּף. מַה דַּעְתְּכֶם
Mah lanu od tzorech be'edim? hinneh ka'et shema'tem et haggidduf
what further need have we of witnesses? behold, now ye have heard the blasphemy:

מַה דַּעְתְּכֶם? הֵשִׁיבוּ: בֶּן־מָוֶת הוּא.
Mah da'techem? heshivu: ben-mavet hu.
what think ye? They answered and said, He is worthy of death.

אָז יָרְקוּ בְּפָנָיו וְהִכּוּהוּ בְּאֶגְרוֹף; גַּם סָטְרוּ לוֹ
az yareku befanav vehikkuhu be'egrof; gam sateru lo
Then did they spit in his face and buffet him: and some smote him with the palms of their hands,

וְאָמְרוּ: נַבֵּא לָנוּ, הַמָּשִׁיחַ, מִיהוּ הַמַּכֶּה אוֹתְךָ
ve'ameru. Nabbei lanu, hammashiach, mihu hammakkeh otecha
saying, Prophesy unto us, thou Christ: who is he that struck thee?

אוֹתָהּ שָׁעָה יָשַׁב כֵּיפָא מִחוּץ לַבַּיִת, בֶּחָצֵר. נִגְּשָׁה אֵלָיו שִׁפְחָה אַחַת וְאָמְרָה
otah sha'ah yashav keifa michutz labbayit, bechatzer. niggshah elav shifchah achat ve'amerah
Now Peter was sitting without in the court: and a maid came unto him, saying,

גַּם אַתָּה הָיִיתָ עִם יֵשׁוּעַ הַגְּלִילִי
gam attah hayita im yeshua haggelili
Thou also wast with Jesus the Galilæan.

אַךְ הוּא הִכְחִישׁ בִּפְנֵי הַכֹּל בְּאָמְרוֹ: אֵינֶנִּי יוֹדֵעַ מָה אַתְּ אוֹמֶרֶת
ach hu hichchish bifnei hakkol be'amero: einenni yodea mah at omeret
But he denied before them all, saying, I know not what thou sayest.

אוֹתָהּ שָׁעָה אָמַר יֵשׁוּעַ אֶל הֶהָמוֹן: כְּמוֹ עַל שׁוֹדֵד יְצָאתֶם בַּחֲרָבוֹת וּבְמַקְלוֹת לִתְפֹּס אוֹתִי
otah sha'ah amar yeshua el hehamon: kemo al shoded yetzatem bacharavot uvemaklot litpos oti
In that hour said Jesus to the multitudes, Are ye come out as against a robber with swords and staves to seize me?

הֲרֵי יוֹם יוֹם יָשַׁבְתִּי בַּמִּקְדָּשׁ וְלִמַּדְתִּי וְלֹא שְׁלַחְתֶּם יָד לִתְפֹּס אוֹתִי
harei yom yom yashavti bammikdash velimmadti velo shelachtem yad litpos oti
I sat daily in the temple teaching, and ye took me not.

אַךְ כָּל זֶה קָרָה לְמַעַן יִתְקַיְמוּ כִּתְבֵי הַנְּבִיאִים
ach kol zeh karah lema'an yitkayemu kitvei hannevi'im
But all this is come to pass, that the scriptures of the prophets might be fulfilled.

אָז עֲזָבוּהוּ כָּל תַּלְמִידָיו וּבָרְחוּ
az azavuhu kol talmidav uvarechu
Then all the disciples left him, and fled.

הָאֲנָשִׁים אֲשֶׁר עָצְרוּ אֶת יֵשׁוּעַ הוֹלִיכוּהוּ אֶל קַיָּפָא הַכֹּהֵן הַגָּדוֹל
ha'anashim asher atzru et yeshua holichuhu el kayafa hakkohen haggadol
And they that had taken Jesus led him away to the house of Caiaphas the high priest,

וְשָׁם נִקְהֲלוּ הַסּוֹפְרִים וְהַזְּקֵנִים
vesham nik'halu hassoferim vehazzekenim
where the scribes and the elders were gathered together.

כֵּיפָא הָלַךְ אַחֲרָיו בְּמֶרְחָק מָה וּכְשֶׁהִגִּיעַ לַחֲצַר הַכֹּהֵן הַגָּדוֹל
keifa halach acharav bemerchak mah uchshehiggia lachatzar hakkohen haggadol
But Peter followed him afar off, unto the court of the high priest,

נִכְנַס פְּנִימָה וְיָשַׁב עִם הַמְשָׁרְתִים לִרְאוֹת מַה יִּהְיֶה הַסּוֹף
nichnas penimah veyashav im hamsharetim lir'ot mah yihyeh hassof
and entered in, and sat with the officers, to see the end.

אָז חִפְּשׂוּ רָאשֵׁי הַכֹּהֲנִים וְכָל הַסַּנְהֶדְרִין עֵדוּת שֶׁקֶר עַל יֵשׁוּעַ כְּדֵי לְהָמִית אוֹתוֹ
az chippesu rashei hakkohanim vechol hassanhedrin edut sheker al yeshua kedei lehamit oto
Now the chief priests and the whole council sought false witness against Jesus, that they might put him to death;

אַךְ לֹא מָצְאוּ, אַף שֶׁבָּאוּ לְשָׁם עֵדֵי שֶׁקֶר רַבִּים. אַחֲרֵי כֵן נִגְּשׁוּ שְׁנֵי עֵדֵי שֶׁקֶר וְאָמְרוּ
ach lo matze'u, af shebba'u lesham edei sheker rabbim. Acharei chen niggshu shnei edei sheker ve'ameru
and they found it not, though many false witnesses came. But afterward came two,

זֶה אָמַר, אֲנִי יָכוֹל לַהֲרֹס אֶת הֵיכַל הָאֱלֹהִים וּבִשְׁלוֹשָׁה יָמִים לִבְנוֹת אוֹתוֹ
zeh amar, ani yachol laharos et heichal ha'elohim uvishloshah yamim livnot oto
and said, This man said, I am able to destroy the temple of God, and to build it in three days.

קָם הַכֹּהֵן הַגָּדוֹל וְשָׁאַל אוֹתוֹ: אֵינְךָ מֵשִׁיב דָּבָר עַל מַה שֶּׁאֵלֶּה מְעִידִים נֶגְדְּךָ
kam hakkohen haggadol vesha'al oto. Eincha meshiv davar al mah she'elleh me'idim negdecha
And the high priest stood up, and said unto him, Answerest thou nothing? what is it which these witness against thee?

עוֹדְכֶם יְשֵׁנִים וְנָחִים? הִנֵּה בָּאָה הַשָּׁעָה וּבֶן־הָאָדָם יִמָּסֵר לִידֵי אֲנָשִׁים חוֹטְאִים
odechem yeshenim venachim? hinneh ba'ah hasha'ah uven-ha'adam yimmaser lidei anashim chote'im
Sleep on now, and take your rest: behold, the hour is at hand, and the Son of man is betrayed into the hands of sinners.

קוּמוּ וְנֵלֵךְ. הִנֵּה מִתְקָרֵב הַמַּסְגִּיר אוֹתִי
kumu venelech. hinneh mitkarev hammasgir oti
Arise, let us be going: behold, he is at hand that betrayeth me.

עוֹדֶנּוּ מְדַבֵּר וְהִנֵּה בָּא יְהוּדָה, אֶחָד מִן הַשְּׁנֵים־עָשָׂר
odennu medabber vehinneh ba yehudah, echad min hashneim-'asar
And while he yet spake, lo, Judas, one of the twelve, came,

וְאִתּוֹ הָמוֹן רַב, בַּחֲרָבוֹת וּבְמַקְלוֹת מֵאֵת רָאשֵׁי הַכֹּהֲנִים וְזִקְנֵי הָעָם
ve'itto hamon rav, bacharavot uvemaklot, me'et rashei hakkohanim veziknei ha'am,
and with him a great multitude with swords and staves, from the chief priests and elders of the people.

הַמַּסְגִּיר אוֹתוֹ הִקְדִּים לָתֵת סִימָן בְּאָמְרוֹ: מִי שֶׁאֶתֵּן לוֹ נְשִׁיקָה זֶה הוּא; תִּפְסוּ אוֹתוֹ
hammasgir oto hikdim latet siman be'amero: mi she'etten lo neshikah zeh hu; tifsu oto
Now he that betrayed him gave them a sign, saying, Whomsoever I shall kiss, that is he: take him.

מִיָּד נִגַּשׁ אֶל יֵשׁוּעַ וְאָמַר: שָׁלוֹם, רַבִּי, וְנִשֵּׁק אוֹתוֹ
miyad niggash el yeshua ve'amar: shalom, rabbi, venishek oto
And straightway he came to Jesus, and said, Hail, Rabbi; and kissed him.

אָמַר לוֹ יֵשׁוּעַ: חָבֵר, לְשֵׁם מָה אַתָּה כָּאן? אָז נִגְּשׁוּ אֶל יֵשׁוּעַ, אָחֲזוּ בּוֹ בִּידֵיהֶם וְעָצְרוּ אוֹתוֹ
amar lo yeshua. chaver, leshem mah attah kan? az niggeshu el yeshua', achazu bo bideihem ve'atzeru oto
And Jesus said unto him, Friend, do that for which thou art come. Then they came and laid hands on Jesus, and took him.

אֶחָד מֵהָאֲנָשִׁים שֶׁהָיוּ עִם יֵשׁוּעַ שָׁלַח יָדוֹ וְשָׁלַף אֶת חַרְבּוֹ
echad meha'anashim shehayu im yeshua shalach yado veshalaf et charbo
And behold, one of them that were with Jesus stretched out his hand, and drew his sword,

וּבְהַכּוֹתוֹ אֶת עֶבֶד הַכֹּהֵן הַגָּדוֹל קִצֵּץ אֶת אָזְנוֹ
uvehakkoto et eved hakkohen haggadol kitzetz et ozno
and smote the servant of the high priest, and struck off his ear.

אָמַר אֵלָיו יֵשׁוּעַ: הָשֵׁב אֶת חַרְבְּךָ אֶל מְקוֹמָהּ, כִּי כָּל הָאוֹחֲזִים בַּחֶרֶב, בַּחֶרֶב יֹאבֵדוּ
amar elav yeshua: hashev et charbecha el mekomah, ki kol ha'ochazim bacherev, bacherev yovedu
Then saith Jesus unto him, Put up again thy sword into its place: for all they that take the sword shall perish with the sword.

שֶׁמָּא חוֹשֵׁב אַתָּה שֶׁאֵינֶנִּי יָכוֹל לְבַקֵּשׁ מֵאָבִי וּמִיָּד יַמְצִיא לִי יוֹתֵר מִשְּׁנֵים־עָשָׂר לִגְיוֹנוֹת מַלְאָכִים
shemma choshev attah she'einenni yachol levakkesh me'avi umiyad yamtzi li yoter misheneim-'asar ligyonot mal'achim
Or thinkest thou that I cannot beseech my Father, and he shall even now send me more than twelve legions of angels?

אֲבָל כֵּיצַד יִתְקַיְּמוּ דִּבְרֵי הַכְּתוּבִים שֶׁכָּךְ צָרִיךְ לִהְיוֹת
aval keitzad yitkayemu divrei hakketuvim shekkach tzarich lihyot
How then should the scriptures be fulfilled, that thus it must be?

שְׁבוּ לָכֶם פֹּה עַד שֶׁאֵלֵךְ לְשָׁם וְאֶתְפַּלֵּל
shevu lachem poh ad she'elech lesham ve'etpallel
Sit ye here, while I go yonder and pray.

הוּא לָקַח אִתּוֹ אֶת כֵּיפָא וְאֶת שְׁנֵי בְּנֵי זַבְדַּי וְהֵחֵל מִתְמַלֵּא עֶצֶב וּמוּעָקָה
hu lakach itto et keifa ve'et shenei benei zavdai vehechel mitmallei etzev umu'akah
And he took with him Peter and the two sons of Zebedee, and began to be sorrowful and sore troubled.

אָמַר לָהֶם: נַפְשִׁי מָרָה עָלַי עַד מָוֶת, הִשָּׁאֲרוּ פֹּה וֶהֱיוּ עֵרִים אִתִּי
amar lahem: nafshi marah alai ad mavet, hisha'aru poh veheyu erim itti
Then saith he unto them, My soul is exceeding sorrowful, even unto death: abide ye here, and watch with me.

אָז הָלַךְ מְעַט הָלְאָה, נָפַל עַל פָּנָיו וְהִתְפַּלֵּל בְּאָמְרוֹ
az halach me'at hale'ah, nafal al panav vehitpallel be'omro
And he went forward a little, and fell on his face, and prayed, saying,

אָבִי, אִם אֶפְשָׁר הַדָּבָר, הַעֲבֵר נָא מִמֶּנִּי אֶת הַכּוֹס הַזֹּאת, אַךְ לֹא כִּרְצוֹנִי אֲנִי כִּי אִם כִּרְצוֹנְךָ אַתָּה
avi, im efshar haddavar, ha'aver na mimmenni et hakkos hazzot, ach lo kirtzoni ani ki im kirtzonecha attah
My Father, if it be possible, let this cup pass away from me: nevertheless, not as I will, but as thou wilt.

לְאַחַר מִכֵּן בָּא אֶל הַתַּלְמִידִים וּמְצָאָם יְשֵׁנִים. אָמַר אֶל כֵּיפָא
le'achar mikken ba el hattalmidim umetza'am yeshenim. amar el keifa
And he cometh unto the disciples, and findeth them sleeping, and saith unto Peter,

וּבְכֵן לֹא יְכָלְתֶּם לְהִשָּׁאֵר עֵרִים אִתִּי שָׁעָה אַחַת
uvechen lo yechaletem lehisha'er erim itti sha'ah achat
What, could ye not watch with me one hour?

הֱיוּ עֵרִים וְהִתְפַּלְּלוּ כְּדֵי שֶׁלֹּא תָּבוֹאוּ לִידֵי נִסָּיוֹן. אָמְנָם הָרוּחַ חֲפֵצָה, אֲבָל הַבָּשָׂר חַלָּשׁ
heyu erim vehitpallelu kedei shello tavo'u lidei nissayon. omnam haruach chafetzah, aval habbasar chalash
Watch and pray, that ye enter not into temptation: the spirit indeed is willing, but the flesh is weak.

הָלַךְ שֵׁנִית וְהִתְפַּלֵּל בְּאָמְרוֹ. אָבִי, אִם אִי אֶפְשָׁר שֶׁהַכּוֹס תַּעֲבֹר מִבְּלִי שֶׁאֶשְׁתֶּה אוֹתָהּ, יְהִי נָא כִּרְצוֹנְךָ
halach shenit vehitpallel be'omro. Avi, im i efshar shehakkos ta'avor mibbeli she'eshteh otah, yehi na kirtzonecha
Again a second time he went away, and prayed, saying, My Father, if this cannot pass away, except I drink it, thy will be done.

הוּא חָזַר וְשׁוּב מָצָא אוֹתָם יְשֵׁנִים, כִּי עֵינֵיהֶם הָיוּ כְּבֵדוֹת
hu chazar veshuv matza otam yeshenim, ki eineihem hayu kevedot
And he came again and found them sleeping, for their eyes were heavy.

עוֹד פַּעַם עָזַב אוֹתָם וְהָלַךְ לְהִתְפַּלֵּל בַּשְּׁלִישִׁית בְּאָמְרוֹ שׁוּב אֶת אוֹתָן הַמִּלִּים
od pa'am azav otam vehalach lehitpallel bashelishit be'amero shuv et otan hammillim
And he left them again, and went away, and prayed a third time, saying again the same words.

אַחֲרֵי כֵן בָּא אֶל הַתַּלְמִידִים וְאָמַר לָהֶם
acharei chen ba el hattalmidim ve'amar lahem
Then cometh he to the disciples, and saith unto them,

לָקַח אֶת הַכּוֹס, בֵּרַךְ וְנָתַן לָהֶם בְּאָמְרוֹ: שְׁתוּ מִמֶּנָּה כֻּלְּכֶם
lakach et hakkos, berech venatan lahem be'amero. Shtu mimmennah kullchem
And he took a cup, and gave thanks, and gave to them, saying, Drink ye all of it;

כִּי זֶה דָּמִי, דַּם הַבְּרִית [הַחֲדָשָׁה] הַנִּשְׁפָּךְ בְּעַד רַבִּים לִסְלִיחַת חֲטָאִים
ki zeh dami, dam habberit [hachadashah] hannishpach be'ad rabbim lislichat chata'im
for this is my blood of the covenant, which is poured out for many unto remission of sins.

וַאֲנִי אוֹמֵר לָכֶם, מֵעַתָּה לֹא אֶשְׁתֶּה מִפְּרִי הַגֶּפֶן הַזֶּה
va'ani omer lachem, me'attah lo eshteh mipperi haggefen hazzeh
But I say unto you, I shall not drink henceforth of this fruit of the vine,

עַד אוֹתוֹ הַיּוֹם אֲשֶׁר אֶשְׁתֵּהוּ חָדָשׁ עִמָּכֶם בְּמַלְכוּת אָבִי
ad oto hayom asher eshtehu chadash immachem bemalchut avi
until that day when I drink it new with you in my Father's kingdom.

לְאַחַר שֶׁשָּׁרוּ אֶת הַהַלֵּל יָצְאוּ אֶל הַר הַזֵּיתִים
le'achar shesharu et hahallel yatze'u el har hazzeitim
And when they had sung a hymn, they went out into the mount of Olives.

אָמַר לָהֶם יֵשׁוּעַ: אַתֶּם כֻּלְּכֶם תִּכָּשְׁלוּ בִּגְלָלִי הַלַּיְלָה
amar lahem yeshua. attem kullechem tikkashelu biglali hallaylah
Then saith Jesus unto them, All ye shall be offended in me this night:

שֶׁהֲרֵי כָּתוּב, אַכֶּה אֶת־הָרֹעֶה וּתְפוּצֶין הַצֹּאן
sheharei katuv, akkeh et-haro'eh utefutzein hatzon
for it is written, I will smite the shepherd, and the sheep of the flock shall be scattered abroad.

אֲבָל אַחֲרֵי שֶׁאָקוּם אֵלֵךְ לִפְנֵיכֶם לַגָּלִיל
aval acharei she'akum elech lifneichem laggalil
But after I am raised up, I will go before you into Galilee.

הֵשִׁיב לוֹ כֵּיפָא וְאָמַר: אִם הַכֹּל יִכָּשְׁלוּ בִּגְלָלְךָ, אֲנִי לְעוֹלָם לֹא אֶכָּשֵׁל
heshiv lo keifa ve'amar. im hakkol yikkashelu biglalecha, ani le'olam lo ekkashel
But Peter answered and said unto him, If all shall be offended in thee, I will never be offended.

אָמַר לוֹ יֵשׁוּעַ: אָמֵן אוֹמֵר אֲנִי לְךָ כִּי בַּלַּיְלָה הַזֶּה, בְּטֶרֶם יִקְרָא הַתַּרְנְגוֹל, שָׁלוֹשׁ פְּעָמִים תִּתְכַּחֵשׁ לִי
amar lo yeshua: amen omer ani lecha ki ballaylah hazzeh, beterem yikra hattarnegol, shalosh pe'amim titkachesh li
Jesus said unto him, Verily I say unto thee, that this night, before the cock crow, thou shalt deny me thrice.

אָמַר כֵּיפָא: גַּם אִם עָלַי לָמוּת אִתְּךָ לֹא אֶתְכַּחֵשׁ לְךָ. וְכֵן אָמְרוּ כָּל הַתַּלְמִידִים
amar keifa: gam im alai lamut ittecha lo etkachesh lecha. vechen ameru kol hattalmidim
Peter saith unto him, Even if I must die with thee, yet will I not deny thee. Likewise also said all the disciples.

אַחֲרֵי כֵן בָּא אִתָּם יֵשׁוּעַ אֶל מָקוֹם הַנִּקְרָא גַּת שְׁמָנִים וְאָמַר אֶל הַתַּלְמִידִים
acharei chen ba ittam yeshua el makom hannikra gat shemanim ve'amar el hattalmidim
Then cometh Jesus with them unto a place called Gethsemane, and saith unto his disciples,

הֵשִׁיב לָהֶם: לְכוּ הָעִירָה, אֶל פְּלוֹנִי וְאִמְרוּ לוֹ
heshiv lahem: lechu ha'irah, el peloni ve'imru lo
And he said, Go into the city to such a man, and say unto him,

כֹּה אָמַר רַבֵּנוּ, עִתִּי קְרוֹבָה. אֶצְלְךָ אֶעֱשֶׂה אֶת הַפֶּסַח עִם תַּלְמִידַי
koh amar rabbenu, itti kerovah. etzlecha e'eseh et happesach im talmidai
The Teacher saith, My time is at hand; I keep the passover at thy house with my disciples.

הַתַּלְמִידִים עָשׂוּ כְּמִצְוַת יֵשׁוּעַ וְהֵכִינוּ אֶת הַפֶּסַח
hattalmidim asu kemitzvat yeshua vehechinu et happesach
And the disciples did as Jesus appointed them; and they made ready the passover.

בָּעֶרֶב הֵסֵב עִם הַשְׁנֵים-עָשָׂר
ba'erev hesev im hasheneim-'asar
Now when even was come, he was sitting at meat with the twelve disciples;

וְכַאֲשֶׁר אָכְלוּ אָמַר: אָמֵן אוֹמֵר אֲנִי לָכֶם, אֶחָד מִכֶּם יַסְגִּירֵנִי
vecha'asher achelu amar: amen omer ani lachem, echad mikkem yasgireni
and as they were eating, he said, Verily I say unto you, that one of you shall betray me.

הֵם הִתְעַצְּבוּ מְאֹד וְהֵחֵלּוּ אִישׁ אִישׁ לִשְׁאֹל אוֹתוֹ: זֶה אֲנִי, אֲדוֹנִי
hem hit'atzevu me'od vehechellu ish ish lish'ol oto. zeh ani, adoni
And they were exceeding sorrowful, and began to say unto him every one, Is it I, Lord?

הֵשִׁיב וְאָמַר: הַטּוֹבֵל אִתִּי אֶת יָדוֹ בַּקְּעָרָה הוּא יַסְגִּירֵנִי
heshiv ve'amar. Hattovel itti et yado bakke'arah hu yasgireni
And he answered and said, He that dipped his hand with me in the dish, the same shall betray me.

בֶּן-הָאָדָם אָמְנָם הוֹלֵךְ כַּכָּתוּב עָלָיו
ben-ha'adam omnam holech kakkatuv alav
The Son of man goeth, even as it is written of him:

אַךְ אוֹי לָאִישׁ אֲשֶׁר יַסְגִּיר אֶת בֶּן-הָאָדָם. הָאִישׁ הַהוּא, מוּטָב הָיָה לוֹ אִלּוּלֵא נוֹלַד
ach oy la'ish asher yasgir et ben-ha'adam. ha'ish hahu, mutav hayah lo illulei nolad
but woe unto that man through whom the Son of man is betrayed! good were it for that man if he had not been born.

הֵגִיב יְהוּדָה שֶׁהָיָה עָתִיד לְהַסְגִּירוֹ - וְשָׁאַל: זֶה אֲנִי, רַבִּי? הֵשִׁיב לוֹ: אַתָּה אָמַרְתָּ
hegiv yehudah shehayah atid lehasgiro - vesha'al. zeh ani, rabbi? heshiv lo. attah amarta
And Judas, who betrayed him, answered and said, Is it I, Rabbi? He saith unto him, Thou hast said.

כַּאֲשֶׁר אָכְלוּ לָקַח יֵשׁוּעַ לֶחֶם, בֵּרֵךְ וּבָצַע
ka'asher achelu lakach yeshua lechem, berech uvatza
And as they were eating, Jesus took bread, and blessed, and brake it;

וְנָתַן לַתַּלְמִידִים בְּאָמְרוֹ: קְחוּ וְאִכְלוּ, זֶה גּוּפִי
venatan lattalmidim be'omro: kechu ve'ichlu, zeh gufi
and he gave to the disciples, and said, Take, eat; this is my body.

כִּרְאוֹתָם זֹאת כָּעֲסוּ הַתַּלְמִידִים וְאָמְרוּ: לָמָה הַבִּזְבּוּז הַזֶּה
kir'otam zot ka'asu hattalmidim ve'ameru. Lammah habbizbuz hazzeh
But when the disciples saw it, they had indignation, saying, To what purpose is this waste?

הֲלֹא אֶפְשָׁר הָיָה לִמְכֹּר אֶת זֶה בִּמְחִיר רַב וְלָתֵת לָעֲנִיִּים
halo efshar hayah limkor et zeh bimchir rav velatet la'aniyim
For this ointment might have been sold for much, and given to the poor.

כְּשֶׁהִבְחִין בָּזֶה יֵשׁוּעַ, אָמַר לָהֶם: מַדּוּעַ תָּצִיקוּ לָאִשָּׁה? הֲרֵי מַעֲשֶׂה טוֹב עָשְׂתָה לִי
keshehivchin bazeh yeshua', amar lahem: maddua tatziku la'ishah? harei ma'aseh tov asetah li
But Jesus perceiving it said unto them, Why trouble ye the woman? for she hath wrought a good work upon me.

הָעֲנִיִּים אִתְּכֶם תָּמִיד, אֲבָל אֲנִי, לֹא תָּמִיד אֲנִי אִתְּכֶם
ha'aniyim ittechem tamid, aval ani, lo tamid ani ittechem
For ye have the poor always with you; but me ye have not always.

וְהִיא כְּשֶׁיָּצְקָה אֶת שֶׁמֶן הַבֹּשֶׂם הַזֶּה עַל גּוּפִי עָשְׂתָה זֹאת בִּשְׁבִיל קְבוּרָתִי
vehi kesheyatzekah et shemen habbosem hazzeh al gufi asetah zot bishvil kevurati
For in that she poured this ointment upon my body, she did it to prepare me for burial.

אָמֵן אוֹמֵר אֲנִי לָכֶם, בְּכָל מָקוֹם שֶׁתֻּכְרַז הַבְּשׂוֹרָה הַזֹּאת, בְּכָל הָעוֹלָם,
amen omer ani lachem, bechol makom shettuchraz habbesorah hazzot, bechol ha'olam,
Verily I say unto you, Wheresoever this gospel shall be preached in the whole world,

יְסֻפַּר גַּם מַה שֶּׁעָשְׂתָה הִיא, וְזֶה לְזִכְרָהּ
yesuppar gam mah she'asetah hi, vezeh lezichrah
that also which this woman hath done shall be spoken of for a memorial of her.

לְאַחַר מִכֵּן הָלַךְ אֶחָד מִן הַשְּׁנֵים־עָשָׂר, יְהוּדָה אִישׁ קְרִיּוֹת שְׁמוֹ, אֶל רָאשֵׁי הַכֹּהֲנִים
le'achar mikken halach echad min hasheneim-'asar, yehudah ish keriyot shemo, el rashei hakkohanim
Then one of the twelve, who was called Judas Iscariot, went unto the chief priests,

וְאָמַר: מָה אַתֶּם רוֹצִים לָתֵת לִי וַאֲנִי אֶמְסֹר אוֹתוֹ לָכֶם? נָתְנוּ לוֹ שְׁלוֹשִׁים שִׁקְלֵי כֶּסֶף
ve'amar: mah attem rotzim latet li va'ani emsor oto lachem? natenu lo sheloshim shiklei kesef
and said, What are ye willing to give me, and I will deliver him unto you? And they weighed unto him thirty pieces of silver.

וּמֵאוֹתָהּ עֵת חִפֵּשׂ הִזְדַּמְּנוּת לְהַסְגִּיר אוֹתוֹ
ume'otah et chippes hizdammenut lehasgir oto
And from that time he sought opportunity to deliver him unto them.

בָּרִאשׁוֹן לְחַג הַמַּצּוֹת נִגְּשׁוּ הַתַּלְמִידִים אֶל יֵשׁוּעַ וְשָׁאֲלוּ:
barishon lechag hammatzot niggeshu hattalmidim el yeshua vesha'alu
Now on the first day of unleavened bread the disciples came to Jesus, saying,

הֵיכָן אַתָּה רוֹצֶה שֶׁנָּכִין לְךָ לֶאֱכֹל אֶת הַפֶּסַח
heichan attah rotzeh shennachin lecha le'echol et happesach
Where wilt thou that we make ready for thee to eat the passover?

אָמֵן, אוֹמֵר אֲנִי לָכֶם, מַה שֶּׁלֹּא עֲשִׂיתֶם לְאֶחָד מִן הַקְּטַנִּים הָאֵלֶּה גַּם לִי לֹא עֲשִׂיתֶם
amen, omer ani lachem, mah shello asitem le'echad min hakketannim ha'elleh gam li lo asitem
Verily I say unto you, Inasmuch as ye did it not unto one of these least, ye did it not unto me.

וּבְכֵן אֵלֶּה יֵלְכוּ לְעֹנֶשׁ עוֹלָם וְהַצַּדִּיקִים לְחַיֵּי עוֹלָם
uvechen elleh yelechu le'onesh olam vehatzaddikim lechayei olam
And these shall go away into eternal punishment: but the righteous into eternal life.

כו

לְאַחַר שֶׁדִּבֶּר יֵשׁוּעַ אֶת כָּל הַדְּבָרִים הָאֵלֶּה אָמַר לְתַלְמִידָיו
le'achar sheddibber yeshua et kol haddevarim ha'elleh amar letalmidav
And it came to pass, when Jesus had finished all these words, he said unto his disciples,

אַתֶּם יוֹדְעִים כִּי בְּעוֹד יוֹמַיִם הַפֶּסַח בָּא וּבֶן־הָאָדָם יִמָּסֵר לְהִצָּלֵב
attem yode'im ki be'od yomayim happesach ba uven-ha'adam yimmaser lehitzalev
Ye know that after two days the passover cometh, and the Son of man is delivered up to be crucified.

בְּאוֹתָהּ עֵת נִקְהֲלוּ רָאשֵׁי הַכֹּהֲנִים וְזִקְנֵי הָעָם
be'otah et nik'halu rashei hakkohanim veziknei ha'am
Then were gathered together the chief priests, and the elders of the people,

אֶל חֲצַר הַכֹּהֵן הַגָּדוֹל, קַיָּפָא שְׁמוֹ
el chatzar hakkohen haggadol, kayafa shemo
unto the court of the high priest, who was called Caiaphas;

וְהֶחְלִיטוּ לִתְפֹּס אֶת יֵשׁוּעַ בְּעָרְמָה וּלְהָמִית אוֹתוֹ
vehechlitu litpos et yeshua be'aremah ulehamit oto
and they took counsel together that they might take Jesus by subtlety, and kill him.

אַךְ אָמְרוּ: לֹא בֶּחָג, שֶׁמָּא תִּהְיֶה מְהוּמָה בָּעָם
ach ameru: lo bechag, shemma tihyeh mehumah ba'am
But they said, Not during the feast, lest a tumult arise among the people.

כְּשֶׁהָיָה יֵשׁוּעַ בְּבֵית עַנְיָה בְּבֵיתוֹ שֶׁל שִׁמְעוֹן הַמְצֹרָע
keshehayah yeshua beveit anyah beveito shel shim'on hamtzora
Now when Jesus was in Bethany, in the house of Simon the leper,

נִגְּשָׁה אֵלָיו אִשָּׁה שֶׁהֶחֱזִיקָה פַּךְ שֶׁמֶן וּבוֹ בֹּשֶׂם יָקָר מְאֹד
niggeshah elav ishah shehechezikah pach shemen uvo bosem yakar me'od
there came unto him a woman having an alabaster cruse of exceeding precious ointment,

וַיָּצְקָה אוֹתוֹ עַל רֹאשׁוֹ בִּהְיוֹתוֹ מֵסֵב לְיַד הַשֻּׁלְחָן
veyatzekah oto al rosho bihyoto mesev leyad hashulchan
and she poured it upon his head, as he sat at meat.

יַעֲנוּ הַצַּדִּיקִים וְיֹאמְרוּ אֵלָיו, אֲדוֹנֵנוּ, מָתַי רְאִינוּ אוֹתְךָ רָעֵב וְהֶאֱכַלְנוּ אוֹתְךָ, אוֹ צָמֵא וְהִשְׁקֵינוּ אוֹתְךָ
ya'anu hatzaddikim veyomeru elav, adonenu, matai ra'inu otcha ra'ev vehe'echalnu otecha, o tzamei vehishkeinu otcha
Then shall the righteous answer him, saying, Lord, when saw we thee hungry, and fed thee? or athirst, and gave thee drink?

מָתַי רְאִינוּךָ עוֹבֵר אֹרַח וְאָסַפְנוּ אוֹתְךָ, אוֹ עָרוֹם וְהִלְבַּשְׁנוּ אוֹתְךָ
matai re'inucha over orach ve'asafnu otcha, o arom vehilbashnu otcha
And when saw we thee a stranger, and took thee in? or naked, and clothed thee?

וּמָתַי רְאִינוּ אוֹתְךָ חוֹלֶה אוֹ בְּמַאֲסָר וּבָאנוּ אֵלֶיךָ
umatai ra'inu otcha choleh o bema'asar uvanu eleicha
And when saw we thee sick, or in prison, and came unto thee?

יָשִׁיב הַמֶּלֶךְ וְיֹאמַר לָהֶם
yashiv hammelech veyomar lahem
And the King shall answer and say unto them,

אָמֵן, אוֹמֵר אֲנִי לָכֶם, מַה שֶּׁעֲשִׂיתֶם לְאֶחָד מֵאַחַי הַקְּטַנִּים הָאֵלֶּה לִי עֲשִׂיתֶם
amen, omer ani lachem, mah she'asitem le'echad me'achai hakketannim ha'elleh li asitem
Verily I say unto you, Inasmuch as ye did it unto one of these my brethren, even these least, ye did it unto me.

אַחֲרֵי כֵן יֹאמַר אֶל הַנִּצָּבִים לִשְׂמֹאלוֹ
acharei chen yomar el hannitzavim lismolo
Then shall he say also unto them on the left hand,

לְכוּ מִמֶּנִּי, אֲרוּרִים, אֶל אֵשׁ עוֹלָם הַמּוּכָנָה לַשָּׂטָן וּלְמַלְאָכָיו
lechu mimmenni, arurim, el esh olam hammuchanah lashotan ulemal'achav
Depart from me, ye cursed, into the eternal fire which is prepared for the devil and his angels:

כִּי רָעֵב הָיִיתִי וְלֹא נְתַתֶּם לִי לֶאֱכֹל, צָמֵא הָיִיתִי וְלֹא הִשְׁקִיתֶם אוֹתִי
ki ra'ev hayiti velo netattem li le'echol, tzamei hayiti velo hishkeitem oti
for I was hungry, and ye did not give me to eat; I was thirsty, and ye gave me no drink;

עוֹבֵר אֹרַח הָיִיתִי וְלֹא אֲסַפְתֶּם אוֹתִי, עָרוֹם - וְלֹא הִלְבַּשְׁתֶּם אוֹתִי, חוֹלֶה וּבְמַאֲסָר - וְלֹא בִּקַּרְתֶּם אוֹתִי
over orach hayiti velo asaftem oti, arom - velo hilbashtem oti, choleh uvema'asar - velo bikkartem oti
I was a stranger, and ye took me not in; naked, and ye clothed me not; sick, and in prison, and ye visited me not.

יָשִׁיבוּ גַּם הֵם וְיֹאמְרוּ, אֲדוֹנֵנוּ, מָתַי רְאִינוּ אוֹתְךָ רָעֵב
yashivu gam hem veyomeru, adonenu, matai ra'inu otcha ra'ev
Then shall they also answer, saying, Lord, when saw we thee hungry,

אוֹ צָמֵא אוֹ עוֹבֵר אֹרַח אוֹ עָרוֹם אוֹ חוֹלֶה אוֹ בְּמַאֲסָר וְלֹא שֵׁרַתְנוּ אוֹתְךָ
o tzamei o over orach o arom o choleh o bema'asar velo sheratnu otcha
or athirst, or a stranger, or naked, or sick, or in prison, and did not minister unto thee?

אָז יַעֲנֶה לָהֶם וְיֹאמַר
az ya'aneh lahem veyomar
Then shall he answer them, saying,

עַל כֵּן קְחוּ אֶת הַכִּכָּר וּתְנוּ לָאִישׁ אֲשֶׁר לוֹ עֶשֶׂר הַכִּכָּרִים
al ken kchu et hakkikkar utnu la'ish asher lo eser hakkikkarim
Take ye away therefore the talent from him, and give it unto him that hath the ten talents.

כִּי כָּל מִי שֶׁיֵּשׁ לוֹ נָתוֹן יִנָּתֵן לוֹ וְשֶׁפַע יִהְיֶה לוֹ
ki kol mi sheyesh lo naton yinnaten lo veshefa yihyeh lo
For unto every one that hath shall be given, and he shall have abundance:

אַךְ מִי שֶׁאֵין לוֹ גַּם מַה שֶּׁיֵּשׁ לוֹ יִלָּקַח מִמֶּנּוּ
ach mi she'ein lo gam mah sheyesh lo yillakach mimmennu
but from him that hath not, even that which he hath shall be taken away.

וְאֶת הָעֶבֶד הַבִּלְתִּי מוֹעִיל הַשְׁלִיכוּ אֶל הַחֹשֶׁךְ הַחִיצוֹן; שָׁם יִהְיוּ הַיְלָלָה וַחֲרוֹק הַשִּׁנַּיִם
ve'et ha'eved habbilti mo'il hashlichu el hachoshech hachitzon; sham yihyu haylalah vacharok hashinnayim
And cast ye out the unprofitable servant into the outer darkness: there shall be the weeping and the gnashing of teeth.

כַּאֲשֶׁר יָבוֹא בֶּן־הָאָדָם בִּכְבוֹדוֹ וְכָל הַמַּלְאָכִים אִתּוֹ, יֵשֵׁב עַל כִּסֵּא כְבוֹדוֹ
ka'asher yavo ben-ha'adam bichvodo vechol hammal'achim itto, yeshev al kissei kevodo
But when the Son of man shall come in his glory, and all the angels with him, then shall he sit on the throne of his glory:

וְיֵאָסְפוּ לְפָנָיו כָּל הַגּוֹיִים אָז יַפְרִידֵם זֶה מִזֶּה
veye'asefu lefanav kol haggoyim az yafridem zeh mizzeh
and before him shall be gathered all the nations: and he shall separate them one from another,

כְּרוֹעֶה הַמַּפְרִיד אֶת הַכְּבָשִׂים מִן הָעִזִּים
kero'eh hammafrid et hakkevasim min ha'izzim
as the shepherd separateth the sheep from the goats;

וְיַצִּיב אֶת הַכְּבָשִׂים לִימִינוֹ וְאֶת הָעִזִּים לִשְׂמֹאלוֹ
veyatziv et hakkevasim liymino ve'et ha'izzim lismolo
and he shall set the sheep on his right hand, but the goats on the left.

יֹאמַר הַמֶּלֶךְ אֶל הַנִּצָּבִים לִימִינוֹ
yomar hammelech el hannitzavim liymino
Then shall the King say unto them on his right hand,

בֹּאוּ בְּרוּכֵי אָבִי וּרְשׁוּ אֶת הַמַּלְכוּת הַמּוּכָנָה לָכֶם מֵאָז הִוָּסֵד תֵּבֵל
bo'u bruchei avi ureshu et hammalchut hammuchanah lachem me'az hivvased tevel
Come, ye blessed of my Father, inherit the kingdom prepared for you from the foundation of the world:

כִּי רָעֵב הָיִיתִי וּנְתַתֶּם לִי לֶאֱכֹל, צָמֵא הָיִיתִי וְהִשְׁקֵיתֶם אוֹתִי, עוֹבֵר אֹרַח הָיִיתִי וַאֲסַפְתֶּם אוֹתִי
ki ra'ev hayiti unetattem li le'echol, tzamei hayiti vehishkeitem oti, over orach hayiti va'asaftem oti
for I was hungry, and ye gave me to eat; I was thirsty, and ye gave me drink; I was a stranger, and ye took me in;

עָרוֹם וְהִלְבַּשְׁתֶּם אוֹתִי, חוֹלֶה הָיִיתִי וּבִקַּרְתֶּם אוֹתִי, בְּמַאֲסָר הָיִיתִי וּבָאתֶם אֵלַי
arom vehilbashtem oti, choleh hayiti uvikkartem oti, bema'asar hayiti uvatem elai
naked, and ye clothed me; I was sick, and ye visited me; I was in prison, and ye came unto me.

הָיִיתָ נֶאֱמָן בִּמְעַט, אַפְקִיד אוֹתְךָ עַל הַרְבֵּה. בּוֹא אֶל שִׂמְחַת אֲדוֹנְךָ
hayita ne'eman bim'at, afkid otecha al harbeh. bo el simchat adoncha
thou hast been faithful over a few things, I will set thee over many things; enter thou into the joy of thy lord.

נִגַּשׁ גַּם זֶה שֶׁקִּבֵּל שְׁתֵּי כִּכָּרִים וְאָמַר
niggash gam zeh shekkibbel shtei kikkarim ve'amar
And he also that received the two talents came and said,

שְׁתֵּי כִּכָּרִים הִפְקַדְתָּ בְּיָדִי, הִנֵּה הִרְוַחְתִּי שְׁתֵּי כִּכָּרִים נוֹסָפוֹת
shtei kikkarim hifkadta beyadi, hinneh hirvachti shetei kikkarim nosafot
Lord, thou deliveredst unto me two talents: lo, I have gained other two talents.

הֵשִׁיב לוֹ אֲדוֹנָיו, יָפֶה, עֶבֶד טוֹב וְנֶאֱמָן
heshiv lo adonav, yafeh, eved tov vene'eman
His lord said unto him, Well done, good and faithful servant:

הָיִיתָ נֶאֱמֶן בִּמְעַט, אַפְקִיד אוֹתְךָ עַל הַרְבֵּה. בּוֹא אֶל שִׂמְחַת אֲדוֹנְךָ
hayita ne'emen bim'at, afkid otecha al harbeh. bo el simchat adonecha
thou hast been faithful over a few things, I will set thee over many things; enter thou into the joy of thy lord.

נִגַּשׁ גַּם זֶה שֶׁקִּבֵּל כִּכָּר אַחַת וְאָמַר
niggash gam zeh shekkibbel kikkar achat ve'amar
And he also that had received the one talent came and said,

אֲדוֹנִי, יָדַעְתִּי שֶׁאַתָּה אִישׁ קָשֶׁה, הַקּוֹצֵר בְּמָקוֹם שֶׁלֹּא זָרַעְתָּ וְאוֹסֵף בְּמָקוֹם שֶׁלֹּא פִּזַּרְתָּ
adoni, yada'ti she'attah ish kasheh, hakkotzer bemakom shello zara'ta ve'osef bemakom shello pizzarta
Lord, I knew thee that thou art a hard man, reaping where thou didst not sow, and gathering where thou didst not scatter;

וּמֵאַחַר שֶׁפָּחַדְתִּי הָלַכְתִּי וְהִטְמַנְתִּי אֶת כִּכָּרְךָ בָּאֲדָמָה. הִנֵּהִי אֲשֶׁר לְךָ
ume'achar sheppachadti halachti vehitmanti et kikkarecha ba'adamah. hinnehi asher lecha
and I was afraid, and went away and hid thy talent in the earth: lo, thou hast thine own.

הֵשִׁיב אֲדוֹנָיו וְאָמַר אֵלָיו
heshiv adonav ve'amar elav
But his lord answered and said unto him,

עֶבֶד רַע וְעָצֵל! יָדַעְתָּ שֶׁאֲנִי קוֹצֵר בְּמָקוֹם שֶׁלֹּא זָרַעְתִּי וְאוֹסֵף בְּמָקוֹם שֶׁלֹּא פִּזַּרְתִּי
eved ra ve'atzel! yada'ta she'ani kotzer bemakom shello zara'ti ve'osef bemakom shello pizzarti
Thou wicked and slothful servant, thou knewest that I reap where I sowed not, and gather where I did not scatter;

לָכֵן הָיִיתָ צָרִיךְ לְהַפְקִיד אֶת כַּסְפִּי אֵצֶל הַשֻּׁלְחָנִים
lachen hayita tzarich lehafkid et kaspi etzel hashulchanim
thou oughtest therefore to have put my money to the bankers,

וַאֲנִי בְּבוֹאִי הָיִיתִי מְקַבֵּל אֶת שֶׁלִּי עִם הָרִבִּית
va'ani bevo'i hayiti mekabbel et shelli im haribbit
and at my coming I should have received back mine own with interest.

אַךְ הוּא הֵשִׁיב, אָמֵן אוֹמֵר אֲנִי לָכֶן, אֵינֶנִּי מַכִּיר אֶתְכֶן
ach hu heshiv, amen omer ani lachen, einenni makkir etchen
But he answered and said, Verily I say unto you, I know you not.

לָכֵן עִמְדוּ עַל הַמִּשְׁמָר, כִּי אֵינְכֶם יוֹדְעִים אֶת הַיּוֹם אַף לֹא אֶת הַשָּׁעָה
lachen imdu al hammishmar, ki einechem yode'im et hayom af lo et hasha'ah
Watch therefore, for ye know not the day nor the hour.

דּוֹמֶה הַדָּבָר לְאִישׁ הַיּוֹצֵא לְמַסָּע. קֹדֶם לָכֵן קָרָא לַעֲבָדָיו וְהִפְקִיד בְּיָדָם אֶת הוֹנוֹ
domeh haddavar le'ish hayotzei lemassa. Kodem lachen kara la'avadav vehifkid beyadam et hono
For it is as when a man, going into another country, called his own servants, and delivered unto them his goods.

לְאֶחָד נָתַן חָמֵשׁ כִּכְּרֵי כֶסֶף, לְאַחֵר שְׁתַּיִם וּלְאַחֵר אַחַת
le'echad natan chamesh kikkerei kesef, le'acher shetayim ule'acher achat
And unto one he gave five talents, to another two, to another one;

לְכָל אִישׁ לְפִי כִּשְׁרוֹנוֹ, וְנָסַע
lechol ish lefi kishrono, venasa
to each according to his several ability; and he went on his journey.

זֶה שֶׁקִּבֵּל חָמֵשׁ כִּכָּרִים הָלַךְ מִיָּד, סָחַר בָּהֶן וְהִרְוִיחַ חָמֵשׁ אֲחֵרוֹת
zeh shekkibbel chamesh kikkarim halach miyad, sachar bahen vehirviach chamesh acherot
Straightway he that received the five talents went and traded with them, and made other five talents.

כְּמוֹ כֵן זֶה שֶׁקִּבֵּל שְׁתַּיִם הִרְוִיחַ שְׁתַּיִם אֲחֵרוֹת
kemo chen zeh shekkibbel shtayim hirviach shtayim acherot
In like manner he also that received the two gained other two.

אַךְ זֶה שֶׁקִּבֵּל אַחַת הָלַךְ וְחָפַר בָּאֲדָמָה וְהִטְמִין אֶת כֶּסֶף אֲדוֹנָיו
ach zeh shekkibbel achat halach vechafar ba'adamah vehitmin et kesef adonav
But he that received the one went away and digged in the earth, and hid his lord's money.

אַחֲרֵי זְמַן רַב בָּא הָאָדוֹן שֶׁל הָעֲבָדִים הָהֵם וְעָרַךְ עִמָּהֶם חֶשְׁבּוֹן
acharei zeman rav ba ha'adon shel ha'avadim hahem ve'arach immahem cheshbon
Now after a long time the lord of those servants cometh, and maketh a reckoning with them.

כַּאֲשֶׁר נִגַּשׁ זֶה שֶׁקִּבֵּל חָמֵשׁ כִּכָּרִים הֵבִיא חָמֵשׁ כִּכָּרִים נוֹסָפוֹת וְאָמַר
ka'asher niggash zeh shekkibbel chamesh kikkarim hevi chamesh kikkarim nosafot ve'amar
And he that received the five talents came and brought other five talents, saying,

אֲדוֹנִי, חָמֵשׁ כִּכָּרִים הִפְקַדְתָּ בְּיָדִי, הִנֵּה הִרְוַחְתִּי חָמֵשׁ כִּכָּרִים נוֹסָפוֹת
adoni, chamesh kikkarim hifkadta beyadi, hinneh hirvachti chamesh kikkarim nosafot
Lord, thou deliveredst unto me five talents: lo, I have gained other five talents.

הֵשִׁיב לוֹ אֲדוֹנָיו, יָפֶה, עֶבֶד טוֹב וְנֶאֱמָן
heshiv lo adonav, yafeh, eved tov vene'eman
His lord said unto him, Well done, good and faithful servant:

חָמֵשׁ מֵהֶן הָיוּ כְּסִילוֹת וְחָמֵשׁ הָיוּ נְבוֹנוֹת
chamesh mehen hayu kesilot vechamesh hayu nevonot
And five of them were foolish, and five were wise.

שֶׁכֵּן הַכְּסִילוֹת לָקְחוּ אֶת הַמְּנוֹרוֹת וְלֹא לָקְחוּ אִתָּן שֶׁמֶן
shekken hakkesilot lakechu et hammenorot velo lakechu ittan shemen
For the foolish, when they took their lamps, took no oil with them:

אֲבָל הַנְּבוֹנוֹת לָקְחוּ שֶׁמֶן בִּכְלֵיהֶן יַחַד עִם מְנוֹרוֹתֵיהֶן
aval hannevonot lakechu shemen bichleihen yachad im menoroteihen
but the wise took oil in their vessels with their lamps.

כֵּיוָן שֶׁהִתְמַהְמַהּ הֶחָתָן נִמְנְמוּ כֻּלָּן וְנִרְדְּמוּ
keivan shehitmahmah hechatan nimnemu kullan venirdemu
Now while the bridegroom tarried, they all slumbered and slept.

בַּחֲצוֹת הַלַּיְלָה נִשְׁמְעָה קְרִיאָה, הִנֵּה הֶחָתָן, צְאֶינָה לִקְרָאתוֹ
bachatzot hallaylah nishme'ah keri'ah, hinneh hechatan, tze'einah likrato
But at midnight there is a cry, Behold, the bridegroom! Come ye forth to meet him.

אָז הִתְעוֹרְרוּ הָעֲלָמוֹת הָהֵן וְהֵכִינוּ אֶת מְנוֹרוֹתֵיהֶן
az hit'oreru ha'alamot hahen vehechinu et menoroteihen
Then all those virgins arose, and trimmed their lamps.

אָמְרוּ הַכְּסִילוֹת לַנְּבוֹנוֹת, תֵּנָּה לָנוּ מִן הַשֶּׁמֶן שֶׁלָּכֶן, כִּי מְנוֹרוֹתֵינוּ דּוֹעֲכוֹת
ameru hakkesilot lannevonot, tennah lanu min hashemen shellachen, ki menoroteinu do'achot
And the foolish said unto the wise, Give us of your oil; for our lamps are going out.

עָנוּ הַנְּבוֹנוֹת וְאָמְרוּ
anu hannevonot ve'ameru
But the wise answered, saying,

שֶׁמָּא לֹא יַסְפִּיק לָנוּ וְלָכֶן. לֵכְנָה אֶל הַמּוֹכְרִים וּקְנֶינָה בִּשְׁבִילְכֶן
shemma lo yaspik lanu velachen. Lechenah el hammocherim ukeneinah bishvilechen
Peradventure there will not be enough for us and you: go ye rather to them that sell, and buy for yourselves.

בְּשָׁעָה שֶׁהָלְכוּ לִקְנוֹת בָּא הֶחָתָן
besha'ah shehalechu liknot ba hechatan
And while they went away to buy, the bridegroom came;

הָעֲלָמוֹת הַמּוּכָנוֹת נִכְנְסוּ אִתּוֹ לַחֲתֻנָּה וְהַדֶּלֶת נִסְגְּרָה
ha'alamot hammuchanot nichnesu itto lachatunnah vehaddelet nisgerah
and they that were ready went in with him to the marriage feast: and the door was shut.

לְאַחַר מִכֵּן בָּאוּ גַּם שְׁאָר הָעֲלָמוֹת וְאָמְרוּ, אֲדוֹנֵנוּ אֲדוֹנֵנוּ, פְּתַח לָנוּ
le'achar mikken ba'u gam she'ar ha'alamot ve'ameru, adonenu adonenu, ptach lanu
Afterward came also the other virgins, saying, Lord, Lord, open to us.

וְזֹאת דְּעוּ: אִלּוּ יָדַע בַּעַל הַבַּיִת בְּאֵיזוֹ אַשְׁמוּרָה יָבוֹא הַגַּנָּב
vezot de'u. illu yada ba'al habbayit be'eizo ashmurah yavo haggannav
But know this, that if the master of the house had known in what watch the thief was coming,

הָיָה שׁוֹקֵד וְלֹא מַנִּיחַ לוֹ לַחְדֹּר לְבֵיתוֹ
hayah shoked velo mannich lo lachdor leveito
he would have watched, and would not have suffered his house to be broken through.

לָכֵן הֱיוּ מוּכָנִים גַּם אַתֶּם, כִּי בְּשָׁעָה שֶׁלֹּא תַעֲלֶה עַל דַּעְתְּכֶם יָבוֹא בֶּן־הָאָדָם
lachen heyu muchanim gam attem, ki besha'ah shello ta'aleh al da'techem yavo ben-ha'adam
Therefore be ye also ready; for in an hour that ye think not the Son of man cometh.

מִי הוּא אֵפוֹא הָעֶבֶד הַנֶּאֱמָן שֶׁהִפְקִידוֹ הָאָדוֹן עַל בְּנֵי בֵיתוֹ לָתֵת לָהֶם אֶת אָכְלָם בְּעִתּוֹ
mi hu efo ha'eved hanne'eman shehifkido ha'adon al benei beito latet lahem et achelam be'itto
Who then is the faithful and wise servant, whom his lord hath set over his household, to give them their food in due season?

אַשְׁרֵי הָעֶבֶד שֶׁיָּבוֹא אֲדוֹנָיו וְיִמְצָא אוֹתוֹ עוֹשֶׂה כֵן
ashrei ha'eved sheyavo adonav veyimtza oto oseh ken
Blessed is that servant, whom his lord when he cometh shall find so doing.

אָמֵן אוֹמֵר אֲנִי לָכֶם, הוּא יַפְקִיד אוֹתוֹ עַל כָּל אֲשֶׁר לוֹ
amen omer ani lachem, hu yafkid oto al kol asher lo
Verily I say unto you, that he will set him over all that he hath.

אֲבָל אִם הָעֶבֶד הָרַע יֹאמַר בְּלִבּוֹ אֲדוֹנִי מִתְמַהְמֵהַּ
aval im ha'eved hara yomar belibbo adoni mitmahmeah
But if that evil servant shall say in his heart, My lord tarrieth;

וְיַתְחִיל לְהַכּוֹת אֶת חֲבֵרָיו הָעֲבָדִים וְיֹאכַל וְיִשְׁתֶּה עִם הַשִּׁכּוֹרִים
veyatchil lehakkot et chaverav ha'avadim veyochal veyishteh im hashikkorim
and shall begin to beat his fellow-servants, and shall eat and drink with the drunken;

בּוֹא יָבוֹא אֲדוֹנָיו שֶׁל הָעֶבֶד הַהוּא בְּיוֹם שֶׁאֵינוֹ מְצַפֶּה לוֹ וּבְשָׁעָה שֶׁאֵינוֹ יוֹדֵעַ
bo yavo adonav shel ha'eved hahu beyom she'eino metzappeh lo uvesha'ah she'eino yodea
the lord of that servant shall come in a day when he expecteth not, and in an hour when he knoweth not,

יְשַׁסֵּף אוֹתוֹ וְיָשִׂים חֶלְקוֹ עִם הַצְּבוּעִים; שָׁם יִהְיוּ הַיְלָלָה וַחֲרוֹק הַשִּׁנַּיִם
yeshassef oto veyasim chelko im hatzevu'im; sham yihyu haylalah vacharok hashinnayim
and shall cut him asunder, and appoint his portion with the hypocrites: there shall be the weeping and the gnashing of teeth.

כה

אָז תִּדְמֶה מַלְכוּת הַשָּׁמַיִם לְעֶשֶׂר עֲלָמוֹת אֲשֶׁר לָקְחוּ אֶת מְנוֹרוֹתֵיהֶן וְיָצְאוּ לִקְרַאת הֶחָתָן
az tidmeh malchut hashamayim le'eser alamot asher lakchu et menoroteihen veyatze'u likrat hechatan
Then shall the kingdom of heaven be likened unto ten virgins, who took their lamps, and went forth to meet the bridegroom.

וְהֶעָלִים צָצִים יוֹדְעִים אַתֶּם שֶׁהַקַּיִץ קָרוֹב
vehe'alim tzatzim yode'im attem shehakkayitz karov
and putteth forth its leaves, ye know that the summer is nigh;

כֵּן גַּם אַתֶּם, כִּרְאוֹתְכֶם אֶת כָּל אֵלֶּה דְּעוּ כִּי קָרוֹב הוּא בַּפֶּתַח
ken gam attem, kir'otechem et kol elleh de'u ki karov hu bappetach
even so ye also, when ye see all these things, know ye that he is nigh, even at the doors.

אָמֵן אוֹמֵר אֲנִי לָכֶם שֶׁלֹּא יַעֲבֹר הַדּוֹר הַזֶּה עַד אֲשֶׁר יִהְיוּ כָּל אֵלֶּה
amen omer ani lachem shello ya'avor haddor hazzeh ad asher yihyu kol elleh
Verily I say unto you, This generation shall not pass away, till all these things be accomplished.

הַשָּׁמַיִם וְהָאָרֶץ יַעַבְרוּ וּדְבָרַי לֹא יַעַבְרוּ
hashamayim veha'aretz ya'avru udevarai lo ya'avru
Heaven and earth shall pass away, but my words shall not pass away.

אֲבָל אֶת הַיּוֹם הַהוּא וְהַשָּׁעָה אֵין אִישׁ יוֹדֵעַ, גַּם לֹא מַלְאֲכֵי הַשָּׁמַיִם וְגַם לֹא הַבֵּן, אֶלָּא הָאָב לְבַדּוֹ
aval et hayom hahu vehasha'ah ein ish yodea', gam lo mal'achei hashamayim vegam lo habben, ella ha'av levaddo
But of that day and hour knoweth no one, not even the angels of heaven, neither the Son, but the Father only.

כִּימֵי נֹחַ כֵּן יִהְיֶה בּוֹאוֹ שֶׁל בֶּן-הָאָדָם
kiymei noach ken yihyeh bo'o shel ben-ha'adam
And as were the days of Noah, so shall be the coming of the Son of man.

כְּמוֹ שֶׁבַּיָּמִים קֹדֶם לַמַּבּוּל
kemo shebbayamim kodem lammabbul
For as in those days which were before the flood

הָיוּ אוֹכְלִים וְשׁוֹתִים וּמִתְחַתְּנִים עַד הַיּוֹם שֶׁנִּכְנַס נֹחַ לַתֵּבָה
hayu ochelim veshotim umitchattenim ad hayom shennichnas noach lattevah
they were eating and drinking, marrying and giving in marriage, until the day that Noah entered into the ark,

וְלֹא יָדְעוּ עַד שֶׁבָּא הַמַּבּוּל וְסָחַף אֶת הַכֹּל, כָּךְ יִהְיֶה גַּם בּוֹאוֹ שֶׁל בֶּן-הָאָדָם
velo yade'u ad shebba hammabbul vesachaf et hakkol, kach yihyeh gam bo'o shel ben-ha'adam
and they knew not until the flood came, and took them all away; so shall be the coming of the Son of man.

אוֹתָהּ עֵת יִהְיוּ שְׁנַיִם בַּשָּׂדֶה, אֶחָד יִלָּקַח וְאֶחָד יֵעָזֵב
otah et yihyu shenayim bassadeh, echad yillakach ve'echad ye'azev
Then shall two men be in the field; one is taken, and one is left:

שְׁתַּיִם טוֹחֲנוֹת בָּרֵחַיִם - אַחַת תִּלָּקַח וְאַחַת תֵּעָזֵב
shetayim tochanot barechayim - achat tillakach ve'achat te'azev
two women shall be grinding at the mill; one is taken, and one is left.

עַל כֵּן עִמְדוּ עַל הַמִּשְׁמָר, כִּי אֵינְכֶם יוֹדְעִים בְּאֵיזֶה יוֹם יָבוֹא אֲדוֹנְכֶם
al ken imdu al hammishmar, ki einechem yode'im be'eizeh yom yavo adonchem
Watch therefore: for ye know not on what day your Lord cometh.

הִנֵּה מֵרֹאשׁ אָמַרְתִּי לָכֶם
hinneh merosh amarti lachem
Behold, I have told you beforehand.

לָכֵן אִם יֹאמְרוּ לָכֶם הִנְהוּ בַּמִּדְבָּר, אַל תֵּצְאוּ
lachen im yomeru lachem hinehu bammidbar, al tetze'u
If therefore they shall say unto you, Behold, he is in the wilderness; go not forth:

הִנְהוּ בְּחַדְרֵי חֲדָרִים, אַל תַּאֲמִינוּ
hinnehu bechadrei chadarim, al ta'aminu
Behold, he is in the inner chambers; believe it not.

כִּי כַּבָּרָק הַיּוֹצֵא מִמִּזְרָח וּמֵאִיר עַד מַעֲרָב כֵּן יִהְיֶה בּוֹאוֹ שֶׁל בֶּן־הָאָדָם
ki kabbarak hayotzei mimmizrach ume'ir ad ma'arav ken yihyeh bo'o shel ben-ha'adam
For as the lightning cometh forth from the east, and is seen even unto the west; so shall be the coming of the Son of man.

בַּמָּקוֹם שֶׁהַגְּוִיָּה נִמְצֵאת, שָׁם יִקָּבְצוּ הַנְּשָׁרִים
bammakom shehaggeviyah nimtzet, sham yikkavetzu hannesharim
Wheresoever the carcase is, there will the eagles be gathered together.

מִיָּד אַחֲרֵי צָרַת הַיָּמִים הָהֵם תֶּחְשַׁךְ הַשֶּׁמֶשׁ וְהַיָּרֵחַ לֹא יַגִּיהַּ אוֹרוֹ
miyad acharei tzarat hayamim hahem techshach hashemesh vehayareach lo yaggiah oro
But immediately after the tribulation of those days the sun shall be darkened, and the moon shall not give her light,

הַכּוֹכָבִים יִפְּלוּ מִן הַשָּׁמַיִם וְכֹחוֹת הַשָּׁמַיִם יִזְדַּעְזְעוּ
hakkochavim yippelu min hashamayim vechochot hashamayim yizda'ze'u
and the stars shall fall from heaven, and the powers of the heavens shall be shaken:

אָז יֵרָאֶה אוֹת בֶּן־הָאָדָם בַּשָּׁמַיִם וְאָז יִסְפְּדוּ כָּל מִשְׁפְּחוֹת הָאָרֶץ
az yera'eh ot ben-ha'adam bashamayim ve'az yispedu kol mishpechot ha'aretz
and then shall appear the sign of the Son of man in heaven: and then shall all the tribes of the earth mourn,

וְיִרְאוּ אֶת בֶּן־הָאָדָם בָּא עִם עַנְנֵי הַשָּׁמַיִם בִּגְבוּרָה וּבְכָבוֹד רָב
veyir'u et ben-ha'adam ba im anenei hashamayim bigvurah uvechavod rav
and they shall see the Son of man coming on the clouds of heaven with power and great glory.

וְהוּא יִשְׁלַח אֶת מַלְאָכָיו בְּשׁוֹפָר גָּדוֹל
vehu yishlach et mal'achav beshofar gadol
And he shall send forth his angels with a great sound of a trumpet,

וִיקַבְּצוּ אֶת בְּחִירָיו מֵאַרְבַּע הָרוּחוֹת, מִקְצוֹת הַשָּׁמַיִם עַד קְצוֹתָם
viykabbetzu et bechirav me'arba haruchot, miktzot hashamayim ad ketzotam
and they shall gather together his elect from the four winds, from one end of heaven to the other.

לִמְדוּ אֶת הַמָּשָׁל מִן הַתְּאֵנָה: כַּאֲשֶׁר עֲנָפֶיהָ מִתְרַכְּכִים
limdu et hammashal min hatte'enah: ka'asher anafeiha mitrakkechim
Now from the fig tree learn her parable: when her branch is now become tender,

אֲזַי הַנִּמְצָאִים בִּיהוּדָה, שֶׁיָּנוּסוּ אֶל הֶהָרִים
azai hannimtza'im biyehudah, sheyanusu el heharim
then let them that are in Judæa flee unto the mountains:

מִי שֶׁעַל הַגָג אַל יֵרֵד לָקַחַת חֲפָצִים מִבֵּיתוֹ
mi she'al haggag al yered lakachat chafatzim mibbeito
let him that is on the housetop not go down to take out the things that are in his house:

וּמִי שֶׁבַּשָּׂדֶה אַל יַחֲזֹר לָקַחַת אֶת בִּגְדוֹ
umi shebbassadeh al yachazor lakachat et bigdo
and let him that is in the field not return back to take his cloak.

וְאוֹי לְהָרוֹת וְלַמֵּינִיקוֹת בַּיָּמִים הָהֵם
ve'oy leharot velammeinikot bayamim hahem
But woe unto them that are with child and to them that give suck in those days!

בְּרַם הִתְפַּלְּלוּ שֶׁלֹּא תִּהְיֶה מְנוּסַתְכֶם בַּחוֹרֶף אַף לֹא בְּשַׁבָּת
beram hitpallelu shello tihyeh menusatchem bachoref af lo beshabbat
And pray ye that your flight be not in the winter, neither on a sabbath:

כִּי אָז תִּהְיֶה צָרָה גְדוֹלָה
ki az tihyeh tzarah gedolah
for then shall be great tribulation,

אֲשֶׁר לֹא הָיְתָה כָּמוֹהָ מֵרֵאשִׁית הָעוֹלָם וְעַד עַתָּה, אַף לֹא תִּהְיֶה כָּמוֹהָ
asher lo hayetah kamoha mereshit ha'olam ve'ad attah, af lo tihiyeh kamoha
such as hath not been from the beginning of the world until now, no, nor ever shall be.

וְאִלּוּלֵא קֻצְּרוּ הַיָּמִים הָהֵם לֹא הָיָה נִצָּל כָּל בָּשָׂר
ve'illulei kutzeru hayamim hahem lo hayah nitzal kol basar
And except those days had been shortened, no flesh would have been saved:

אַךְ לְמַעַן הַבְּחִירִים יְקֻצְּרוּ הַיָּמִים הָהֵם
ach lema'an habbchirim yekutzeru hayamim hahem
but for the elect's sake those days shall be shortened.

אִם יֹאמַר לָכֶם אִישׁ בָּעֵת הַהִיא, הִנֵּה פֹּה הַמָּשִׁיחַ אוֹ הִנֵּהוּ שָׁם, אַל תַּאֲמִינוּ
im yomar lachem ish ba'et hahi, hinneh poh hammashiach o hinnehu sham, al ta'aminu
Then if any man shall say unto you, Lo, here is the Christ, or, Here; believe it not.

כִּי יָקוּמוּ מְשִׁיחֵי שֶׁקֶר וּנְבִיאֵי שֶׁקֶר
ki yakumu meshichei sheker unevi'ei sheker
For there shall arise false Christs, and false prophets,

וְיִתְּנוּ אוֹתוֹת גְּדוֹלִים וּמוֹפְתִים כְּדֵי לְהַתְעוֹת, אִם אֶפְשָׁר, גַּם אֶת הַבְּחִירִים
veyittenu otot gedolim umofetim kedei lehat'ot, im efshar, gam et habbchirim
and shall show great signs and wonders; so as to lead astray, if possible, even the elect.

וְיִהְיוּ רָעָב וּרְעִידוֹת אֲדָמָה בִּמְקוֹמוֹת רַבִּים
veyihyu ra'av ure'idot adamah bimkomot rabbim
and there shall be famines and earthquakes in divers places.

אַךְ כָּל אֵלֶּה רֵאשִׁית הַצָּרוֹת
ach kol elleh reshit hatzarot
But all these things are the beginning of travail.

אָז יִמְסְרוּ אֶתְכֶם לָרוֹדְפִים וְיַהַרְגוּ אֶתְכֶם
az yimseru etchem larodefim veyahargu etchem
Then shall they deliver you up unto tribulation, and shall kill you:

וְתִהְיוּ שְׂנוּאִים עַל כָּל הַגּוֹיִים בִּגְלַל שְׁמִי
vetihyu senu'im al kol haggoyim biglal shemi
and ye shall be hated of all the nations for my name's sake.

רַבִּים יִכָּשְׁלוּ בְּאוֹתָהּ עֵת וְיַסְגִּירוּ זֶה אֶת זֶה וְיִשְׂנְאוּ זֶה אֶת זֶה
rabbim yikkashelu be'otah et veyasgiru zeh et zeh veyisne'u zeh et zeh
And then shall many stumble, and shall deliver up one another, and shall hate one another.

נְבִיאֵי שֶׁקֶר יָקוּמוּ וְיַתְעוּ רַבִּים
nevi'ei sheker yakumu veyat'u rabbim
And many false prophets shall arise, and shall lead many astray.

וּמֵאַחַר שֶׁתִּרְבֶּה הַהֶפְקֵרוּת תִּתְקָרֵר אַהֲבַת רַבִּים
ume'achar shettirbeh hahefkerut titkarer ahavat rabbim
And because iniquity shall be multiplied, the love of the many shall wax cold.

אֲבָל הַמַּחֲזִיק מַעֲמָד עַד קֵץ הוּא יִוָּשַׁע
aval hammachazik ma'amad ad ketz hu yivvasha
But he that endureth to the end, the same shall be saved.

וּבְשׂוֹרָה זוֹ שֶׁל הַמַּלְכוּת תֻּכְרַז בְּכָל הָעוֹלָם לְעֵדוּת לְכָל הַגּוֹיִים
uvesorah zo shel hammalchut tuchraz bechol ha'olam le'edut lechol haggoyim
And this gospel of the kingdom shall be preached in the whole world for a testimony unto all the nations;

וְאַחֲרֵי כֵן יָבוֹא הַקֵּץ
ve'acharei chen yavo hakketz
and then shall the end come.

לָכֵן כַּאֲשֶׁר תִּרְאוּ אֶת הַשִּׁקּוּץ הַמְשׁוֹמֵם, כַּנֶּאֱמַר בְּפִי דָּנִיֵּאל הַנָּבִיא
lachen ka'asher tir'u et hashikkutz hammeshomem, kanne'emar befi dani'el hannavi
When therefore ye see the abomination of desolation, which was spoken of through Daniel the prophet,

עוֹמֵד בְּמָקוֹם קָדוֹשׁ - עַל הַקּוֹרֵא לְהָבִין
omed bemakom kadosh - al hakkorei lehavin
standing in the holy place (let him that readeth understand),

כד

בְּצֵאתוֹ מִבֵּית הַמִּקְדָּשׁ לָלֶכֶת לְדַרְכּוֹ
betzeto mibbeit hammikdash lalechet ledarko
And Jesus went out from the temple, and was going on his way;

נִגְּשׁוּ תַּלְמִידָיו לְהַרְאוֹת לוֹ אֶת בִּנְיְנֵי הַמִּקְדָּשׁ
niggshu talmidav lehar'ot lo et binyenei hammikdash
and his disciples came to him to show him the buildings of the temple.

הֵגִיב יֵשׁוּעַ וְאָמַר לָהֶם: רוֹאִים אַתֶּם אֶת כָּל אֵלֶּה? אָמֵן אוֹמֵר אֲנִי לָכֶם
hegiv yeshua ve'amar lahem: ro'im attem et kol elleh? amen omer ani lachem
But he answered and said unto them, See ye not all these things? verily I say unto you,

לֹא תִשָּׁאֵר פֹּה אֶבֶן עַל אֶבֶן אֲשֶׁר לֹא תֻּפַּל אַרְצָה
lo tisha'er poh even al even asher lo tuppal artzah
There shall not be left here one stone upon another, that shall not be thrown down.

כַּאֲשֶׁר יָשַׁב עַל הַר הַזֵּיתִים נִגְּשׁוּ אֵלָיו הַתַּלְמִידִים לְבַדָּם וְאָמְרוּ
ka'asher yashav al har hazzeitim niggshu elav hattalmidim levaddam ve'ameru
And as he sat on the mount of Olives, the disciples came unto him privately, saying,

הַגֶּד נָא לָנוּ מָתַי יִהְיֶה הַדָּבָר הַזֶּה וּמַה הוּא אוֹת בּוֹאֲךָ וְקֵץ הָעוֹלָם
hagged na lanu matai yihyeh haddavar hazzeh umah hu ot bo'acha veketz ha'olam
Tell us, when shall these things be? and what shall be the sign of thy coming, and of the end of the world?

הֵשִׁיב יֵשׁוּעַ וְאָמַר לָהֶם: הִזָּהֲרוּ שֶׁלֹּא יַתְעֶה אֶתְכֶם אִישׁ
heshiv yeshua ve'amar lahem: hizzaharu shello yat'eh etchem ish
And Jesus answered and said unto them, Take heed that no man lead you astray.

כִּי רַבִּים יָבוֹאוּ בִּשְׁמִי וְיֹאמְרוּ אֲנִי הַמָּשִׁיחַ וְיַתְעוּ רַבִּים
ki rabbim yavo'u bishmi veyomeru ani hammashiach veyat'u rabbim
For many shall come in my name, saying, I am the Christ; and shall lead many astray.

וְאַתֶּם עֲתִידִים לִשְׁמֹעַ מִלְחָמוֹת וּשְׁמוּעוֹת מִלְחָמָה. שִׂימוּ לֵב, אַל תִּבָּהֲלוּ
ve'attem atidim lishmoa milchamot ushemu'ot milchamah. Simu lev, al tibbahalu
And ye shall hear of wars and rumors of wars; see that ye be not troubled:

כִּי צָרִיךְ לִהְיוֹת הַדָּבָר הַזֶּה, וּבְכָל זֹאת עוֹד לֹא בָּא הַקֵּץ
ki tzarich lihyot haddavar hazzeh, uvechol zot od lo ba hakketz
for these things must needs come to pass; but the end is not yet.

גּוֹי יָקוּם עַל גּוֹי וּמַמְלָכָה עַל מַמְלָכָה
goy yakum al goy umamlachah al mamlachah
For nation shall rise against nation, and kingdom against kingdom;

וּמֵהֶם תַּלְקוּ בְּבָתֵּי הַכְּנֶסֶת שֶׁלָּכֶם וְתִרְדְּפוּם מֵעִיר לָעִיר
umehem talku bevattei hakkneset shellachem vetirdefum me'ir le'ir
and some of them shall ye scourge in your synagogues, and persecute from city to city:

לְמַעַן יָבוֹא עֲלֵיכֶם כָּל דָּם נָקִי שֶׁנִשְׁפַּךְ עַל הָאָרֶץ
lema'an yavo aleichem kol dam naki shenishpach al ha'aretz
that upon you may come all the righteous blood shed on the earth,

מִדַּם הֶבֶל הַצַּדִּיק עַד דַּם זְכַרְיָה בֶּן בֶּרֶכְיָה
middam hevel hatzaddik ad dam zecharyah ben berechyah
from the blood of Abel the righteous unto the blood of Zachariah son of Barachiah,

אֲשֶׁר רְצַחְתֶּם אוֹתוֹ בֵּין הַהֵיכָל לַמִּזְבֵּחַ
asher retzachtem oto bein haheichal lamizbeach
whom ye slew between the sanctuary and the altar.

אָמֵן אוֹמֵר אֲנִי לָכֶם, בּוֹא יָבוֹא כָּל זֶה עַל הַדּוֹר הַזֶּה
amen omer ani lachem, bo yavo kol zeh al haddor hazzeh
Verily I say unto you, All these things shall come upon this generation.

יְרוּשָׁלַיִם, יְרוּשָׁלַיִם, הַהוֹרֶגֶת אֶת הַנְּבִיאִים וְסוֹקֶלֶת אֶת הַשְּׁלוּחִים אֵלֶיהָ
yerushalayim, yerushalayim, hahoreget et hannevi'im vesokelet et hasheluchim eleiha
O Jerusalem, Jerusalem, that killeth the prophets, and stoneth them that are sent unto her!

כַּמָּה פְּעָמִים חָפַצְתִּי לְקַבֵּץ אֶת בָּנַיִךְ
kamah pe'amim chafatzti lekabbetz et banayich
how often would I have gathered thy children together,

כְּתַרְנְגֹלֶת הַמְקַבֶּצֶת אֶת אֶפְרוֹחֶיהָ תַּחַת כְּנָפֶיהָ וְלֹא רְצִיתֶם
ketarnegolet hamkabbetzet et efrocheiha tachat kenafeiha velo retzitem
even as a hen gathereth her chickens under her wings, and ye would not!

הִנֵּה בֵּיתְכֶם יִנָּטֵשׁ לָכֶם
hinneh beitchem yinnatesh lachem
Behold, your house is left unto you desolate.

וַאֲנִי אוֹמֵר לָכֶם: מֵעַתָּה לֹא תִרְאוּנִי עַד אֲשֶׁר תֹּאמְרוּ
va'ani omer lachem: me'attah lo tir'uni ad asher tomru
For I say unto you, Ye shall not see me henceforth, till ye shall say,

בָּרוּךְ הַבָּא בְּשֵׁם יְהוָה
baruch habba beshem hashem
Blessed is he that cometh in the name of the Lord.

וְתוֹכָן מָלֵא גָזֵל וְתַאֲוְתָנוּת
vetochan malei gezel veta'avtanut
but within they are full from extortion and excess.

פָּרוּשׁ עִוֵּר, טַהֵר תְּחִלָּה אֶת תּוֹךְ הַכּוֹס כְּדֵי שֶׁתִּהְיֶה טְהוֹרָה גַּם מִבַּחוּץ
parush ivver, taher techillah et toch hakkos kdei shettihyeh tehorah gam mibbachutz
Thou blind Pharisee, cleanse first the inside of the cup and of the platter, that the outside thereof may become clean also.

אוֹי לָכֶם סוֹפְרִים וּפְרוּשִׁים צְבוּעִים, כִּי דּוֹמִים אַתֶּם לִקְבָרִים מְסֻיָּדִים
oy lachem soferim uferushim tzevu'im, ki domim attem likvarim mesuyadim
Woe unto you, scribes and Pharisees, hypocrites! for ye are like unto whited sepulchres,

הַנִּרְאִים יָפִים מִבַּחוּץ וְאִלּוּ תּוֹכָם מָלֵא עַצְמוֹת מֵתִים וְכָל טֻמְאָה
hannir'im yafim mibbachutz ve'illu tocham malei atzmot metim vechol tum'ah
which outwardly appear beautiful, but inwardly are full of dead men's bones, and of all uncleanness.

כָּךְ גַּם אַתֶּם: מִבַּחוּץ אַתֶּם נִרְאִים צַדִּיקִים לְעֵינֵי הַבְּרִיּוֹת, אֲבָל בִּפְנִים מְלֵאֵי צְבִיעוּת וָעָוֶל
kach gam attem. mibbachutz attem nir'im tzaddikim le'einei habberiyot, aval bifnim mele'ei tzevi'ut ve'avel
Even so ye also outwardly appear righteous unto men, but inwardly ye are full of hypocrisy and iniquity.

אוֹי לָכֶם סוֹפְרִים וּפְרוּשִׁים צְבוּעִים, כִּי בּוֹנִים אַתֶּם אֶת קִבְרֵי הַנְּבִיאִים
oy lachem soferim uferushim tzevu'im, ki bonim attem et kivrei hannevi'im
Woe unto you, scribes and Pharisees, hypocrites! for ye build the sepulchres of the prophets,

וּמְיַפִּים אֶת מַצְבוֹת הַצַּדִּיקִים
umeyappim et matzevot hatzaddikim
and garnish the tombs of the righteous,

אוֹמְרִים אַתֶּם: אִלּוּ חָיִינוּ בִּימֵי אֲבוֹתֵינוּ לֹא הָיִינוּ שֻׁתָּפִים עִמָּהֶם לִשְׁפֹּךְ אֶת דַּם הַנְּבִיאִים
omerim attem: illu chayinu bimei avoteinu lo hayinu shuttafim immahem lishpoch et dam hannevi'im
and say, If we had been in the days of our fathers, we should not have been partakers with them in the blood of the prophets.

כָּךְ אַתֶּם מְעִידִים עַל עַצְמְכֶם שֶׁבָּנִים אַתֶּם לְרוֹצְחֵי הַנְּבִיאִים
kach attem me'idim al atzmechem shebbanim attem lerotzchei hannevi'im
Wherefore ye witness to yourselves, that ye are sons of them that slew the prophets.

אַף אַתֶּם מִלְאוּ אֶת סְאַת אֲבוֹתֵיכֶם
af attem malle'u et se'at avoteichem
Fill ye up then the measure of your fathers.

נְחָשִׁים בְּנֵי צִפְעוֹנִים, אֵיךְ תִּמָּלְטוּ מִדִּין גֵּיהִנֹּם
nechashim benei tzif'onim, eich timmaltu middin geihinnom
Ye serpents, ye offspring of vipers, how shall ye escape the judgment of hell?

לָכֵן הִנְנִי שׁוֹלֵחַ לָכֶם נְבִיאִים וַחֲכָמִים וְסוֹפְרִים וּמֵהֶם תַּהַרְגוּ וְתִצְלְבוּ
lachen hineni sholeach lachem nevi'im vachachamim vesoferim umehem tahargu vetitzlevu
Therefore, behold, I send unto you prophets, and wise men, and scribes: some of them shall ye kill and crucify;

הַנִּשְׁבָּע בַּהֵיכָל אֵין בְּךָ כְּלוּם, אֲבָל הַנִּשְׁבָּע בִּזְהַב הַהֵיכָל חַיָּב
hannishba baheichal ein bechach kelum, aval hannishba bizhav haheichal chayav
Whosoever shall swear by the temple, it is nothing; but whosoever shall swear by the gold of the temple, he is a debtor.

כְּסִילִים וְעִוְרִים! מַה גָּדוֹל יוֹתֵר, הַזָּהָב אוֹ הַהֵיכָל הַמְקַדֵּשׁ אֶת הַזָּהָב
kesilim ve'ivrim! mah gadol yoter, hazzahav o haheichal hamekaddesh et hazzahav
Ye fools and blind: for which is greater, the gold, or the temple that hath sanctified the gold?

וְכֵן גַּם אוֹמְרִים אַתֶּם, הַנִּשְׁבָּע בַּמִּזְבֵּחַ אֵין בְּךָ כְּלוּם, אֲבָל הַנִּשְׁבָּע בַּקָּרְבָּן שֶׁעָלָיו - חַיָּב
vechen gam omerim attem, hannishba bammizbeach ein bechach kelum, aval hannishba bakkareban she'alav - chayav
And, Whosoever shall swear by the altar, it is nothing; but whosoever shall swear by the gift that is upon it, he is a debtor.

עִוְרִים: מַה גָּדוֹל יוֹתֵר, הַקָּרְבָּן אוֹ הַמִּזְבֵּחַ הַמְקַדֵּשׁ אֶת הַקָּרְבָּן
Ivrim: mah gadol yoter, hakkareban o hammizbeach hamkaddesh et hakkareban
Ye blind: for which is greater, the gift, or the altar that sanctifieth the gift?

לָכֵן הַנִּשְׁבָּע בַּמִּזְבֵּחַ נִשְׁבָּע בּוֹ וּבְכֹל אֲשֶׁר עָלָיו
lachen hannishba bammizbeach nishba bo uvechol asher alav
He therefore that sweareth by the altar, sweareth by it, and by all things thereon.

וְהַנִּשְׁבָּע בַּהֵיכָל נִשְׁבָּע בּוֹ וּבַשׁוֹכֵן בּוֹ
vehannishba baheichal nishba bo uvashochen bo
And he that sweareth by the temple, sweareth by it, and by him that dwelleth therein.

וְהַנִּשְׁבָּע בַּשָּׁמַיִם נִשְׁבָּע בְּכִסֵּא אֱלֹהִים וּבַיּוֹשֵׁב עָלָיו
vehannishba bashamayim nishba bechissei elohim uvayoshev alav
And he that sweareth by the heaven, sweareth by the throne of God, and by him that sitteth thereon.

אוֹי לָכֶם סוֹפְרִים וּפְרוּשִׁים צְבוּעִים, כִּי נוֹתְנִים אַתֶּם מַעַשְׂרוֹת מִמִּנְתָּה וְשֶׁבֶת וְכַמּוֹן
oy lachem soferim uferushim tzevu'im, ki notenim attem ma'asrot mimmintah veshevet vechammon
Woe unto you, scribes and Pharisees, hypocrites! for ye tithe mint and anise and cummin,

וּמַזְנִיחִים אֶת הַדְּבָרִים הַחֲשׁוּבִים יוֹתֵר שֶׁבַּתּוֹרָה - אֶת הַמִּשְׁפָּט, אֶת הַחֶסֶד וְאֶת הָאֱמוּנָה
umaznichim et haddevarim hachashuvim yoter shebbattorah - et hammishpat, et hachesed ve'et ha'emunah
and have left undone the weightier matters of the law, justice, and mercy, and faith:

צָרִיךְ הָיָה לַעֲשׂוֹת אֶת אֵלֶּה הָאַחֲרוֹנִים וְאֵין לַעֲזֹב אֶת הַדְּבָרִים הָאֲחֵרִים
tzarich hayah la'asot et elleh ha'acharonim ve'ein la'azov et haddevarim ha'acherim
but these ye ought to have done, and not to have left the other undone.

מוֹרֵי דֶרֶךְ עִוְרִים הָעוֹצְרִים אֶת הַיַּתּוּשׁ בְּמִסְנֶנֶת וּבוֹלְעִים אֶת הַגָּמָל
morei derech ivrim ha'otzerim et hayattush bemisnenet uvole'im et haggamal
Ye blind guides, that strain out the gnat, and swallow the camel!

אוֹי לָכֶם סוֹפְרִים וּפְרוּשִׁים צְבוּעִים, כִּי מְטַהֲרִים אַתֶּם אֶת הַכּוֹס וְאֶת הַקְּעָרָה מִבַּחוּץ
oy lachem soferim uferushim tzevu'im, ki metaharim attem et hakkos ve'et hakke'arah mibbachutz
Woe unto you, scribes and Pharisees, hypocrites! for ye cleanse the outside of the cup and of the platter,

אוֹהֲבִים הֵם אֶת מוֹשַׁב הָרֹאשׁ בַּסְּעוּדוֹת וְאֶת הַמּוֹשָׁבִים הָרִאשׁוֹנִים בְּבָתֵּי הַכְּנֶסֶת
ohavim hem et moshav harosh basse'udot ve'et hammoshavim harishonim bevattei hakkeneset
and love the chief place at feasts, and the chief seats in the synagogues,

וּבְרְכוֹת שָׁלוֹם בַּשְׁוָקִים וּלְהִקָּרֵא רַבִּי עַל־יְדֵי אֲנָשִׁים
uvirchot shalom bashvakim ulehikkarei rabbi al-yedei anashim
and the salutations in the marketplaces, and to be called of men, Rabbi.

אַךְ אַתֶּם אַל יִקָּרֵא לָכֶם רַבִּי, כִּי אֶחָד הוּא רַבְּכֶם וְאַתֶּם אַחִים כֻּלְּכֶם
ach attem al yikkarei lachem rabbi, ki echad hu rabbechem ve'attem achim kullchem
But be not ye called Rabbi: for one is your teacher, and all ye are brethren.

וְאַל תִּקְרְאוּ אָב לְאִישׁ מִכֶּם בָּאָרֶץ, כִּי אֶחָד הוּא אֲבִיכֶם שֶׁבַּשָּׁמַיִם
ve'al tikre'u av le'ish mikkem ba'aretz, ki echad hu avichem shebbashamayim
And call no man your father on the earth: for one is your Father, even he who is in heaven.

גַּם אַל תִּקָּרְאוּ מוֹרֵי תּוֹרָה, כִּי אֶחָד הוּא הַמּוֹרֶה שֶׁלָּכֶם - הַמָּשִׁיחַ
gam al tikkare'u morei torah, ki echad hu hammoreh shellachem - hammashiach
Neither be ye called masters: for one is your master, even the Christ.

הַגָּדוֹל בָּכֶם יִהְיֶה מְשָׁרֶתְכֶם
haggadol bachem yihyeh mesharetchem
But he that is greatest among you shall be your servant.

הַמְרוֹמֵם אֶת עַצְמוֹ יֻשְׁפַּל וְהַמַּשְׁפִּיל אֶת עַצְמוֹ יְרוֹמָם
hameromem et atzmo yushpal vehammashpil et atzmo yeromam
And whosoever shall exalt himself shall be humbled; and whosoever shall humble himself shall be exalted.

אוֹי לָכֶם סוֹפְרִים וּפְרוּשִׁים צְבוּעִים, כִּי סוֹגְרִים אַתֶּם אֶת מַלְכוּת הַשָּׁמַיִם בִּפְנֵי בְּנֵי אָדָם
oy lachem soferim uferushim tzevu'im, ki sogerim attem et malchut hashamayim bifnei benei adam
But woe unto you, scribes and Pharisees, hypocrites! because ye shut the kingdom of heaven against men:

הֵן אַתֶּם אֵינְכֶם נִכְנָסִים לְתוֹכָהּ וְגַם לַבָּאִים אֵינְכֶם מַנִּיחִים לְהִכָּנֵס
hen attem einehem nichnasim letochah vegam labba'im einchem mannichim lehikkanes
for ye enter not in yourselves, neither suffer ye them that are entering in to enter.

אוֹי לָכֶם סוֹפְרִים וּפְרוּשִׁים צְבוּעִים, כִּי סוֹבְבִים אַתֶּם בַּיָּם וּבַיַּבָּשָׁה כְּדֵי לְגַיֵּר אִישׁ אֶחָד
oy lachem soferim uferushim tzevu'im, ki sovevim attem bayam uvayabbashah kedei legayer ish echad
Woe unto you, scribes and Pharisees, hypocrites! for ye compass sea and land to make one proselyte;

וְכַאֲשֶׁר יִתְגַּיֵּר אַתֶּם עוֹשִׂים אוֹתוֹ לְבֶן גֵּיהִנּוֹם כִּפְלַיִם מִכֶּם
vecha'asher yitgayer attem osim oto leven geihinnom kiflayim mikkem
and when he is become so, ye make him twofold more a son of hell than yourselves.

אוֹי לָכֶם מוֹרֵי דֶרֶךְ עִוְרִים הָאוֹמְרִים
oy lachem morei derech ivrim ha'omerim
Woe unto you, ye blind guides, that say,

נְאֻם יְהוָה לַאדֹנִי: שֵׁב לִימִינִי עַד־אָשִׁית אֹיְבֶיךָ הֲדֹם לְרַגְלֶיךָ
ne'um hashem ladoni: shev limini ad-'ashit oyeveicha hadom leragleicha
The Lord said unto my Lord, Sit thou on my right hand, Till I put thine enemies underneath thy feet?

וּבְכֵן אִם דָּוִד קוֹרֵא לוֹ אָדוֹן כֵּיצַד הוּא בְּנוֹ
uvechen im david korei lo adon keitzad hu beno
If David then calleth him Lord, how is he his son?

אַף אֶחָד לֹא הָיָה יָכוֹל לַעֲנוֹת לוֹ דָּבָר, וּמֵאוֹתוֹ יוֹם גַּם לֹא הֵעֵז אִישׁ לְהוֹסִיף לִשְׁאֹל אוֹתוֹ
af echad lo hayah yachol la'anot lo davar, ume'oto yom gam lo he'ez ish lehosif lish'ol oto
And no one was able to answer him a word, neither durst any man from that day forth ask him any more questions.

כג

אָז דִּבֶּר יֵשׁוּעַ אֶל הֲמוֹן הָעָם וְאֶל תַּלְמִידָיו
az dibber yeshua el hamon ha'am ve'el talmidav
Then spake Jesus to the multitudes and to his disciples,

אָמַר לָהֶם: הַסּוֹפְרִים וְהַפְּרוּשִׁים יוֹשְׁבִים עַל כִּסֵּא מֹשֶׁה
amar lahem: hassoferim vehapperushim yoshevim al kissei mosheh
saying, The scribes and the Pharisees sit on Moses' seat:

לָכֵן כָּל אֲשֶׁר יֹאמְרוּ לָכֶם עֲשׂוּ וְשִׁמְרוּ
lachen kol asher yomeru lachem asu veshimru
all things therefore whatsoever they bid you, these do and observe:

אַךְ כְּמַעֲשֵׂיהֶם אַל תַּעֲשׂוּ, כִּי אוֹמְרִים הֵם וְאֵינָם עוֹשִׂים
ach kema'aseihem al ta'asu, ki omerim hem ve'einam osim
but do not ye after their works; for they say, and do not.

הֵם קוֹשְׁרִים מַשָּׂאוֹת כְּבֵדִים וּמַעֲמִיסִים אוֹתָם עַל שִׁכְמֵי הָאֲנָשִׁים
hem kosherim masho'ot kevedim uma'amisim otam al shichmei ha'anashim
Yea, they bind heavy burdens and grievous to be borne, and lay them on men's shoulders;

אַךְ אֵינָם רוֹצִים לְהָנִיעַ אוֹתָם אַף בְּאֶצְבָּעָם
ach einam rotzim lehania otam af be'etzba'am
but they themselves will not move them with their finger.

וְעוֹשִׂים אֶת כָּל מַעֲשֵׂיהֶם כְּדֵי לְהֵרָאוֹת לִבְנֵי אָדָם
ve'osim et kol ma'aseihem kedei lehera'ot livnei adam
But all their works they do to be seen of men:

בְּהַרְחִיבָם אֶת תְּפִלֵּיהֶם וּבְהַאֲרִיכָם אֶת צִיצִיּוֹתֵיהֶם
beharchivam et tefilleihem uveha'aricham et tzitziyoteihem
for they make broad their phylacteries, and enlarge the borders of their garments,

אָנֹכִי אֱלֹהֵי אַבְרָהָם, אֱלֹהֵי יִצְחָק וֵאלֹהֵי יַעֲקֹב? אֵין הוּא אֱלֹהֵי הַמֵּתִים כִּי אִם אֱלֹהֵי הַחַיִּים
anochi elohei avraham, elohei yitzchak velohei ya'akov? ein hu elohei hammetim ki im elohei hachayim
I am the God of Abraham, and the God of Isaac, and the God of Jacob? God is not the God of the dead, but of the living.

שָׁמְעוּ זֹאת הַהֲמוֹנִים וְהִשְׁתּוֹמְמוּ עַל תּוֹרָתוֹ
shame'u zot hahamonim vehishtomemu al torato
And when the multitudes heard it, they were astonished at his teaching.

כַּאֲשֶׁר שָׁמְעוּ הַפְּרוּשִׁים כִּי הִשְׁתִּיק אֶת הַצְּדוֹקִים, נֶאֶסְפוּ יַחְדָּיו
ka'asher shame'u happerushim ki hishtik et hatzedokim, ne'esfu yachdav
But the Pharisees, when they heard that he had put the Sadducees to silence, gathered themselves together.

וְאֶחָד מִבַּעֲלֵי הַתּוֹרָה שֶׁבֵּינֵיהֶם שָׁאַל אוֹתוֹ כְּדֵי לְנַסּוֹתוֹ
ve'echad mibba'alei hattorah shebbeineihem sha'al oto kedei lenassoto
And one of them, a lawyer, asked him a question, trying him:

רַבִּי, אֵיזוֹהִי הַמִּצְוָה הַגְּדוֹלָה שֶׁבַּתּוֹרָה
rabbi, eizohi hammitzvah haggedolah shebbattorah
Teacher, which is the great commandment in the law?

הֵשִׁיב לוֹ יֵשׁוּעַ: וְאָהַבְתָּ אֵת יְהוָה אֱלֹהֶיךָ בְּכָל-לְבָבְךָ וּבְכָל-נַפְשְׁךָ וּבְכָל מְאֹדֶךָ
heshiv lo yeshua: ve'ahavta et hashem eloheicha bechol-levavecha uvechol-nafshecha uvechol me'odecha
And he said unto him, Thou shalt love the Lord thy God with all thy heart, and with all thy soul, and with all thy mind.

זֹאת הַמִּצְוָה הַגְּדוֹלָה וְהָרִאשׁוֹנָה
zot hammitzvah haggedolah veharishonah
This is the great and first commandment.

הַשְּׁנִיָּה דּוֹמָה לָהּ: וְאָהַבְתָּ לְרֵעֲךָ כָּמוֹךָ
hasheniyah domah lah. ve'ahavta lere'acha kamocha
And a second like unto it is this, Thou shalt love thy neighbor as thyself.

בִּשְׁתֵּי מִצְווֹת אֵלֶּה תְּלוּיָה כָּל הַתּוֹרָה וְהַנְּבִיאִים
bishtei mitzvot elleh teluyah kol hattorah vehannevi'im
On these two commandments the whole law hangeth, and the prophets.

כְּשֶׁנִּקְהֲלוּ הַפְּרוּשִׁים שָׁאַל אוֹתָם יֵשׁוּעַ
keshennik'halu happerushim sha'al otam yeshua
Now while the Pharisees were gathered together, Jesus asked them a question,

מַה דַּעְתְּכֶם עַל הַמָּשִׁיחַ? בֶּן מִי הוּא? הֵשִׁיבוּ לוֹ: בֶּן-דָּוִד
mah da'techem al hammashiach? ben mi hu? heshivu lo. ben-david
saying, What think ye of the Christ? whose son is he? They say unto him, The son of David.

אָמַר לָהֶם: אִם כֵּן כֵּיצַד, בְּהַשְׁרָאַת הָרוּחַ, קוֹרֵא לוֹ דָּוִד אָדוֹן בְּאָמְרוֹ
amar lahem. im ken keitzad, behashra'at haruach, korei lo david adon be'omro
He saith unto them, How then doth David in the Spirit call him Lord, saying,

אָמַר לָהֶם: אִם כֵּן, תְּנוּ לַקֵּיסָר אֶת אֲשֶׁר לַקֵּיסָר וְלֵאלֹהִים אֶת אֲשֶׁר לֵאלֹהִים
'amar lahem. Im ken, tenu lakkeisar et asher lakkeisar vele'elohim et asher lelohim
Then saith he unto them, Render therefore unto Cæsar the things that are Cæsar's; and unto God the things that are God's.

כְּשָׁמְעָם זֹאת הִשְׁתּוֹמְמוּ, הִנִּיחוּ לוֹ וְהָלְכוּ
keshame'am zot hishtomemu, hinnichu lo vehalechu
And when they heard it, they marvelled, and left him, and went away.

בְּאוֹתוֹ יוֹם נִגְּשׁוּ אֵלָיו צְדוֹקִים, הָאוֹמְרִים שֶׁאֵין תְּחִיַּת מֵתִים, וְשָׁאֲלוּ אוֹתוֹ
be'oto yom niggeshu elav tzedokim, ha'omerim she'ein techiyat metim, vesha'alu oto
On that day there came to him Sadducees, they that say that there is no resurrection: and they asked him,

רַבִּי, מֹשֶׁה אָמַר
rabbi, mosheh amar
saying, Teacher, Moses said

אִישׁ אִם יָמוּת וּבָנִים אֵין לוֹ, יִקַּח אָחִיו אֶת אִשְׁתּוֹ וְיָקִים זֶרַע לְאָחִיו
ish im yamut uvanim ein lo, yikkach achiv et ishto veyakim zera le'achiv
If a man die, having no children, his brother shall marry his wife, and raise up seed unto his brother.

וּבְכֵן הָיוּ עִמָּנוּ שִׁבְעָה אַחִים. הָרִאשׁוֹן הִתְחַתֵּן וּמֵת, וְכֵיוָן שֶׁלֹּא הָיוּ לוֹ יְלָדִים הִשְׁאִיר אֶת אִשְׁתּוֹ לְאָחִיו
uvechen hayu immanu shiv'ah achim. harishon hitchatten umet, vecheivan shello hayu lo yeladim hish'ir et ishto le'achiv
Now there were with us seven brethren: and the first married and deceased, and having no seed left his wife unto his brother;

כָּךְ גַּם הַשֵּׁנִי וְהַשְּׁלִישִׁי עַד הַשְּׁבִיעִי
kach gam hasheni vehashelishi ad hashevi'i
in like manner the second also, and the third, unto the seventh.

וְאַחֲרֵי כֻלָּם מֵתָה הָאִשָּׁה
ve'acharei kullam metah ha'ishah
And after them all, the woman died.

אִם כֵּן לְמִי מֵהַשִּׁבְעָה תִּהְיֶה לְאִשָּׁה בִּתְחִיַּת הַמֵּתִים, שֶׁהֲרֵי הָיְתָה שַׁיֶּכֶת לְכֻלָּם
im ken lemi mehashiv'ah tihyeh le'ishah bitchiyat hammetim, sheharei hayetah shayechet lechullam
In the resurrection therefore whose wife shall she be of the seven? for they all had her.

הֵשִׁיב לָהֶם יֵשׁוּעַ וְאָמַר: אַתֶּם טוֹעִים מִשּׁוּם שֶׁאֵינְכֶם יוֹדְעִים אֶת הַכְּתוּבִים, אַף לֹא אֶת גְּבוּרַת הָאֱלֹהִים
heshiv lahem yeshua ve'amar: attem to'im mishum she'einechem yode'im et hakketuvim, af lo et gevurat ha'elohim
But Jesus answered and said unto them, Ye do err, not knowing the scriptures, nor the power of God.

בַּתְּחִיָּה אֵין הָאֲנָשִׁים מִתְחַתְּנִים, אֶלָּא שֶׁהֵם כְּמַלְאֲכֵי שָׁמַיִם
battechiyah ein ha'anashim mitchattenim, ella shehem kemal'achei shamayim
For in the resurrection they neither marry, nor are given in marriage, but are as angels in heaven.

וַאֲשֶׁר לִתְחִיַּת הַמֵּתִים, הַאִם לֹא קְרָאתֶם מַה שֶּׁנֶּאֱמַר לָכֶם מִפִּי אֱלֹהִים
va'asher litchiyat hammetim, ha'im lo keratem mah shenne'emar lachem mippi elohim
But as touching the resurrection of the dead, have ye not read that which was spoken unto you by God, saying,

אָמַר הַמֶּלֶךְ לַמְשָׁרְתִים, קִשְׁרוּ אֶת יָדָיו וְרַגְלָיו וְהַשְׁלִיכוּהוּ אֶל הַחֹשֶׁךְ הַחִיצוֹן
amar hammelech lamsharetim, kishru et yadav veraglav vehashlichuhu el hachoshech hachitzon
Then the king said to the servants, Bind him hand and foot, and cast him out into the outer darkness;

שָׁם יִהְיוּ הַיְלָלָה וַחֲרֹק הַשִּׁנַּיִם
sham yihyu haylalah vacharok hashinnayim
there shall be the weeping and the gnashing of teeth.

הֵן רַבִּים הַקְּרוּאִים וּמְעַטִּים הַנִּבְחָרִים
hen rabbim hakkeru'im ume'attim hannivcharim
For many are called, but few chosen.

הָלְכוּ הַפְּרוּשִׁים וְהִתְיָעֲצוּ לְהַכְשִׁיל אוֹתוֹ בִּדְבָרוֹ
halechu happerushim vehitya'atzu lehachshil oto bidvaro
Then went the Pharisees, and took counsel how they might ensnare him in his talk.

שָׁלְחוּ אֵלָיו אֶת תַּלְמִידֵיהֶם יַחַד עִם חֲסִידֵי בֵּית הוֹרְדוֹס וְהַלְלוּ אָמְרוּ
shalchu elav et talmideihem yachad im chasidei beit horedos vehallalu ameru
And they send to him their disciples, with the Herodians, saying,

רַבִּי, אֲנַחְנוּ יוֹדְעִים שֶׁאַתָּה אִישׁ אֱמֶת וְאֶת דֶּרֶךְ אֱלֹהִים אַתָּה מוֹרֶה עַל-פִּי הָאֱמֶת. גַּם אֵינְךָ חוֹשֵׁשׁ מֵאִישׁ
rabbi, anachnu yode'im she'attah ish emet ve'et derech elohim attah moreh al-pi ha'emet. gam einecha choshesh me'ish
Teacher, we know that thou art true, and teachest the way of God in truth, and carest not for any one:

כִּי אֵינְךָ נוֹשֵׂא פָנִים לָאֲנָשִׁים
ki eincha nosei panim la'anashim
for thou regardest not the person of men.

עַל כֵּן אֱמֹר נָא לָנוּ, מַה דַּעְתְּךָ: הַאִם מֻתָּר לָתֵת מַס לַקֵּיסָר אוֹ לֹא
al ken emor na lanu, mah da'techa: ha'im muttar latet mas lakkeisar o lo
Tell us therefore, What thinkest thou? Is it lawful to give tribute unto Cæsar, or not?

הִבְחִין יֵשׁוּעַ בְּרִשְׁעָתָם וְאָמַר: לָמָּה אַתֶּם מְנַסִּים אוֹתִי? צְבוּעִים
hivchin yeshua berish'atam ve'amar: lammah attem menassim oti? tzevu'im
But Jesus perceived their wickedness, and said, Why make ye trial of me, ye hypocrites?

הַרְאוּ לִי אֶת מַטְבֵּעַ הַמַּס. הִגִּישׁוּ לוֹ דִּינָר
har'u li et matbea hammas. higgishu lo dinar
Show me the tribute money. And they brought unto him a denarius.

שָׁאַל אוֹתָם: שֶׁל מִי הַדְּמוּת הַזֹּאת וְהַכְּתֹבֶת
sha'al otam. shel mi haddemut hazzot vehakketovet
And he saith unto them, Whose is this image and superscription?

הֵשִׁיבוּ: שֶׁל הַקֵּיסָר
heshivu. shel hakkeisar.
They say unto him, Cæsar's.

שָׁלַח אֶת עֲבָדָיו לִקְרֹא אֶת הַמֻּזְמָנִים אֶל הַחֲתֻנָּה וְלֹא רָצוּ לָבוֹא
shalach et avadav likro et hammuzmanim el hachatunnah velo ratzu lavo
and sent forth his servants to call them that were bidden to the marriage feast: and they would not come.

הוֹסִיף לִשְׁלֹחַ עֲבָדִים אֲחֵרִים שֶׁיֹּאמְרוּ לַמֻּזְמָנִים, הִנֵּה עָרַכְתִּי אֶת סְעוּדָתִי
hosif lishloach avadim acherim sheyomeru lammuzmanim, hinneh arachti et se'udati
Again he sent forth other servants, saying, Tell them that are bidden, Behold, I have made ready my dinner;

הַשְּׁוָרִים וְהַבָּקָר הַמְפֻטָּם טְבוּחִים וְהַכֹּל מוּכָן. בֹּאוּ לַחֲתֻנָּה
hashevarim vehabbakar hamfuttam tevuchim vehakkol muchan. Bo'u lachatunnah
my oxen and my fatlings are killed, and all things are ready: come to the marriage feast.

אַךְ הֵם לֹא שָׂמוּ לֵב וְהָלְכוּ לָהֶם זֶה אֶל שָׂדֵהוּ וְזֶה אֶל מִסְחָרוֹ
ach hem lo samu lev vehalechu lahem zeh el sadehu vezeh el mischaro
But they made light of it, and went their ways, one to his own farm, another to his merchandise;

וְהַנּוֹתָרִים תָּפְסוּ אֶת עֲבָדָיו, הִתְעַלְּלוּ בָּהֶם וַהֲרָגוּם
vehannotarim tafesu et avadav, hit'allelu bahem vaharagum
and the rest laid hold on his servants, and treated them shamefully, and killed them.

הַמֶּלֶךְ נִתְמַלֵּא חֵמָה; שָׁלַח אֶת חֲיָלָיו וְהִשְׁמִיד אֶת הַמְרַצְּחִים הָהֵם וְשָׂרַף אֶת עִירָם בָּאֵשׁ
hammelech nitmallei chemah; shalach et chayalav vehishmid et hamratzechim hahem vesaraf et iram ba'esh
But the king was wroth; and he sent his armies, and destroyed those murderers, and burned their city.

אָז אָמַר אֶל עֲבָדָיו, הִנֵּה הַחֲתֻנָּה מוּכָנָה, אַךְ אֵלֶּה שֶׁהֻזְמְנוּ לֹא הָיוּ רְאוּיִים
az amar el avadav, hinneh hachatunnah muchanah, ach elleh shehuzmenu lo hayu re'uyim
Then saith he to his servants, The wedding is ready, but they that were bidden were not worthy.

לָכֵן לְכוּ אֶל פָּרָשׁוֹת הַדְּרָכִים וְכָל מִי שֶׁתִּמְצְאוּ קִרְאוּ אוֹתוֹ לַחֲתֻנָּה
lachen lechu el parashot hadderachim vechol mi shettimtze'u kir'u oto lachatunnah
Go ye therefore unto the partings of the highways, and as many as ye shall find, bid to the marriage feast.

יָצְאוּ הָעֲבָדִים הָהֵם אֶל הַדְּרָכִים וְאָסְפוּ אֶת כָּל מִי שֶׁמָּצְאוּ, גַּם רָעִים וְגַם טוֹבִים
yatze'u ha'avadim hahem el hadderachim ve'asefu et kol mi shemmatze'u, gam ra'im vegam tovim
And those servants went out into the highways, and gathered together all as many as they found, both bad and good:

וְנִתְמַלֵּא אוּלָם הַחֲתֻנָּה מְסֻבִּים
venitmallei ulam hachatunnah mesubbim
and the wedding was filled with guests.

כְּשֶׁבָּא הַמֶּלֶךְ לִרְאוֹת אֶת הַמְסֻבִּים רָאָה שָׁם אִישׁ שֶׁאֵינֶנּוּ לָבוּשׁ בִּגְדֵי חֲתֻנָּה
kshebba hammelech lir'ot et hamsubbim ra'ah sham ish she'einennu lavush bigdei chatunnah
But when the king came in to behold the guests, he saw there a man who had not on a wedding-garment:

אָמַר אֵלָיו, חָבֵר, אֵיךְ בָּאתָ לְכָאן בְּלִי בִּגְדֵי חֲתֻנָּה? הַלָּה הֶחֱרִישׁ
amar elav, chaver, eich bata lechan beli bigdei chatunnah? hallah hecherish
and he saith unto him, Friend, how camest thou in hither not having a wedding-garment? And he was speechless.

הֵשִׁיבוּ לוֹ: הַשְׁמֵד יַשְׁמִיד אֶת הָרְשָׁעִים הָהֵם
heshivu lo: hashmed yashmid et haresha'im hahem
They say unto him, He will miserably destroy those miserable men,

וְאֶת הַכֶּרֶם יַחְכִּיר לְכוֹרְמִים אֲחֵרִים אֲשֶׁר יָשִׁיבוּ לוֹ אֶת הַפְּרִי בְּעִתּוֹ
ve'et hakkerem yachkir lechoremim acherim asher yashivu lo et happeri be'itto
and will let out the vineyard unto other husbandmen, who shall render him the fruits in their seasons.

אָמַר לָהֶם יֵשׁוּעַ: הַאִם לֹא קְרָאתֶם בַּכְּתוּבִים, אֶבֶן מָאֲסוּ הַבּוֹנִים
amar lahem yeshua: ha'im lo keratem bakketuvim, even ma'asu habbonim
Jesus saith unto them, Did ye never read in the scriptures, The stone which the builders rejected,

הָיְתָה לְרֹאשׁ פִּנָּה; מֵאֵת יְהוָה הָיְתָה זֹּאת, הִיא נִפְלָאת בְּעֵינֵינוּ
hayetah lerosh pinnah; me'et hashem hayetah zot, hi niflat be'eineinu
The same was made the head of the corner; This was from the Lord, And it is marvellous in our eyes?

עַל כֵּן אֲנִי אוֹמֵר לָכֶם
al ken ani omer lachem
Therefore say I unto you,

כִּי תִּלָּקַח מִכֶּם מַלְכוּת הָאֱלֹהִים וְתִנָּתֵן לְגוֹי אֲשֶׁר יָפִיק אֶת פִּרְיָהּ
ki tillakach mikkem malchut ha'elohim vetinnaten legoy asher yafik et piryah
The kingdom of God shall be taken away from you, and shall be given to a nation bringing forth the fruits thereof.

וְהַנּוֹפֵל עַל הָאֶבֶן הַזֹּאת יִשָּׁבֵר לִרְסִיסִים, וְכֹל מִי שֶׁתִּפֹּל עָלָיו תִּכְתֹּשׁ אוֹתוֹ
vehannofel al ha'even hazzot yishaver liresisim, vechol mi shettippol alav tichtosh oto
And he that falleth on this stone shall be broken to pieces: but on whomsoever it shall fall, it will scatter him as dust.

כַּאֲשֶׁר שָׁמְעוּ רָאשֵׁי הַכֹּהֲנִים וְהַפְּרוּשִׁים אֶת מְשָׁלָיו הֵבִינוּ כִּי עֲלֵיהֶם הוּא מְדַבֵּר
ka'asher shame'u rashei hakkohanim vhapperushim et meshalav hevinu ki aleihem hu medabber
And when the chief priests and the Pharisees heard his parables, they perceived that he spake of them.

הֵם בִּקְשׁוּ לִתְפֹּס אוֹתוֹ, אֲבָל חָשְׁשׁוּ מִפְּנֵי הֲמוֹנֵי הָעָם, שֶׁכֵּן אֵלֶּה חֲשָׁבוּהוּ לְנָבִיא
hem bikshu litpos oto, aval chasheshu mippenei hamonei ha'am, shekken elleh chashavuhu lenavi
And when they sought to lay hold on him, they feared the multitudes, because they took him for a prophet.

כב

יֵשׁוּעַ הוֹסִיף לְדַבֵּר אֲלֵיהֶם בִּמְשָׁלִים וְאָמַר
yeshua hosif ledabber aleihem bimshalim ve'amar
And Jesus answered and spake again in parables unto them, saying,

דּוֹמָה מַלְכוּת הַשָּׁמַיִם לְמֶלֶךְ בָּשָׂר וָדָם שֶׁעָשָׂה חֲתֻנָּה לִבְנוֹ
domah malchut hashamayim lemelech basar vadam she'asah chatunnah livno
The kingdom of heaven is likened unto a certain king, who made a marriage feast for his son,

אַתֶּם לְעֻמַּת זֹאת רְאִיתֶם וְלֹא חֲזַרְתֶּם בָּכֶם אַחֲרֵי כֵן לְהַאֲמִין לוֹ
attem le'ummat zot re'item velo chazartem bachem acharei chen leha'amin lo
and ye, when ye saw it, did not even repent yourselves afterward, that ye might believe him.

שִׁמְעוּ מָשָׁל אַחֵר: אִישׁ בַּעַל אֲחֻזָּה נָטַע כֶּרֶם
shim'u mashal acher. ish ba'al achuzzah nata kerem
Hear another parable: There was a man that was a householder, who planted a vineyard,

הוּא גִּדֵּר אוֹתוֹ מִסָּבִיב, חָצַב בּוֹ יֶקֶב וּבָנָה מִגְדָּל
hu gidder oto missaviv, chatzav bo yekev uvanah migdal
and set a hedge about it, and digged a winepress in it, and built a tower,

וּלְאַחַר שֶׁהֶחְכִּיר אוֹתוֹ לְכוֹרְמִים נָסַע
ule'achar shehechkir oto lechoremim nasa
and let it out to husbandmen, and went into another country.

בְּהַגִּיעַ עֵת הַבָּצִיר שָׁלַח אֶת עֲבָדָיו אֶל הַכּוֹרְמִים לְקַבֵּל אֶת הַפְּרִי שֶׁלּוֹ
behaggia et habbatzir shalach et avadav el hakkoremim lekabbel et happeri shello
And when the season of the fruits drew near, he sent his servants to the husbandmen, to receive his fruits.

תָּפְסוּ הַכּוֹרְמִים אֶת עֲבָדָיו, אֶת זֶה הִלְקוּ, אֶת זֶה הָרְגוּ וְאֶת זֶה סָקְלוּ
tafesu hakkoremim et avadav, et zeh hilku, et zeh haregu ve'et zeh sakelu
And the husbandmen took his servants, and beat one, and killed another, and stoned another.

הוֹסִיף וְשָׁלַח עֲבָדִים אֲחֵרִים, רַבִּים מִן הָרִאשׁוֹנִים, וְגַם לָהֶם עָשׂוּ כָּךְ
hosif veshalach avadim acherim, rabbim min harishonim, vegam lahem asu kach
Again, he sent other servants more than the first: and they did unto them in like manner.

לְבַסּוֹף שָׁלַח אֲלֵיהֶם אֶת בְּנוֹ בְּאָמְרוֹ, אֶת בְּנִי יְכַבְּדוּ
levassof shalach aleihem et beno be'omro, et beni yechabbdu
But afterward he sent unto them his son, saying, They will reverence my son.

כְּשֶׁרָאוּ הַכּוֹרְמִים אֶת הַבֵּן אָמְרוּ אִישׁ אֶל רֵעֵהוּ
keshera'u hakkoremim et habben ameru ish el re'ehu
But the husbandmen, when they saw the son, said among themselves,

זֶה הַיּוֹרֵשׁ, בּוֹאוּ נַהֲרֹג אוֹתוֹ וְנִקַּח לָנוּ אֶת נַחֲלָתוֹ
zeh hayoresh, bo'u naharog oto venikkach lanu et nachalato
This is the heir; come, let us kill him, and take his inheritance.

הֵם תָּפְסוּ אוֹתוֹ, גֵּרְשׁוּהוּ אֶל מִחוּץ לַכֶּרֶם וַהֲרָגוּהוּ
hem tafesu oto, gereshuhu el michutz lakkerem vaharaguhu
And they took him, and cast him forth out of the vineyard, and killed him.

וּבְכֵן, כְּשֶׁיָּבוֹא בַּעַל הַכֶּרֶם מַה יַּעֲשֶׂה לַכּוֹרְמִים הָהֵם
uvechen, kesheyavo ba'al hakkerem mah ya'aseh lakkoremim hahem
When therefore the lord of the vineyard shall come, what will he do unto those husbandmen?

אָז חָשְׁבוּ בְּלִבָבָם: אִם נֹאמַר מִן הַשָּׁמַיִם, יֹאמַר לָנוּ
az chashevu bilvavam: im nomar min hashamayim, yomar lanu
And they reasoned with themselves, saying, If we shall say, From heaven; he will say unto us,

אִם כֵּן מַדּוּעַ לֹא הֶאֱמַנְתֶּם לוֹ
im ken maddua lo he'emantem lo
Why then did ye not believe him?

וְאִם נֹאמַר מִבְּנֵי אָדָם, חוֹשְׁשִׁים אָנוּ מִן הָעָם, כִּי כֻּלָּם חוֹשְׁבִים אֶת יוֹחָנָן לְנָבִיא
ve'im nomar mibbenei adam, chosheshim anu min ha'am, ki kullam choshevim et yochanan lenavi
But if we shall say, From men; we fear the multitude; for all hold John as a prophet.

הֵשִׁיבוּ וְאָמְרוּ לְיֵשׁוּעַ: אֵין אָנוּ יוֹדְעִים
heshivu ve'ameru leyeshua. Ein anu yode'im.
And they answered Jesus, and said, We know not.

אָמַר לָהֶם: גַּם אֲנִי לֹא אֹמַר לָכֶם בְּאֵיזוֹ סַמְכוּת אֲנִי עוֹשֶׂה אֶת הַדְּבָרִים הָאֵלֶּה
amar lahem. Gam ani lo omar lachem be'eizo samchut ani oseh et haddevarim
He also said unto them, Neither tell I you by what authority I do these things.

אֲבָל מַה דַּעְתְּכֶם: לְאִישׁ הָיוּ שְׁנֵי בָנִים. הוּא נִגַּשׁ אֶל הָרִאשׁוֹן וְאָמַר, בְּנִי, לֵךְ לַעֲבֹד הַיּוֹם בַּכֶּרֶם
aval mah da'techem. Le'ish hayu shenei banim. hu niggash el harishon ve'amar, beni, lech la'avod hayom bakkerem
But what think ye? A man had two sons; and he came to the first, and said, Son, go work to-day in the vineyard.

הֵשִׁיב הָרִאשׁוֹן, אֵינֶנִּי רוֹצֶה, אֲבָל לְאַחַר מִכֵּן הִתְחָרֵט וְהָלַךְ
heshiv harishon, einenni rotzeh, aval le'achar mikken hitcharet vehalach
And he answered and said, I will not: but afterward he repented himself, and went.

נִגַּשׁ אֶל הַשֵּׁנִי וְאָמַר לוֹ אוֹתוֹ דָּבָר. הֵשִׁיב הַשֵּׁנִי, 'כֵּן, אֲדוֹנִי' וְלֹא הָלַךְ
niggash el hasheni ve'amar lo oto davar. heshiv hasheni, ken, adoni velo halach
And he came to the second, and said likewise. And he answered and said, I go, sir: and went not.

מִי מִשְּׁנֵיהֶם עָשָׂה אֶת רְצוֹן הָאָב? הֵשִׁיבוּ: הָרִאשׁוֹן. אָמַר לָהֶם יֵשׁוּעַ
mi misheneihem asah et retzon ha'av? heshivu. harishon. amar lahem yeshua
Which of the two did the will of his father? They say, The first. Jesus saith unto them,

אָמֵן אוֹמֵר אֲנִי לָכֶם, הַמּוֹכְסִים וְהַזּוֹנוֹת יָבוֹאוּ לִפְנֵיכֶם לְמַלְכוּת הָאֱלֹהִים
amen omer ani lachem, hammochesim vehazzonot yavo'u lifneichem lemalchut ha'elohim
Verily I say unto you, that the publicans and the harlots go into the kingdom of God before you.

כִּי יוֹחָנָן בָּא אֲלֵיכֶם בְּדֶרֶךְ צְדָקָה וְלֹא הֶאֱמַנְתֶּם לוֹ
ki yochanan ba aleichem bederech tzedakah velo he'emantem lo
For John came unto you in the way of righteousness, and ye believed him not;

אֲבָל הַמּוֹכְסִים וְהַזּוֹנוֹת הֶאֱמִינוּ לוֹ
aval hammochesim vehazzonot he'eminu lo
but the publicans and the harlots believed him:

כְּשֶׁרָאָה עֵץ תְּאֵנָה אֶחָד בַּדֶּרֶךְ הִתְקָרֵב אֵלָיו וְלֹא מָצָא בּוֹ מְאוּמָה מִלְּבַד עָלִים. אָמַר אֵלָיו
keshera'ah etz te'enah echad badderech hitkarev elav velo matza bo me'umah millevad alim. amar elav
And seeing a fig tree by the way side, he came to it, and found nothing thereon, but leaves only; and he saith unto it,

מֵעַתָּה לֹא יִהְיֶה מִמְּךָ פְּרִי לְעוֹלָם! וּבוֹ בָרֶגַע הִתְיַבֵּשׁ עֵץ הַתְּאֵנָה
me'attah lo yihyeh mimmecha peri le'olam! uvo barega hityabbesh etz hatte'enah
Let there be no fruit from thee henceforward for ever. And immediately the fig tree withered away.

כִּרְאוֹתָם זֹאת תָּמְהוּ הַתַּלְמִידִים וְאָמְרוּ: אֵיךְ יָבֵשׁ עֵץ הַתְּאֵנָה פִּתְאוֹם
kir'otam zot tamehu hattalmidim ve'ameru. Eich yavash etz hatte'enah pit'om
And when the disciples saw it, they marvelled, saying, How did the fig tree immediately wither away?

הֵשִׁיב לָהֶם יֵשׁוּעַ
heshiv lahem yeshua
And Jesus answered and said unto them,

אָמֵן אוֹמֵר אֲנִי לָכֶם, אִם יֵשׁ לָכֶם אֱמוּנָה וְאֵינְכֶם מְפַקְפְּקִים, לֹא רַק כְּמַעֲשֵׂה הַתְּאֵנָה הַזֹּאת תַּעֲשׂוּ
amen omer ani lachem, im yesh lachem emunah ve'einechem mefakpekim, lo rak kema'aseh hatte'enah hazzot ta'asu
Verily I say unto you, If ye have faith, and doubt not, ye shall not only do what is done to the fig tree,

אֶלָּא גַּם אִם תַּגִּידוּ לָהָר הַזֶּה הֵעָקֵר וְהִזָּרֵק לְתוֹךְ הַיָּם, יִתְקַיֵּם הַדָּבָר
ella gam im taggidu lahar hazzeh he'aker vehizzarek letoch hayam, yitkayem haddavar
but even if ye shall say unto this mountain, Be thou taken up and cast into the sea, it shall be done.

וְכָל מַה שֶּׁתְּבַקְשׁוּ בִּתְפִלָּה וְאַתֶּם מַאֲמִינִים תְּקַבְּלוּהוּ
vechol mah shettevakshu bitfillah ve'attem ma'aminim tekabbeluhu
And all things, whatsoever ye shall ask in prayer, believing, ye shall receive.

כְּשֶׁנִּכְנַס לְבֵית הַמִּקְדָּשׁ וְלִמֵּד שָׁם נִגְּשׁוּ אֵלָיו רָאשֵׁי הַכֹּהֲנִים וְזִקְנֵי הָעָם
keshennichnas leveit hammikdash velimmed sham niggshu elav rashei hakkohanim veziknei ha'am
And when he was come into the temple, the chief priests and the elders of the people came unto him as he was teaching,

וְשָׁאֲלוּ: בְּאֵיזוֹ סַמְכוּת אַתָּה עוֹשֶׂה אֶת הַדְּבָרִים הָאֵלֶּה וּמִי נָתַן לְךָ אֶת הַסַּמְכוּת הַזֹּאת
vesha'alu: be'eizo samchut attah oseh et hadevarim ha'elleh umi natan lecha et hassamchut hazzot
and said, By what authority doest thou these things? and who gave thee this authority?

הֵשִׁיב יֵשׁוּעַ וְאָמַר לָהֶם: גַּם אֲנִי אֶשְׁאַל אֶתְכֶם דָּבָר אֶחָד
heshiv yeshua ve'amar lahem: gam ani esh'al etchem davar echad
And Jesus answered and said unto them, I also will ask you one question,

אֲשֶׁר אִם תַּגִּידוּ לִי אוֹתוֹ, גַּם אֲנִי אַגִּיד לָכֶם בְּאֵיזוֹ סַמְכוּת אֲנִי עוֹשֶׂה אֶת הַדְּבָרִים הָאֵלֶּה
asher im taggidu li oto, gam ani aggid lachem be'eizo samchut ani oseh et haddevarim ha'elleh
which if ye tell me, I likewise will tell you by what authority I do these things.

טְבִילַת יוֹחָנָן מֵאַיִן הָיְתָה, מִן הַשָּׁמַיִם אוֹ מִבְּנֵי אָדָם
tevilat yochanan me'ayin hayetah, min hashamayim o mibbnei adam
The baptism of John, whence was it? from heaven or from men?

בְּהִכָּנְסוֹ לִירוּשָׁלַיִם הָמְתָה כָּל הָעִיר וְהַכֹּל שָׁאֲלוּ: מִי הוּא זֶה
behikkaneso liyerushalayim hametah kol ha'ir vehakkol sha'alu. mi hu zeh
And when he was come into Jerusalem, all the city was stirred, saying, Who is this?

הֵשִׁיבוּ הֲמוֹנֵי הָעָם: זֶה הַנָּבִיא יֵשׁוּעַ מִנַּצְרַת אֲשֶׁר בַּגָּלִיל
heshivu hamonei ha'am: zeh hannavi yeshua minnatzerat asher baggalil
And the multitudes said, This is the prophet, Jesus, from Nazareth of Galilee.

יֵשׁוּעַ נִכְנַס לְבֵית הַמִּקְדָּשׁ וְגֵרֵשׁ אֶת כָּל הַמּוֹכְרִים וְהַקּוֹנִים בְּבֵית הַמִּקְדָּשׁ
yeshua nichnas leveit hammikdash vegeresh et kol hammocherim vehakkonim beveit hammikdash
And Jesus entered into the temple of God, and cast out all them that sold and bought in the temple,

וְהָפַךְ אֶת שֻׁלְחֲנוֹת מַחֲלִיפֵי־הַכְּסָפִים וְאֶת כִּסְאוֹת מוֹכְרֵי הַיּוֹנִים
vehafach et shulchanot machalifei-hakkesafim ve'et kis'ot mocherei hayonim
and overthrew the tables of the money-changers, and the seats of them that sold the doves;

אָמַר לָהֶם: הֵן כָּתוּב, בֵּיתִי בֵּית־תְּפִלָּה יִקָּרֵא, אַךְ אַתֶּם הוֹפְכִים אוֹתוֹ לִמְעָרַת פָּרִיצִים
amar lahem: hen katuv, beiti beit-tefillah yikkare, ach attem hofechim oto lim'arat paritzim
and he saith unto them, It is written, My house shall be called a house of prayer: but ye make it a den of robbers.

נִגְּשׁוּ אֵלָיו עִוְרִים וּפִסְחִים בְּבֵית הַמִּקְדָּשׁ וְהוּא רִפֵּא אוֹתָם
niggeshu elav ivrim ufischim beveit hammikdash vehu rippei otam
And the blind and the lame came to him in the temple; and he healed them.

כִּרְאוֹת רָאשֵׁי הַכֹּהֲנִים וְהַסּוֹפְרִים אֶת הַנִּפְלָאוֹת אֲשֶׁר עָשָׂה
kir'ot rashei hakkohanim vehassoferim et hannifla'ot asher asah
But when the chief priests and the scribes saw the wonderful things that he did,

וְאֶת הַיְלָדִים הַצּוֹעֲקִים בַּמִּקְדָּשׁ, הוֹשַׁע־נָא לְבֶן־דָּוִד!, נִתְמַלְּאוּ כַּעַס
ve'et hayladim hatzo'akim bammikdash, hosha'-na leven-david!, nitmalle'u ka'as
and the children that were crying in the temple and saying, Hosanna to the son of David; they were moved with indignation,

וְאָמְרוּ לוֹ: אַתָּה שׁוֹמֵעַ מַה שֶּׁאֵלֶּה אוֹמְרִים
ve'ameru lo: attah shomea mah she'elleh omerim
and said unto him, Hearest thou what these are saying?

הֵשִׁיב לָהֶם יֵשׁוּעַ: כֵּן, הַאִם מֵעוֹדְכֶם לֹא קְרָאתֶם, מִפִּי עוֹלְלִים וְיוֹנְקִים יִסַּדְתָּ עֹז
heshiv lahem yeshua: ken, ha'im me'odechem lo keratem, mippi olelim veyonekim yissadta oz
And Jesus saith unto them, Yea: did ye never read, Out of the mouth of babes and sucklings thou hast perfected praise?

לְאַחַר מִכֵּן עָזַב אוֹתָם וְיָצָא אֶל מִחוּץ לָעִיר, אֶל בֵּית עַנְיָה, וְלָן שָׁם
le'achar mikken azav otam veyatza el michutz la'ir, el beit anyah, velan sham
And he left them, and went forth out of the city to Bethany, and lodged there.

בַּבֹּקֶר שָׁב אֶל הָעִיר וְהוּא רָעֵב
babboker shav el ha'ir vehu ra'ev
Now in the morning as he returned to the city, he hungered.

בְּאָמְרוֹ לָהֶם: לְכוּ אֶל הַכְּפָר אֲשֶׁר מִמּוּלְכֶם
be'amero lahem: lechu el hakkefar asher mimmulechem
saying unto them, Go into the village that is over against you,

וּמִיָּד תִּמְצְאוּ אָתוֹן קְשׁוּרָה וְעַיִר אִתָּהּ. הַתִּירוּ אוֹתָם וְהָבִיאוּ אֵלַי
umiyad timtze'u aton keshurah ve'ayir ittah. hattiru otam vehavi'u elai
and straightway ye shall find an ass tied, and a colt with her: loose them, and bring them unto me.

וְאִם מִישֶׁהוּ יֹאמַר לָכֶם דָּבָר, תֹּאמְרוּ הָאָדוֹן זָקוּק לָהֶם וּמִיָּד יִשְׁלַח אוֹתָם
ve'im mishehu yomar lachem davar, tomeru ha'adon zakuk lahem umiyad yishlach otam
And if any one say aught unto you, ye shall say, The Lord hath need of them; and straightway he will send them.

כָּל זֶה קָרָה כְּדֵי שֶׁיִּתְקַיֵּם דְּבַר הַנָּבִיא
kol zeh karah kedei sheyitkayem devar hannavi
Now this is come to pass, that it might be fulfilled which was spoken through the prophet, saying,

אִמְרוּ לְבַת־צִיּוֹן: הִנֵּה מַלְכֵּךְ יָבוֹא לָךְ
imru levat-tziyon. hinneh malkech yavo lach
Tell ye the daughter of Zion, Behold, thy King cometh unto thee,

עָנִי וְרֹכֵב עַל־חֲמוֹר וְעַל־עַיִר בֶּן־אֲתֹנוֹת
ani verochev al-chamor ve'al-'ayir ben-'atonot
Meek, and riding upon an ass, And upon a colt the foal of an ass.

הַתַּלְמִידִים הָלְכוּ וְעָשׂוּ כְּמִצְוַת יֵשׁוּעַ
hattalmidim halechu ve'asu kemitzvat yeshua
And the disciples went, and did even as Jesus appointed them,

הֵם הֵבִיאוּ אֶת הָאָתוֹן וְאֶת הָעַיִר וּלְאַחַר שֶׁשָּׂמוּ עֲלֵיהֶם אֶת בִּגְדֵיהֶם הוּא יָשַׁב עֲלֵיהֶם
hem hevi'u et ha'aton ve'et ha'ayir ule'achar shesamu aleihem et bigdeihem hu yashav aleihem
and brought the ass, and the colt, and put on them their garments; and he sat thereon.

רַבִּים מִן הֶהָמוֹן פָּרְשׂוּ אֶת בִּגְדֵיהֶם עַל הַדֶּרֶךְ
rabbim min hehamon paresu et bigdeihem al hadderech
And the most part of the multitude spread their garments in the way;

וַאֲחֵרִים כָּרְתוּ עֲנָפִים מִן הָעֵצִים וְשָׁטְחוּ אוֹתָם עַל הַדֶּרֶךְ
va'acherim karetu anafim min ha'etzim veshatechu otam al hadderech
and others cut branches from the trees, and spread them in the way.

וַהֲמוֹן הָעָם שֶׁהָלְכוּ לְפָנָיו וְאַחֲרָיו קָרְאוּ: הוֹשַׁע־נָא לְבֶן־דָּוִד
vahamon ha'am shehalechu lefanav ve'acharav kare'u: hosha'-na leven-david
And the multitudes that went before him, and that followed, cried, saying, Hosanna to the son of David:

בָּרוּךְ הַבָּא בְּשֵׁם יְהוָה! הוֹשַׁע־נָא בַּמְּרוֹמִים
baruch habba beshem hashem! hosha'-na bammeromim
Blessed is he that cometh in the name of the Lord; Hosanna in the highest.

כְּשֵׁם שֶׁבֶּן־הָאָדָם לֹא בָּא כְּדֵי שֶׁיְשָׁרְתוּהוּ אֶלָּא כְּדֵי לְשָׁרֵת וְלָתֵת אֶת נַפְשׁוֹ כֹּפֶר בְּעַד רַבִּים
keshem shebben-ha'adam lo ba kedei sheyesharetuhu ella kedei lesharet velatet et nafsho kofer be'ad rabbim
even as the Son of man came not to be ministered unto, but to minister, and to give his life a ransom for many.

בְּצֵאתָם מִירִיחוֹ הָלְכוּ אַחֲרָיו הָמוֹן עַם רָב.
betzetam miricho halechu acharav hamon am rav
And as they went out from Jericho, a great multitude followed him.

וְהִנֵּה שְׁנֵי עִוְרִים, שֶׁיָּשְׁבוּ בְּצַד הַדֶּרֶךְ וְשָׁמְעוּ כִּי יֵשׁוּעַ עוֹבֵר
vehinneh shenei ivrim, sheyashevu betzad hadderech veshame'u ki yeshua over
And behold, two blind men sitting by the way side, when they heard that Jesus was passing by,

הֵחֵלּוּ לִצְעֹק: אֲדוֹנֵנוּ בֶּן־דָּוִד, רַחֵם עָלֵינוּ
hechellu litz'ok: adonenu ben-david, rachem aleinu
cried out, saying, Lord, have mercy on us, thou son of David.

הָעָם גָּעַר בָּהֶם לְהַשְׁתִּיקָם
ha'am ga'ar bahem lehashtikam
And the multitude rebuked them, that they should hold their peace:

אַךְ הֵם צָעֲקוּ בְּיֶתֶר שְׂאֵת: אֲדוֹנֵנוּ בֶּן־דָּוִד, רַחֵם עָלֵינוּ
ach hem tza'aku beyeter se'et: adonenu ben-david, rachem aleinu
but they cried out the more, saying, Lord, have mercy on us, thou son of David.

יֵשׁוּעַ נֶעֱצַר, קָרָא לָהֶם וְשָׁאַל: מָה רְצוֹנְכֶם שֶׁאֶעֱשֶׂה לָכֶם
yeshua ne'etzar, kara lahem vesha'al: mah retzonechem she'e'eseh lachem
And Jesus stood still, and called them, and said, What will ye that I should do unto you?

הֵשִׁיבוּ לוֹ: אָדוֹן - שֶׁתִּפָּקַחְנָה עֵינֵינוּ
heshivu lo: Adon - shettippakachnah eineinu
They say unto him, Lord, that our eyes may be opened.

נִתְמַלֵּא יֵשׁוּעַ רַחֲמִים וְנָגַע בְּעֵינֵיהֶם
nitmallei yeshua rachamim venaga be'eineihem
And Jesus, being moved with compassion, touched their eyes;

מִיָּד רָאוּ וְהָלְכוּ אַחֲרָיו
miyad ra'u vehalechu acharav
and straightway they received their sight, and followed him.

כא

כַּאֲשֶׁר הִתְקָרְבוּ לִירוּשָׁלַיִם וּבָאוּ אֶל בֵּית־פַּגֵּי, אֶל הַר הַזֵּיתִים, שָׁלַח יֵשׁוּעַ שְׁנֵי תַּלְמִידִים
Ka'asher hitkarevu liyerushalayim uva'u el beit-paggei, el har hazzeitim, shalach yeshua shenei talmidim
And when they drew nigh unto Jerusalem, and came unto Bethphage, unto the mount of Olives, then Jesus sent two disciples,

שָׁאַל אוֹתָהּ: מַה בַּקָּשָׁתֵךְ? הֵשִׁיבָה לוֹ
sha'al otah: mah bakkashatech? heshivah lo
And he said unto her, What wouldest thou? She saith unto him,

אֱמֹר נָא שֶׁיֵּשְׁבוּ שְׁנֵי בָנַי אֵלֶּה אֶחָד לִימִינְךָ וְאֶחָד לִשְׂמֹאלְךָ בְּמַלְכוּתְךָ
Emor na sheyeshevu shenei banai elleh echad liminecha ve'echad lismolecha bemalchutcha
Command that these my two sons may sit, one on thy right hand, and one on thy left hand, in thy kingdom.

עָנָה יֵשׁוּעַ וְאָמַר
anah yeshua ve'amar
But Jesus answered and said,

אֵינְכֶם יוֹדְעִים מַה שֶׁאַתֶּם מְבַקְשִׁים. הַאִם יְכוֹלִים אַתֶּם לִשְׁתּוֹת אֶת הַכּוֹס אֲשֶׁר אֲנִי עָתִיד לִשְׁתּוֹת
Einechem yode'im mah she'attem mevakshim. Ha'im yecholim attem lishtot et hakkos asher ani atid lishtot
Ye know not what ye ask. Are ye able to drink the cup that I am about to drink?

הֵשִׁיבוּ לוֹ: יְכוֹלִים אָנוּ
heshivu lo: yecholim anu
They say unto him, We are able.

אָמַר לָהֶם: אָמְנָם אֶת כּוֹסִי תִּשְׁתּוּ, אַךְ לָשֶׁבֶת לִימִינִי וְלִשְׂמֹאלִי אֵין בְּיָדִי לָתֵת
amar lahem: amnam et kosi tishtu, ach lashevet limini velismoli ein beyadi latet
He saith unto them, My cup indeed ye shall drink: but to sit on my right hand, and on my left hand, is not mine to give;

אֶלָּא לַאֲשֶׁר הוּכַן לָהֶם מֵאֵת אָבִי
ella la'asher huchan lahem me'et avi
but it is for them for whom it hath been prepared of my Father.

כַּאֲשֶׁר שָׁמְעוּ זֹאת הָעֲשָׂרָה נִתְמַלְּאוּ כַּעַס עַל שְׁנֵי הָאַחִים
ka'asher shame'u zot ha'asarah nitmalle'u ka'as al shenei ha'achim
And when the ten heard it, they were moved with indignation concerning the two brethren.

קָרָא לָהֶם יֵשׁוּעַ וְאָמַר
kara lahem yeshua ve'amar
But Jesus called them unto him, and said,

אַתֶּם יוֹדְעִים שֶׁהַמּוֹשְׁלִים בַּגּוֹיִים רוֹדִים בָּהֶם וְהַגְּדוֹלִים שׁוֹלְטִים בָּהֶם
Attem yode'im shehammoshelim baggoyim rodim bahem vehaggedolim sholetim bahem
Ye know that the rulers of the Gentiles lord it over them, and their great ones exercise authority over them.

אַל יְהִי כֵן בֵּינֵיכֶם. אַדְּרַבָּא, הֶחָפֵץ לִהְיוֹת גָּדוֹל בָּכֶם יְהֵא מְשָׁרֵת שֶׁלָּכֶם
al yehi chen beineichem. adderabba, hechafetz lihyot gadol bachem yehei mesharet shellachem
Not so shall it be among you: but whosoever would become great among you shall be your minister;

וְהֶחָפֵץ לִהְיוֹת רִאשׁוֹן בֵּינֵיכֶם יְהֵא עֶבֶד לָכֶם
vehechafetz lihyot rishon beineichem yehei eved lachem
and whosoever would be first among you shall be your servant:

אֵלֶּה הָאַחֲרוֹנִים עָבְדוּ שָׁעָה אַחַת וְאַתָּה הִשְׁוִיתָ אוֹתָם אֵלֵינוּ
elleh ha'acharonim avedu sha'ah achat ve'attah hishveita otam eleinu
saying, These last have spent but one hour, and thou hast made them equal unto us,

אֲנַחְנוּ שֶׁסָּבַלְנוּ אֶת כֹּבֶד הַיּוֹם וְאֶת הַחֹם
anachnu shessavalnu et koved hayom ve'et hachom
who have borne the burden of the day and the scorching heat.

הֵשִׁיב וְאָמַר אֶל אֶחָד מֵהֶם, חָבֵר, אֵינֶנִּי עוֹשֵׁק אוֹתָךְ. הֲרֵי עַל שָׂכָר דִּינָר הִסְכַּמְתָּ אִתִּי
heshiv ve'amar el echad mehem, chaver, einenni oshek otcha. harei al sechar dinar hiskamta itti
But he answered and said to one of them, Friend, I do thee no wrong: didst not thou agree with me for a shilling?

קַח אֶת שֶׁלְּךָ וְלֵךְ, וְאוּלָם רְצוֹנִי לָתֵת לָאַחֲרוֹן הַזֶּה כְּמוֹ לְךָ
kach et shellecha velech, ve'ulam retzoni latet la'acharon hazzeh kemo lecha
Take up that which is thine, and go thy way; it is my will to give unto this last, even as unto thee.

הַאִם אָסוּר לִי לַעֲשׂוֹת בְּשֶׁלִּי כִּרְצוֹנִי? אוֹ שֶׁמָּא עֵינְךָ צָרָה עַל שֶׁטּוֹב אֲנִי
ha'im asur li la'asot beshelli kirtzoni? o shemma einecha tzarah al shettov ani
Is it not lawful for me to do what I will with mine own? or is thine eye evil, because I am good?

כָּכָה יִהְיוּ הָאַחֲרוֹנִים רִאשׁוֹנִים וְהָרִאשׁוֹנִים אַחֲרוֹנִים
kachah yihyu ha'acharonim rishonim veharishonim acharonim
So the last shall be first, and the first last.

כְּשֶׁהָיָה יֵשׁוּעַ קָרוֹב לַעֲלוֹת לִירוּשָׁלַיִם לָקַח אֶת הַשְּׁנֵים־עָשָׂר לְבַדָּם וּבַדֶּרֶךְ אָמַר לָהֶם
keshehayah yeshua karov la'alot liyerushalayim lakach et hasheneim-'asar levaddam uvadderech amar lahem
And as Jesus was going up to Jerusalem, he took the twelve disciples apart, and on the way he said unto them,

הִנֵּה אֲנַחְנוּ עוֹלִים לִירוּשָׁלַיִם וּבֶן־הָאָדָם יִמָּסֵר לְרָאשֵׁי הַכֹּהֲנִים וְלַסּוֹפְרִים
hinneh anachnu olim liyerushalayim uven-ha'adam yimmaser lerashei hakkohanim velassoferim
Behold, we go up to Jerusalem; and the Son of man shall be delivered unto the chief priests and scribes;

הֵם יֶחֱרְצוּ אֶת דִּינוֹ לְמָוֶת
hem yechertzu et dino lemavet
and they shall condemn him to death,

וְיִמְסְרוּ אוֹתוֹ לַגּוֹיִים לְהָתֵל בּוֹ וּלְהַלְקוֹתוֹ וְלִצְלֹב אוֹתוֹ, וּבַיּוֹם הַשְּׁלִישִׁי יָקוּם
veyimseru oto laggoyim lehatel bo ulehalkoto velitzlov oto, uvayom hashelishi yakum
and shall deliver him unto the Gentiles to mock, and to scourge, and to crucify: and the third day he shall be raised up.

אַחֲרֵי כֵן נִגְּשָׁה אֵלָיו הָאֵם שֶׁל בְּנֵי זַבְדַּי עִם בָּנֶיהָ
acharei chen niggeshah elav ha'em shel benei zavdai im baneiha
Then came to him the mother of the sons of Zebedee with her sons,

וְהִשְׁתַּחֲוְתָה לוֹ לְבַקֵּשׁ מִמֶּנּוּ דָּבָר
vehishtachavtah lo levakkesh mimmennu davar
worshipping him, and asking a certain thing of him.

וּלְאַחַר שֶׁהִסְכִּים עִם הַפּוֹעֲלִים עַל שְׂכַר דִּינָר לְיוֹם שָׁלַח אוֹתָם אֶל כַּרְמוֹ
ule'achar shehiskim im happo'alim al schar dinar leyom shalach otam el karmo
And when he had agreed with the laborers for a shilling a day, he sent them into his vineyard.

כְּשֶׁיָּצָא בְּשָׁעָה תֵּשַׁע רָאָה אֲחֵרִים עוֹמְדִים בְּטֵלִים בַּשּׁוּק
kesheyatza besha'ah tesha ra'ah acherim omedim betelim bashuk
And he went out about the third hour, and saw others standing in the marketplace idle;

אָמַר לָהֶם, 'לְכוּ גַם אַתֶּם אֶל כַּרְמִי וְאֶתֵּן לָכֶם אֶת הַמַּגִּיעַ לָכֶם'. הֵם הָלְכוּ
amar lahem, lechu gam attem el karmi ve'etten lachem et hammaggia lachem. hem halechu
and to them he said, Go ye also into the vineyard, and whatsoever is right I will give you. And they went their way.

יָצָא גַם בְּשָׁעָה שְׁתֵּים-עֶשְׂרֵה וְגַם בְּשָׁעָה שָׁלוֹשׁ וְעָשָׂה כַּדָּבָר הַזֶּה
yatza gam besha'ah sheteim-'esreh vegam besha'ah shalosh ve'asah kaddavar hazzeh
Again he went out about the sixth and the ninth hour, and did likewise.

אַחֲרֵי כֵן יָצָא בְּשָׁעָה חָמֵשׁ לִפְנוֹת עֶרֶב וּמָצָא אֲחֵרִים עוֹמְדִים
acharei chen yatza besha'ah chamesh lifnot erev umatza acherim omedim
And about the eleventh hour he went out, and found others standing;

שָׁאַל אוֹתָם, לָמָּה אַתֶּם עוֹמְדִים פֹּה בְּטֵלִים כָּל הַיּוֹם
sha'al otam, lammah attem omedim poh betelim kol hayom
and he saith unto them, Why stand ye here all the day idle?

הֵשִׁיבוּ לוֹ, מִפְּנֵי שֶׁלֹּא שָׂכַר אוֹתָנוּ אִישׁ. אָמַר לָהֶם, לְכוּ גַם אַתֶּם אֶל הַכֶּרֶם
heshivu lo, mippenei shello sachar otanu ish. amar lahem, lechu gam attem el hakkerem
They say unto him, Because no man hath hired us. He saith unto them, Go ye also into the vineyard.

לְעֵת עֶרֶב אָמַר בַּעַל הַכֶּרֶם אֶל פְּקִידוֹ
le'et erev amar ba'al hakkerem el pekido
And when even was come, the lord of the vineyard saith unto his steward,

קְרָא אֶת הַפּוֹעֲלִים וְשַׁלֵּם לָהֶם אֶת שְׂכָרָם, הָחֵל בָּאַחֲרוֹנִים וְכַלֵּה בָּרִאשׁוֹנִים
kera et happo'alim veshallem lahem et secharam, hachel ba'acharonim vechalleh barishonim
Call the laborers, and pay them their hire, beginning from the last unto the first.

בָּאוּ אֵלֶּה שֶׁנִּשְׂכְּרוּ בְּשָׁעָה חָמֵשׁ לִפְנוֹת עֶרֶב וְקִבְּלוּ אִישׁ אִישׁ דִּינָר אֶחָד
ba'u elleh shenniskeru besha'ah chamesh lifnot erev vekibbelu ish ish dinar echad
And when they came that were hired about the eleventh hour, they received every man a shilling.

כְּשֶׁבָּאוּ הָרִאשׁוֹנִים דִּמּוּ בְּנַפְשָׁם שֶׁיְּקַבְּלוּ יוֹתֵר, אַךְ גַּם הֵם קִבְּלוּ אִישׁ אִישׁ דִּינָר אֶחָד
keshebba'u harishonim dimmu benafsham sheyekabbelu yoter, ach gam hem kibbelu ish ish dinar echad
And when the first came, they supposed that they would receive more; and they likewise received every man a shilling.

לְאַחַר שֶׁקִּבְּלוּ הִתְלוֹנְנוּ לִפְנֵי בַּעַל הַבַּיִת בְּאָמְרָם
le'achar shekkibbelu hitlonenu lifnei ba'al habbayit be'omram
And when they received it, they murmured against the householder,

שָׁמְעוּ הַתַּלְמִידִים וְתָמְהוּ מְאֹד. אִם כֵּן, מִי יָכוֹל לְהִוָּשֵׁעַ? שָׁאֲלוּ
shame'u hattalmidim vetamehu me'od. im ken, mi yachol lehivvasha'? sha'alu
And when the disciples heard it, they were astonished exceedingly, saying, Who then can be saved?

הִבִּיט בָּהֶם יֵשׁוּעַ וְאָמַר: מִבְּנֵי אָדָם נִבְצַר הַדָּבָר, אֲבָל הָאֱלֹהִים כָּל יָכוֹל
hibbit bahem yeshua ve'amar: mibbenei adam nivtzar haddavar, aval ha'elohim kol yachol
And Jesus looking upon them said to them, With men this is impossible; but with God all things are possible.

הֵגִיב כֵּיפָא וְאָמַר אֵלָיו: הִנֵּה אֲנַחְנוּ עָזַבְנוּ הַכֹּל וְהָלַכְנוּ אַחֲרֶיךָ, אִם כֵּן מַה יִּהְיֶה לָנוּ
hegiv keifa ve'amar elav: hinneh anachnu azavnu hakkol vehalachnu achareicha, im ken mah yihyeh lanu
Then answered Peter and said unto him, Lo, we have left all, and followed thee; what then shall we have?

אָמַר לָהֶם יֵשׁוּעַ: אָמֵן אוֹמֵר אֲנִי לָכֶם, אַתֶּם הַהוֹלְכִים אַחֲרַי
amar lahem yeshua. amen omer ani lachem, attem haholechim acharai
And Jesus said unto them, Verily I say unto you, that ye who have followed me,

כַּאֲשֶׁר תִּתְחַדֵּשׁ הַבְּרִיאָה וּבֶן־הָאָדָם יֵשֵׁב עַל כִּסֵּא כְבוֹדוֹ
ka'asher titchaddesh habberi'ah uven-ha'adam yeshev al kissei kevodo
in the regeneration when the Son of man shall sit on the throne of his glory,

תֵּשְׁבוּ גַּם אַתֶּם עַל שְׁנֵים־עָשָׂר כִּסְאוֹת לִשְׁפֹּט אֶת שְׁנֵים־עָשָׂר שִׁבְטֵי יִשְׂרָאֵל
teshevu gam attem al sheneim-'asar kis'ot lishpot et sheneim-'asar shivtei yisra'el
ye also shall sit upon twelve thrones, judging the twelve tribes of Israel.

וְכָל מִי שֶׁעָזַב בָּתִּים אוֹ אַחִים וַאֲחָיוֹת אוֹ אָב וָאֵם אוֹ אִשָּׁה אוֹ בָּנִים אוֹ שָׂדוֹת
vechol mi she'azav batim o achim va'achayot o av va'em o ishah o banim o sadot
And every one that hath left houses, or brethren, or sisters, or father, or mother, or children, or lands,

לְמַעַן שְׁמִי - יְקַבֵּל פִּי מֵאָה וְיִירַשׁ חַיֵּי עוֹלָם
lema'an shemi - yekabbel pi me'ah veyirash chayei olam
for my name's sake, shall receive a hundredfold, and shall inherit eternal life.

אֲבָל רַבִּים מִן הָרִאשׁוֹנִים יִהְיוּ אַחֲרוֹנִים וּמֵהָאַחֲרוֹנִים - רִאשׁוֹנִים
aval rabbim min harishonim yihyu acharonim umeha'acharonim - rishonim.
But many shall be last that are first; and first that are last.

כ

כִּי דּוֹמָה מַלְכוּת הַשָּׁמַיִם לְאִישׁ בַּעַל אֲחֻזָּה
ki domah malchut hashamayim le'ish ba'al achuzzah
For the kingdom of heaven is like unto a man that was a householder,

שֶׁיָּצָא הַשְׁכֵּם בַּבֹּקֶר לִשְׂכֹּר פּוֹעֲלִים לְכַרְמוֹ
sheyatza hashkem babboker liskor po'alim lecharmo
who went out early in the morning to hire laborers into his vineyard.

אָמַר אֵלָיו: מַדּוּעַ אַתָּה שׁוֹאֵל אוֹתִי בְּנוֹגֵעַ לַטּוֹב
amar elav: maddua attah sho'el oti benogea lattov
And he said unto him, Why askest thou me concerning that which is good?

אֶחָד הוּא הַטּוֹב, אֲבָל אִם רְצוֹנְךָ לָבוֹא לַחַיִּים, שְׁמֹר אֶת הַמִּצְוֹת
echad hu hattov, aval im retzonecha lavo lachayim, shemor et hammitzvot
One there is who is good: but if thou wouldest enter into life, keep the commandments.

שָׁאַל הָאִישׁ: אֵיזֶה? הֵשִׁיב יֵשׁוּעַ
sha'al ha'ish: eizeh? heshiv yeshua:
He saith unto him, Which? And Jesus said,

לֹא תִּרְצַח, לֹא תִּנְאָף, לֹא תִּגְנֹב, לֹא־תַעֲנֶה בְרֵעֲךָ עֵד שָׁקֶר
Lo tirtzach, lo tin'af, lo tignov, lo-ta'aneh bere'acha ed shaker
Thou shalt not kill, Thou shalt not commit adultery, Thou shalt not steal, Thou shalt not bear false witness,

כַּבֵּד אֶת־אָבִיךָ וְאֶת־אִמֶּךָ, וְאָהַבְתָּ לְרֵעֲךָ כָּמוֹךָ
kabbed et-'avicha ve'et-'immecha, ve'ahavta lere'acha kamocha
Honor thy father and thy mother; and, Thou shalt love thy neighbor as thyself.

אָמַר הַבָּחוּר: אֶת כָּל אֵלֶּה שָׁמַרְתִּי; מַה עוֹד חָסֵר לִי
amar habbachur: et kol elleh shamarti; mah od chaser li
The young man saith unto him, All these things have I observed: what lack I yet?

אָמַר לוֹ יֵשׁוּעַ: אִם רְצוֹנְךָ לִהְיוֹת שָׁלֵם, לֵךְ מְכֹר אֶת רְכוּשְׁךָ וְתֵן לָעֲנִיִּים
amar lo yeshua: im retzonecha lihyot shalem, lech mechor et rechushecha veten la'aniyim
Jesus said unto him, If thou wouldest be perfect, go, sell that which thou hast, and give to the poor,

וְיִהְיֶה לְךָ אוֹצָר בַּשָּׁמַיִם; אַחַר כָּךְ בּוֹא וְלֵךְ אַחֲרַי
veyihyeh lecha otzar bashamayim; achar kach bo velech acharai
and thou shalt have treasure in heaven: and come, follow me.

כְּשֶׁשָּׁמַע הַבָּחוּר אֶת הַדָּבָר הַזֶּה הָלַךְ מִשָּׁם עָצוּב, שֶׁכֵּן הָיוּ לוֹ נְכָסִים רַבִּים
kesheshama habbachur et haddavar hazzeh halach misham atzuv, shekken hayu lo nechasim rabbim
But when the young man heard the saying, he went away sorrowful; for he was one that had great possessions.

אָמַר יֵשׁוּעַ לְתַלְמִידָיו: אָמֵן אוֹמֵר אֲנִי לָכֶם, בְּקֹשִׁי יִכָּנֵס עָשִׁיר לְמַלְכוּת הַשָּׁמַיִם
amar yeshua letalmidav: amen omer ani lachem, bekoshi yikkanes ashir lemalchut hashamayim
And Jesus said unto his disciples, Verily I say unto you, It is hard for a rich man to enter into the kingdom of heaven.

וְעוֹד אֲנִי אוֹמֵר לָכֶם
ve'od ani omer lachem
And again I say unto you,

נָקֵל לַגָּמָל לַעֲבֹר דֶּרֶךְ נֶקֶב מַחַט מֵהִכָּנֵס עָשִׁיר אֶל מַלְכוּת הָאֱלֹהִים
nakel laggamal la'avor derech nekev machat mehikkanes ashir el malchut ha'elohim
It is easier for a camel to go through a needle's eye, than for a rich man to enter into the kingdom of God.

וַאֲנִי אוֹמֵר לָכֶם, הַמְגָרֵשׁ אֶת אִשְׁתּוֹ שֶׁלֹּא עַל־דְּבַר זְנוּת וְנוֹשֵׂא אַחֶרֶת
va'ani omer lachem, hamgaresh et ishto shello al-devar zenut venosei acheret
And I say unto you, Whosoever shall put away his wife, except for fornication, and shall marry another,

נוֹאֵף הוּא
no'ef hu
committeth adultery.

אָמְרוּ לוֹ הַתַּלְמִידִים: אִם כָּךְ הוּא דִין הָאִישׁ וְהָאִשָּׁה לֹא כְּדַאי לְהִתְחַתֵּן
ameru lo hattalmidim: im kach hu din ha'ish veha'ishah lo keda lehitchatten
The disciples say unto him, If the case of the man is so with his wife, it is not expedient to marry.

אָמַר לָהֶם: לֹא הַכֹּל מְבִינִים אֶת הַדָּבָר הַזֶּה, רַק אֵלֶּה שֶׁנִּתַּן לָהֶם
amar lahem: lo hakkol mevinim et haddavar hazzeh, rak elleh shennittan lahem
But he said unto them, Not all men can receive this saying, but they to whom it is given.

יֵשׁ סָרִיסִים שֶׁנּוֹלְדוּ כָּךְ מִבֶּטֶן אִמָּם
yesh sarisim shennoledu kach mibbeten immam
For there are eunuchs, that were so born from their mother's womb:

יֵשׁ סָרִיסִים שֶׁנַּעֲשׂוּ סָרִיסִים עַל־יְדֵי בְּנֵי אָדָם, יֵשׁ סָרִיסִים
yesh sarisim shenna'asu sarisim al-yedei benei adam, yesh sarisim
and there are eunuchs, that were made eunuchs by men: and there are eunuchs,

אֲשֶׁר עָשׂוּ עַצְמָם לְסָרִיסִים לְמַעַן מַלְכוּת שָׁמַיִם. מִי שֶׁבִּיכָלְתּוֹ לְקַבֵּל, שֶׁיְּקַבֵּל
asher asu atzmam lesarisim lema'an malchut shamayim. Mi shebbiyecholto lekabbel, sheyekabbel
that made themselves eunuchs for the kingdom of heaven's sake. He that is able to receive it, let him receive it.

אָז הֵבִיאוּ אֵלָיו יְלָדִים כְּדֵי שֶׁיִּסְמֹךְ יָדָיו עֲלֵיהֶם וְיִתְפַּלֵּל בַּעֲדָם
az hevi'u elav yeladim kedei sheyismoch yadav aleihem veyitpallel ba'adam
Then were there brought unto him little children, that he should lay his hands on them, and pray:

אֶלָּא שֶׁהַתַּלְמִידִים גָּעֲרוּ בָּהֶם
ella shehattalmidim ga'aru bahem
and the disciples rebuked them.

אַךְ יֵשׁוּעַ אָמַר: הַנִּיחוּ לַיְלָדִים לָבוֹא אֵלַי וְאַל תִּמְנְעוּ בַּעֲדָם, כִּי לְכָאֵלֶּה מַלְכוּת הַשָּׁמַיִם
ach yeshua amar: hannichu layladim lavo elai ve'al timne'u ba'adam, ki lecha'elleh malchut hashamayim
But Jesus said, Suffer the little children, and forbid them not, to come unto me: for to such belongeth the kingdom of heaven.

הוּא סָמַךְ יָדָיו עֲלֵיהֶם וְאַחֲרֵי כֵן הָלַךְ מִשָּׁם
hu samach yadav aleihem ve'acharei chen halach misham
And he laid his hands on them, and departed thence.

נִגַּשׁ אֵלָיו אִישׁ אֶחָד וְשָׁאַל: רַבִּי, אֵיזֶה טוֹב עָלַי לַעֲשׂוֹת כְּדֵי לְהַשִּׂיג חַיֵּי עוֹלָם
niggash elav ish echad vesha'al: rabbi, eizeh tov alai la'asot kedei lehashg chayei olam
And behold, one came to him and said, Teacher, what good thing shall I do, that I may have eternal life?

יט

כְּשֶׁגָּמַר יֵשׁוּעַ לְדַבֵּר אֶת הַדְּבָרִים הָאֵלֶּה
kesheggamar yeshua ledabber et haddevarim ha'elleh
And it came to pass when Jesus had finished these words,

יָצָא מִן הַגָּלִיל וּבָא לְאֵזוֹר יְהוּדָה שֶׁבְּעֵבֶר הַיַּרְדֵּן
yatza min haggalil uva le'ezor yehudah shebbe'ever hayarden
he departed from Galilee, and came into the borders of Judæa beyond the Jordan;

הֲמוֹן עַם רַב הָלְכוּ אַחֲרָיו וְהוּא רִפֵּא אוֹתָם שָׁם
hamon am rav halechu acharav vehu rippei otam sham
and great multitudes followed him; and he healed them there.

נִגְּשׁוּ אֵלָיו כַּמָּה פְּרוּשִׁים לְנַסּוֹת אוֹתוֹ וְאָמְרוּ: "הַאִם מֻתָּר לְאִישׁ לְגָרֵשׁ אֶת אִשְׁתּוֹ עַל כָּל דָּבָר
niggshu elav kammah perushim lenassot oto ve'ameru: ha'im muttar le'ish legaresh et ishto al kol davar
And there came unto him Pharisees, trying him, and saying, Is it lawful for a man to put away his wife for every cause?

הֵשִׁיב לָהֶם וְאָמַר: הַאִם לֹא קְרָאתֶם שֶׁהַבּוֹרֵא עָשָׂה אוֹתָם זָכָר וּנְקֵבָה מִבְּרֵאשִׁית
heshiv lahem ve'amar: ha'im lo keratem shehabborei asah otam zachar unekevah mibbereshit
And he answered and said, Have ye not read, that he who made them from the beginning made them male and female,

וְגַם אָמַר, עַל־כֵּן יַעֲזָב־אִישׁ אֶת־אָבִיו וְאֶת־אִמּוֹ
vegam amar, al-ken ya'azav-'ish et-'aviv ve'et-'immo
and said, For this cause shall a man leave his father and mother,

וְדָבַק בְּאִשְׁתּוֹ וְהָיוּ לְבָשָׂר אֶחָד
vedavak be'ishto vehayu levasar echad
and shall cleave to his wife; and the two shall become one flesh?

אֵין הֵם עוֹד שְׁנַיִם אֶלָּא בָּשָׂר אֶחָד. לָכֵן מַה שֶׁחִבֵּר הָאֱלֹהִים אַל יַפְרִיד הָאָדָם
ein hem od shenayim ella basar echad. Lachen mah shechibber ha'elohim al yafrid ha'adam
So that they are no more two, but one flesh. What therefore God hath joined together, let not man put asunder.

אִם כֵּן לָמָּה צִוָּה מֹשֶׁה לָתֵת לָהּ סֵפֶר כְּרִיתוּת וּלְשַׁלְּחָהּ שָׁאֲלוּ אוֹתוֹ
'im ken lammah tzivvah mosheh latet lah sefer keritut uleshallechah sha'alu oto
They say unto him, Why then did Moses command to give a bill of divorcement, and to put her away?

הֵשִׁיב לָהֶם: בִּגְלַל קְשִׁי לְבַבְכֶם הִתִּיר לָכֶם מֹשֶׁה לְשַׁלֵּחַ אֶת נְשֵׁיכֶם
heshiv lahem. Biglal keshi levavchem hittir lachem mosheh leshalleach et nesheichem
He saith unto them, Moses for your hardness of heart suffered you to put away your wives:

אַךְ מֵרֵאשִׁית לֹא הָיָה כָּךְ
ach mereshit lo hayah kach
but from the beginning it hath not been so.

נִכְמְרוּ רַחֲמֵי הָאָדוֹן עַל הָעֶבֶד הַהוּא, פָּטַר אוֹתוֹ וּוִתֵּר לוֹ עַל הַחוֹב
nichmeru rachamei ha'adon al ha'eved hahu, patar oto uvitter lo al hachov
And the lord of that servant, being moved with compassion, released him, and forgave him the debt.

כְּשֶׁיָּצָא הָעֶבֶד הַהוּא מָצָא אֶת אֶחָד מֵחֲבֵרָיו הָעֲבָדִים שֶׁהָיָה חַיָּב לוֹ מֵאָה דִּינָרִים
kesheyatza ha'eved hahu matza et echad mechaverav ha'avadim shehayah chayav lo me'ah dinarim
But that servant went out, and found one of his fellow-servants, who owed him a hundred shillings:

תָּפַס אוֹתוֹ בִּגְרוֹנוֹ וְאָמַר, שַׁלֵּם מַה שֶׁאַתָּה חַיָּב
tafas oto bigrono ve'amar, shallem mah she'attah chayav
and he laid hold on him, and took him by the throat, saying, Pay what thou owest.

נָפַל חֲבֵרוֹ לְרַגְלָיו וּבִקֵּשׁ מֵאִתּוֹ, אָנָּא, הֱיֵה סַבְלָן כְּלַפַּי וַאֲשַׁלֵּם לְךָ
nafal chavero leraglav uvikkesh me'itto, anna, heyeh savlan kelappai va'ashallem lecha
So his fellow-servant fell down and besought him, saying, Have patience with me, and I will pay thee.

אֶלָּא שֶׁהוּא לֹא הִסְכִּים וְעוֹד הָלַךְ וְהִשְׁלִיךְ אוֹתוֹ לַכֶּלֶא עַד אֲשֶׁר יְשַׁלֵּם אֶת הַחוֹב
ella shehu lo hiskim ve'od halach vehishlich oto lakkelei ad asher yeshallem et hachov
And he would not: but went and cast him into prison, till he should pay that which was due.

כְּשֶׁרָאוּ חֲבֵרָיו הָעֲבָדִים אֶת הַנַּעֲשֶׂה הִתְעַצְּבוּ מְאֹד
keshera'u chaverav ha'avadim et hanna'aseh hit'atzevu me'od
So when his fellow-servants saw what was done, they were exceeding sorry,

וּבָאוּ וְסִפְּרוּ לַאֲדוֹנָם אֶת כָּל אֲשֶׁר הָיָה
uva'u vesipperu la'adonam et kol asher hayah
and came and told unto their lord all that was done.

אָז קָרָא לוֹ אֲדוֹנָיו וְאָמַר לוֹ
az kara lo adonav ve'amar lo
Then his lord called him unto him, and saith to him,

עֶבֶד רֶשַׁע, אֶת כָּל הַחוֹב הַהוּא מָחַלְתִּי לְךָ מִשּׁוּם שֶׁבִּקַּשְׁתָּ מִמֶּנִּי
eved rasha, et kol hachov hahu machalti lecha mishum shebbikkashta mimmenni
Thou wicked servant, I forgave thee all that debt, because thou besoughtest me:

הַאִם לֹא הָיִיתָ צָרִיךְ גַּם אַתָּה לְרַחֵם עַל חֲבֵרְךָ הָעֶבֶד כְּשֵׁם שֶׁאֲנִי רִחַמְתִּי עָלֶיךָ
ha'im lo hayita tzarich gam attah lerachem al chaverecha ha'eved keshem she'ani richamti aleicha
shouldest not thou also have had mercy on thy fellow-servant, even as I had mercy on thee?

וּבְכַעֲסוֹ מָסַר אוֹתוֹ אֲדוֹנָיו לַנּוֹגְשִׂים עַד אֲשֶׁר יְשַׁלֵּם אֶת הַחוֹב כֻּלּוֹ
uvecha'aso masar oto adonav lannogesim ad asher yeshallem et hachov kullo
And his lord was wroth, and delivered him to the tormentors, till he should pay all that was due.

כָּכָה גַּם אָבִי שֶׁבַּשָּׁמַיִם יַעֲשֶׂה לָכֶם אִם לֹא תִּמְחֲלוּ אִישׁ לְאָחִיו בְּכָל לְבַבְכֶם
kachah gam avi shebbashamayim ya'aseh lachem im lo timchalu ish le'achiv bechol levavchem
So shall also my heavenly Father do unto you, if ye forgive not every one his brother from your hearts.

אָמֵן אֲנִי אוֹמֵר לָכֶם, כָּל מַה שֶׁתַּאַסְרוּ עַל הָאָרֶץ אָסוּר יִהְיֶה בַּשָּׁמַיִם
amen ani omer lachem, kol mah shetta'asru al ha'aretz asur yihyeh bashamayim
Verily I say unto you, What things soever ye shall bind on earth shall be bound in heaven;

וְכָל מַה שֶׁתַּתִּירוּ עַל הָאָרֶץ יִהְיֶה מֻתָּר בַּשָּׁמַיִם
vechol mah shettattiru al ha'aretz yihyeh muttar bashamayim
and what things soever ye shall loose on earth shall be loosed in heaven.

עוֹד אוֹמֵר אֲנִי לָכֶם, אִם שְׁנַיִם מִכֶּם יַסְכִּימוּ עֲלֵי אֲדָמוֹת בְּכָל דָּבָר אֲשֶׁר יְבַקְשׁוּ
od omer ani lachem, im shenayim mikkem yaskimu alei adamot bechol davar asher yevakshu
Again I say unto you, that if two of you shall agree on earth as touching anything that they shall ask,

הָיֹה יִהְיֶה לָהֶם מֵאֵת אָבִי שֶׁבַּשָּׁמַיִם
hayoh yihyeh lahem me'et avi shebbashamayim
it shall be done for them of my Father who is in heaven.

כִּי בְּמָקוֹם אֲשֶׁר שְׁנַיִם אוֹ שְׁלוֹשָׁה נֶאֱסָפִים לִשְׁמִי שָׁם אֲנִי בְּתוֹכָם
ki bemakom asher shenayim o sheloshah ne'esafim lishmi sham ani betocham
For where two or three are gathered together in my name, there am I in the midst of them.

כֵּיפָא נִגַּשׁ וְשָׁאַל אוֹתוֹ: אֲדוֹנִי, כַּמָּה פְּעָמִים יֶחֱטָא לִי אָחִי וְאֶסְלַח לוֹ? הַאִם עַד שֶׁבַע פְּעָמִים
keifa niggash vesha'al oto: adoni, kammah pe'amim yecheta li achi ve'eslach lo? ha'im ad sheva pe'amim
Then came Peter and said to him, Lord, how oft shall my brother sin against me, and I forgive him? until seven times?

הֵשִׁיב לוֹ יֵשׁוּעַ: אֵינֶנִּי אוֹמֵר לְךָ עַד שֶׁבַע פְּעָמִים אֶלָּא עַד שִׁבְעִים וְשֶׁבַע
heshiv lo yeshua: einenni omer lecha ad sheva pe'amim ella ad shiv'im vasheva
Jesus saith unto him, I say not unto thee, Until seven times; but, Until seventy times seven.

עַל כֵּן דּוֹמָה מַלְכוּת הַשָּׁמַיִם לְמֶלֶךְ בָּשָׂר וָדָם שֶׁרָצָה לַעֲרֹךְ חֶשְׁבּוֹן עִם עֲבָדָיו
al ken domah malchut hashamayim lemelech basar vadam sheratzah la'aroch cheshbon im avadav
Therefore is the kingdom of heaven likened unto a certain king, who would make a reckoning with his servants.

כַּאֲשֶׁר הֵחֵל לְחַשֵּׁב הוּבָא לְפָנָיו אִישׁ שֶׁהָיָה חַיָּב לוֹ עֲשֶׂרֶת אֲלָפִים כִּכְּרֵי כֶסֶף
ka'asher hechel lechashev huva lefanav ish shehayah chayav lo aseret alafim kikkerei kesef
And when he had begun to reckon, one was brought unto him, that owed him ten thousand talents.

כֵּיוָן שֶׁלֹּא הָיָה לוֹ לְשַׁלֵּם
keivan shello hayah lo leshallem
But forasmuch as he had not wherewith to pay,

צִוָּה אֲדוֹנָיו לִמְכֹּר אוֹתוֹ וְאֶת אִשְׁתּוֹ וְאֶת בָּנָיו וְאֶת כָּל אֲשֶׁר לוֹ כְּדֵי שֶׁיְּשֻׁלַּם הַחוֹב
tzivvah adonav limkor oto ve'et ishto ve'et banav ve'et kol asher lo kedei sheyeshullam hachov
his lord commanded him to be sold, and his wife, and children, and all that he had, and payment to be made.

כָּרַע הָעֶבֶד וְהִשְׁתַּחֲוָה לוֹ בְּאָמְרוֹ, אָנָּא, הֱיֵה סַבְלָן כְּלַפַּי וַאֲשַׁלֵּם לְךָ אֶת הַכֹּל
kara ha'eved vehishtachavah lo be'amero, anna, heyeh savlan kelappai va'ashallem lecha et hakkol
The servant therefore fell down and worshipped him, saying, Lord, have patience with me, and I will pay thee all.

הֲרֵינִי אוֹמֵר לָכֶם כִּי הַמַּלְאָכִים שֶׁלָּהֶם בַּשָּׁמַיִם רוֹאִים תָּמִיד אֶת פְּנֵי אָבִי שֶׁבַּשָּׁמַיִם

hareini omer lachem ki hammal'achim shellahem bashamayim ro'im tamid et penei avi shebbashamayim

for I say unto you, that in heaven their angels do always behold the face of my Father who is in heaven.

מַה דַּעְתְּכֶם? אִם יֵשׁ לְאִישׁ מֵאָה כְּבָשִׂים וְאָבַד אֶחָד מֵהֶם

mah da'techem? im yesh le'ish me'ah kevasim ve'avad echad mehem

How think ye? if any man have a hundred sheep, and one of them be gone astray,

הַאִם לֹא יַעֲזֹב אֶת הַתִּשְׁעִים וְתִשְׁעָה עַל הֶהָרִים וְיֵלֵךְ לְחַפֵּשׂ אֶת הָאוֹבֵד

ha'im lo ya'azov et hattish'im vetish'ah al heharim veyelech lechappes et ha'oved

doth he not leave the ninety and nine, and go unto the mountains, and seek that which goeth astray?

וְכַאֲשֶׁר יִמְצָא אוֹתוֹ, אָמֵן אוֹמֵר אֲנִי לָכֶם

vecha'asher yimtza oto, amen omer ani lachem

And if so be that he find it, verily I say unto you,

יִשְׂמַח עָלָיו יוֹתֵר מֵאֲשֶׁר עַל הַתִּשְׁעִים וְתִשְׁעָה שֶׁלֹּא אָבְדוּ

yismach alav yoter me'asher al hattish'im vetish'ah shello avedu

he rejoiceth over it more than over the ninety and nine which have not gone astray.

כָּךְ אֵין רָצוֹן מִלִּפְנֵי אֲבִיכֶם שֶׁבַּשָּׁמַיִם שֶׁיֹּאבַד אֶחָד מִן הַקְּטַנִּים הָאֵלֶּה

kach ein ratzon millifnei avichem shebbashamayim sheyovad echad min haktannim ha'elleh

Even so it is not the will of your Father who is in heaven, that one of these little ones should perish.

אִם יֶחֱטָא לְךָ אָחִיךָ, לֵךְ וְהוֹכַח אוֹתוֹ בֵּינְךָ וּבֵינוֹ לְבַד

'im yecheta lecha achicha, lech vehocheach oto beinecha uveino levad

And if thy brother sin against thee, go, show him his fault between thee and him alone:

אִם יִשְׁמַע לְךָ, קָנִיתָ לְךָ אֶת אָחִיךָ

im yishma lecha, kanita lecha et achicha

if he hear thee, thou hast gained thy brother.

וְאִם לֹא יִשְׁמַע, קַח אִתְּךָ עוֹד אֶחָד אוֹ שְׁנַיִם

ve'im lo yishma', kach ittcha od echad o shnayim

But if he hear thee not, take with thee one or two more,

כְּדֵי שֶׁעַל-פִּי שְׁנַיִם אוֹ שְׁלוֹשָׁה עֵדִים יָקוּם כָּל דָּבָר

kedei she'al-pi shnayim o shloshah edim yakum kol davar

that at the mouth of two witnesses or three every word may be established.

אִם לֹא יִשְׁמַע לָהֶם, הַגֵּד לַקְּהִלָּה

im lo yishma lahem, hagged lakkehillah

And if he refuse to hear them, tell it unto the church:

וְאִם לֹא יִשְׁמַע גַּם לַקְּהִלָּה, שֶׁיִּהְיֶה לְךָ כַּגּוֹי וְכַמּוֹכֵס

ve'im lo yishma gam lakkehillah, sheyihyeh lecha kaggoy vechammoches

and if he refuse to hear the church also, let him be unto thee as the Gentile and the publican.

לָכֵן מִי שֶׁיַּשְׁפִּיל אֶת עַצְמוֹ לִהְיוֹת כַּיֶּלֶד הַזֶּה הוּא הַגָּדוֹל בְּמַלְכוּת הַשָּׁמַיִם
lachen mi sheyashpil et atzmo lihyot kayeled hazzeh hu haggadol bemalchut hashamayim
Whosoever therefore shall humble himself as this little child, the same is the greatest in the kingdom of heaven.

כָּל הַמְקַבֵּל יֶלֶד אֶחָד כָּזֶה בִּשְׁמִי, אוֹתִי הוּא מְקַבֵּל
kol hamkabbel yeled echad kazeh bishmi, oti hu mekabbel
And whoso shall receive one such little child in my name receiveth me:

אַךְ כָּל הַמַּכְשִׁיל אֶחָד מִן הַקְּטַנִּים הָאֵלֶּה הַמַּאֲמִינִים בִּי
ach kol hammachshil echad min hakketannim ha'elleh hamma'aminim bi
but whoso shall cause one of these little ones that believe on me to stumble,

מוּטָב לוֹ שֶׁתִּתָּלֶה אֶבֶן רֵחַיִם עַל צַוָּארוֹ
mutav lo shettittaleh even rechayim al tzavvaro
it is profitable for him that a great millstone should be hanged about his neck,

וִיטֻבַּע בִּמְצוּלוֹת יָם
viytubba bimtzulot yam
and that he should be sunk in the depth of the sea.

אוֹי לָעוֹלָם מִן הַמִּכְשׁוֹלִים
oy la'olam min hammichsholim
Woe unto the world because of occasions of stumbling!

כִּי מִן הַהֶכְרֵחַ שֶׁיָּבוֹאוּ מִכְשׁוֹלִים, אֲבָל אוֹי לָאִישׁ שֶׁהַמִּכְשׁוֹל יָבוֹא דַּרְכּוֹ
ki min hahechreach sheyavo'u michsholim, aval oy la'ish shehammichshol yavo darko
for it must needs be that the occasions come; but woe to that man through whom the occasion cometh!

אִם יָדְךָ אוֹ רַגְלְךָ תַּכְשִׁיל אוֹתְךָ, קַצֵּץ אוֹתָהּ וְהַשְׁלֵךְ אוֹתָהּ מִמְּךָ
im yadecha o raglecha tachshil otecha, katzetz otah vehashlech otah mimmcha
And if thy hand or thy foot causeth thee to stumble, cut it off, and cast it from thee:

מוּטָב לְךָ לָבוֹא לַחַיִּים גִּדֵּם אוֹ קִטֵּעַ מֵהֱיוֹתְךָ מֻשְׁלָךְ לְאֵשׁ עוֹלָם עִם שְׁתֵּי יָדַיִם אוֹ שְׁתֵּי רַגְלַיִם
mutav lecha lavo lachayim giddem o kittea meheyotecha mushlach le'esh olam im shetei yadayim o shetei raglayim
it is good for thee to enter into life maimed or halt, rather than having two hands or two feet to be cast into the eternal fire.

וְאִם עֵינְךָ תַּכְשִׁיל אוֹתְךָ, נַקֵּר אוֹתָהּ וְהַשְׁלֵךְ אוֹתָהּ מִמְּךָ
ve'im eincha tachshil otecha, nakker otah vehashlech otah mimmcha
And if thine eye causeth thee to stumble, pluck it out, and cast it from thee:

מוּטָב לְךָ לָבוֹא לַחַיִּים עִם עַיִן אַחַת מֵהֱיוֹתְךָ מֻשְׁלָךְ לְגֵיהִנּוֹם הָאֵשׁ עִם שְׁתֵּי עֵינַיִם
mutav lecha lavo lachayim im ayin achat meheyotecha mushlach legeihinnom ha'esh im shetei einayim
it is good for thee to enter into life with one eye, rather than having two eyes to be cast into the hell of fire.

הִזָּהֲרוּ שֶׁלֹּא תָבוּזוּ לְאֶחָד הַקְּטַנִּים הָאֵלֶּה
hizzaharu shello tavuzu le'achad hakketannim ha'elleh
See that ye despise not one of these little ones:

כְּבוֹאָם אֶל כְּפַר נַחוּם נִגְּשׁוּ אֶל כֵּיפָא גּוֹבֵי מַחֲצִית הַשֶּׁקֶל וְשָׁאֲלוּ
kevo'am el kefar nachum niggeshu el keifa govei machatzit hashekel vesha'alu
And when they were come to Capernaum, they that received the half-shekel came to Peter, and said,

הַאִם רַבְּכֶם אֵינוֹ מְשַׁלֵּם אֶת מַחֲצִית הַשֶּׁקֶל
ha'im rabbechem eino meshallem et machatzit hashekel
Doth not your teacher pay the half-shekel?

כֵּן, הֵשִׁיב לָהֶם כַּאֲשֶׁר נִכְנַס הַבַּיְתָה הִקְדִּים יֵשׁוּעַ לִשְׁאֹל אוֹתוֹ מַה דַּעְתְּךָ, שִׁמְעוֹן
ken, heshiv lahem ka'asher nichnas habbaytah hikdim yeshua lish'ol oto mah da'techa, shim'on
He saith, Yea. And when he came into the house, Jesus spake first to him, saying, What thinkest thou, Simon?

מַלְכֵי הָאָרֶץ מִמִּי הֵם לוֹקְחִים מֶכֶס וּמַס, מִבְּנֵיהֶם אוֹ מִן הַזָּרִים
malchei ha'aretz mimmi hem lokchim meches umas, mibbeneihem o min hazzarim
the kings of the earth, from whom do they receive toll or tribute? from their sons, or from strangers?

כְּשֶׁהֵשִׁיב מִן הַזָּרִים, אָמַר לוֹ יֵשׁוּעַ: אִם כֵּן, הַבָּנִים פְּטוּרִים
kesheheshiv min hazzarim, amar lo yeshua: im ken, habbanim peturim
And when he said, From strangers, Jesus said unto him, Therefore the sons are free.

אֲבָל כְּדֵי שֶׁלֹּא נִהְיֶה לָהֶם לְמִכְשׁוֹל, לֵךְ אֶל הַיָּם, הַשְׁלֵךְ חַכָּה וְקַח אֶת הַדָּג שֶׁיַּעֲלֶה רִאשׁוֹנָה
aval kedei shello nihyeh lahem lemichshol, lech el hayam, hashlech chakkah vekach et haddag sheya'aleh rishonah
But, lest we cause them to stumble, go thou to the sea, and cast a hook, and take up the fish that first cometh up;

כְּשֶׁתִּפְתַּח אֶת פִּיו תִּמְצָא מַטְבֵּעַ; קַח אוֹתוֹ וְתֵן לָהֶם בַּעֲדִי וּבַעַדְךָ
keshetiftach et piv timtza matbea'; kach oto veten lahem ba'adi uva'adcha
and when thou hast opened his mouth, thou shalt find a shekel: that take, and give unto them for me and thee.

יח

אוֹתָהּ שָׁעָה נִגְּשׁוּ הַתַּלְמִידִים אֶל יֵשׁוּעַ וְשָׁאֲלוּ: מִי הוּא הַגָּדוֹל בְּמַלְכוּת הַשָּׁמַיִם
otah sha'ah niggeshu hattalmidim el yeshua vesha'alu: mi hu haggadol bemalchut hashamayim
In that hour came the disciples unto Jesus, saying, Who then is greatest in the kingdom of heaven?

יֵשׁוּעַ קָרָא אֵלָיו יֶלֶד, הֶעֱמִידוֹ בֵּינֵיהֶם
yeshua kara elav yeled, he'emido beineihem
And he called to him a little child, and set him in the midst of them,

וְאָמַר: אָמֵן אוֹמֵר אֲנִי לָכֶם
ve'amar: amen omer ani lachem
and said, Verily I say unto you,

אִם לֹא תָּשׁוּבוּ וְתִהְיוּ כִּילָדִים לֹא תִּכָּנְסוּ לְמַלְכוּת הַשָּׁמַיִם
im lo tashuvu vetihyu kiyeladim lo tikkanesu lemalchut hashamayim
Except ye turn, and become as little children, ye shall in no wise enter into the kingdom of heaven.

אָמַר הָאִישׁ: אֲדוֹנִי, רַחֵם נָא עַל בְּנִי. הוּא מֻכֵּה יָרֵחַ וּמַחֲלָתוֹ קָשָׁה
amar ha'ish: adoni, rachem na al beni. Hu mukkeh yareach umachalato kashah
and saying, Lord, have mercy on my son: for he is epileptic, and suffereth grievously;

כִּי לְעִתִּים קְרוֹבוֹת הוּא נוֹפֵל לָאֵשׁ וּלְעִתִּים קְרוֹבוֹת לַמַּיִם
ki le'ittim kerovot hu nofel la'esh ule'ittim kerovot lammayim
for oft-times he falleth into the fire, and oft-times into the water.

הֵבֵאתִי אוֹתוֹ אֶל תַּלְמִידֶיךָ וְהֵם לֹא יָכְלוּ לְרַפְּאוֹ
heveti oto el talmideicha vehem lo yachelu lerappe'o
And I brought him to thy disciples, and they could not cure him.

הֵשִׁיב יֵשׁוּעַ וְאָמַר: הוֹי דּוֹר חֲסַר אֱמוּנָה וּמְעֻוַּת דֶּרֶךְ, עַד מָתַי אֶהְיֶה עִמָּכֶם
heshiv yeshua ve'amar: hoy dor chasar emunah ume'avet derech, ad matai ehyeh immachem
And Jesus answered and said, O faithless and perverse generation, how long shall I be with you?

עַד מָתַי אֶסְבֹּל אֶתְכֶם? הָבִיאוּ אוֹתוֹ הֵנָּה אֵלַי
ad matai esbol etchem? havi'u oto hennah elai
how long shall I bear with you? bring him hither to me.

גָּעַר יֵשׁוּעַ בַּשֵּׁד וְהַשֵּׁד יָצָא מִמֶּנּוּ. מֵאוֹתָהּ שָׁעָה נִרְפָּא הַנַּעַר
ga'ar yeshua bashed vehashed yatza mimmennu. me'otah sha'ah nirpa hanna'ar
And Jesus rebuked him; and the demon went out of him: and the boy was cured from that hour.

לְאַחַר מִכֵּן נִגְּשׁוּ הַתַּלְמִידִים אֶל יֵשׁוּעַ לְבַדָּם וְשָׁאֲלוּ: מַדּוּעַ לֹא יָכֹלְנוּ אֲנַחְנוּ לְגָרֵשׁ אוֹתוֹ
le'achar mikken niggeshu hattalmidim el yeshua levaddam vesha'alu: maddua lo yacholenu anachnu legaresh oto
Then came the disciples to Jesus apart, and said, Why could not we cast it out?

הֵשִׁיב לָהֶם: בִּגְלַל מְעוּט אֱמוּנַתְכֶם. אָמֵן אוֹמֵר אֲנִי לָכֶם, אִם יֵשׁ לָכֶם אֱמוּנָה כְּגַרְגִּיר הַחַרְדָּל
heshiv lahem: Biglal mi'ut emunatchem. amen omer ani lachem, im yesh lachem emunah kegargir hachardal
And he saith unto them, Because of your little faith: for verily I say unto you, If ye have faith as a grain of mustard seed,

וְתֹאמְרוּ לָהָר הַזֶּה זוּז מִפֹּה לְשָׁם - הוּא יָזוּז
vetomeru lahar hazzeh zuz mippoh lesham - hu yazuz
ye shall say unto this mountain, Remove hence to yonder place; and it shall remove;

וְשׁוּם דָּבָר לֹא יִבָּצֵר מִכֶּם
veshum davar lo yibbatzer mikkem
and nothing shall be impossible unto you.

כַּאֲשֶׁר הִתְהַלְּכוּ בַּגָּלִיל אָמַר לָהֶם יֵשׁוּעַ: עָתִיד בֶּן־הָאָדָם לְהִמָּסֵר לִידֵי אֲנָשִׁים
ka'asher hit'hallechu baggalil amar lahem yeshua. atid ben-ha'adam lehimmaser liydei anashim
And while they abode in Galilee, Jesus said unto them, The Son of man shall be delivered up into the hands of men;

וְיַהַרְגוּהוּ וּבַיּוֹם הַשְּׁלִישִׁי יָקוּם. אָז הִתְעַצְּבוּ עֶצֶב רַב
veyaharguhu uvayom hashelishi yakum. az hit'atzevu etzev rav
and they shall kill him, and the third day he shall be raised up. And they were exceeding sorry.

זֶה בְּנִי אֲהוּבִי אֲשֶׁר חָפַצְתִּי בּוֹ; אֵלָיו תִּשְׁמָעוּן
zeh beni ahuvi asher chafatzti bo; elav tishma'un
This is my beloved Son, in whom I am well pleased; hear ye him.

כְּשָׁמְעָם זֹאת נָפְלוּ הַתַּלְמִידִים עַל פְּנֵיהֶם וּפָחֲדוּ עַד מְאֹד
keshom'am zot nafelu hattalmidim al peneihem ufachadu ad me'od
And when the disciples heard it, they fell on their face, and were sore afraid.

יֵשׁוּעַ נִגַּשׁ, נָגַע בָּהֶם וְאָמַר: קוּמוּ וְאַל תִּפְחָדוּ
yeshua niggash, naga bahem ve'amar: kumu ve'al tifchadu
And Jesus came and touched them and said, Arise, and be not afraid.

הֵם נָשְׂאוּ עֵינֵיהֶם וְלֹא רָאוּ אִישׁ זוּלָתִי יֵשׁוּעַ לְבַדּוֹ
hem nase'u eineihem velo ra'u ish zulati yeshua levaddo
And lifting up their eyes, they saw no one, save Jesus only.

כְּשֶׁיָּרְדוּ מִן הָהָר צִוָּה עֲלֵיהֶם יֵשׁוּעַ
kesheyaredu min hahar tzivvah aleihem yeshua
And as they were coming down from the mountain, Jesus commanded them, saying,

אַל תְּסַפְּרוּ אֶת הַמַּרְאֶה לְאִישׁ עַד אֲשֶׁר יָקוּם בֶּן־הָאָדָם מִן הַמֵּתִים
al tesapperu et hammar'eh le'ish ad asher yakum ben-ha'adam min hammetim
Tell the vision to no man, until the Son of man be risen from the dead.

שְׁאָלוּהוּ הַתַּלְמִידִים: מַדּוּעַ זֶה אוֹמְרִים הַסּוֹפְרִים כִּי אֵלִיָּהוּ צָרִיךְ לָבוֹא תְּחִלָּה
she'aluhu hattalmidim: maddua zeh omerim hassoferim ki eliyahu tzarich lavo techillah
And his disciples asked him, saying, Why then say the scribes that Elijah must first come?

הֵשִׁיב יֵשׁוּעַ וְאָמַר: אֵלִיָּהוּ אָמְנָם יָבוֹא וְיָשִׁיב אֶת הַכֹּל
heshiv yeshua ve'amar: eliyahu amnam yavo veyashiv et hakkol
And he answered and said, Elijah indeed cometh, and shall restore all things:

אֲבָל אוֹמֵר אֲנִי לָכֶם שֶׁאֵלִיָּהוּ כְּבָר בָּא וְלֹא הִכִּירוּהוּ אֶלָּא עָשׂוּ בוֹ כִּרְצוֹנָם
aval omer ani lachem she'eliyahu kevar ba velo hikkiruhu ella asu bo kirtzonam
but I say unto you, that Elijah is come already, and they knew him not, but did unto him whatsoever they would.

כָּךְ גַּם בֶּן־הָאָדָם עָתִיד לִסְבֹּל מִיָּדָם
kach gam ben-ha'adam atid lisbol miyadam
Even so shall the Son of man also suffer of them.

אָז הֵבִינוּ הַתַּלְמִידִים כִּי עַל יוֹחָנָן הַמַּטְבִּיל דִּבֶּר אֲלֵיהֶם
az hevinu hattalmidim ki al yochanan hammatbil dibber aleihem
Then understood the disciples that he spake unto them of John the Baptist.

כַּאֲשֶׁר בָּאוּ אֶל הֲמוֹן הָעָם נִגַּשׁ אֵלָיו אִישׁ וְכָרַע עַל בִּרְכָּיו לְפָנָיו
ka'asher ba'u el hamon ha'am niggash elav ish vechara al birkav lefanav
And when they were come to the multitude, there came to him a man, kneeling to him,

הֵן עָתִיד בֶּן־הָאָדָם לָבוֹא בִּכְבוֹד אָבִיו עִם מַלְאָכָיו
hen atid ben-ha'adam lavo bichvod aviv im mal'achav
For the Son of man shall come in the glory of his Father with his angels;

וְאָז יְשַׁלֵּם לְכָל אִישׁ כְּמַעֲשֵׂהוּ
ve'az yeshallem lechol ish kema'asehu
and then shall he render unto every man according to his deeds.

אָמֵן אוֹמֵר אֲנִי לָכֶם, יֵשׁ מִן הָעוֹמְדִים פֹּה
amen mer ani lachem, yesh min ha'omedim poh
Verily I say unto you, There are some of them that stand here,

שֶׁלֹּא יִטְעֲמוּ מָוֶת עַד כִּי יִרְאוּ אֶת בֶּן־הָאָדָם בָּא בְּמַלְכוּתוֹ
shello yit'amu mavet ad ki yir'u et ben-ha'adam ba bemalchuto
who shall in no wise taste of death, till they see the Son of man coming in his kingdom.

יז

לְאַחַר שִׁשָּׁה יָמִים לָקַח יֵשׁוּעַ אֶת כֵּיפָא וְאֶת יַעֲקֹב וְאֶת יוֹחָנָן אָחִיו
le'achar shishah yamim lakach yeshua et keifa ve'et ya'akov ve'et yochanan achiv
And after six days Jesus taketh with him Peter, and James, and John his brother,

הוּא הֶעֱלָה אוֹתָם לְהַר גָּבוֹהַּ לְבַדָּם
hu he'elah otam lehar gavoah levaddam
and bringeth them up into a high mountain apart:

וְהִשְׁתַּנָּה לְעֵינֵיהֶם; פָּנָיו זָהֲרוּ כַּשֶּׁמֶשׁ וּבְגָדָיו הִלְבִּינוּ כָאוֹר
vehishtannah le'eineihem; panav zaharu kashemesh uvegadav hilbinu ka'or
and he was transfigured before them; and his face did shine as the sun, and his garments became white as the light.

לְפֶתַע נִרְאוּ אֲלֵיהֶם מֹשֶׁה וְאֵלִיָּהוּ כְּשֶׁהֵם מְדַבְּרִים אִתּוֹ
lefeta nir'u aleihem mosheh ve'eliyahu keshehem medabberim itto
And behold, there appeared unto them Moses and Elijah talking with him.

הֵגִיב כֵּיפָא וְאָמַר אֶל יֵשׁוּעַ: אֲדוֹנִי, טוֹב שֶׁאֲנַחְנוּ כָּאן
hegiv keifa ve'amar el yeshua: adoni, tov she'anachnu kan
And Peter answered, and said unto Jesus, Lord, it is good for us to be here:

אִם תִּרְצֶה אֶעֱשֶׂה פֹּה שָׁלוֹשׁ סֻכּוֹת, לְךָ אַחַת, לְמֹשֶׁה אַחַת וּלְאֵלִיָּהוּ אַחַת
Im tirtzeh e'eseh poh shalosh sukkot, lecha achat, lemosheh achat ule'eliyahu achat
if thou wilt, I will make here three tabernacles; one for thee, and one for Moses, and one for Elijah.

עוֹדוֹ מְדַבֵּר וְעָנָן בָּהִיר סָכַךְ עֲלֵיהֶם וְהִנֵּה קוֹל אוֹמֵר מִתּוֹךְ הֶעָנָן
odo medabber ve'anan bahir sachach aleihem vehinneh kol omer mittoch he'anan
While he was yet speaking, behold, a bright cloud overshadowed them: and behold, a voice out of the cloud, saying,

וְכָל מַה שֶׁתַּתִּיר עַל הָאָרֶץ יִהְיֶה מֻתָּר בַּשָּׁמַיִם
vechol mah shettattir al ha'aretz yihyeh muttar bashamayim
and whatsoever thou shalt loose on earth shall be loosed in heaven.

אָז הִזְהִיר אֶת תַּלְמִידָיו שֶׁלֹּא יְסַפְּרוּ לְאִישׁ כִּי הוּא הַמָּשִׁיחַ
az hizhir et talmidav shello yesapperu le'ish ki hu hammashiach
Then charged he the disciples that they should tell no man that he was the Christ.

מֵאוֹתָהּ עֵת הֵחֵל יֵשׁוּעַ לְהַבְהִיר לְתַלְמִידָיו כִּי עָלָיו לָלֶכֶת לִירוּשָׁלַיִם
me'otah et hechel yeshua lehavhir letalmidav ki alav lalechet liyerushalayim
From that time began Jesus to show unto his disciples, that he must go unto Jerusalem,

וְלִסְבֹּל הַרְבֵּה מִידֵי הַזְּקֵנִים וְרָאשֵׁי הַכֹּהֲנִים וְהַסּוֹפְרִים, וּלְהֵהָרֵג וּבַיּוֹם הַשְּׁלִישִׁי לָקוּם
velisbol harbeh miydei hazzekenim verashei hakkohanim vehassoferim, ulehehareg uvayom hashelishi lakum
and suffer many things of the elders and chief priests and scribes, and be killed, and the third day be raised up.

לָקַח אוֹתוֹ כֵּיפָא לַצַּד וְהֵחֵל לִגְעֹר בּוֹ בְּאָמְרוֹ: חָלִילָה לְךָ, אֲדוֹנִי. אַל יִהְיֶה הַדָּבָר הַזֶּה לְךָ
lakach oto keifa latzad vehechel lig'or bo be'omro: chalilah lecha, adoni. Al yihyeh haddavar hazzeh lecha
And Peter took him, and began to rebuke him, saying, Be it far from thee, Lord: this shall never be unto thee.

פָּנָה יֵשׁוּעַ וְאָמַר לְכֵיפָא: סוּר מִלְּפָנַי, שָׂטָן. מִכְשׁוֹל אַתָּה לִי
panah yeshua ve'amar lekeifa: sur millefanai, satan. michshol attah li
But he turned, and said unto Peter, Get thee behind me, Satan: thou art a stumbling-block unto me:

כִּי אֵין לִבְּךָ לְדִבְרֵי אֱלֹהִים אֶלָּא לְדִבְרֵי בְּנֵי אָדָם
ki ein libbecha ledivrei elohim ella ledivrei benei adam
for thou mindest not the things of God, but the things of men.

אָז אָמַר יֵשׁוּעַ לְתַלְמִידָיו
az amar yeshua letalmidav
Then said Jesus unto his disciples,

מִי שֶׁרוֹצֶה לָבוֹא אַחֲרַי, שֶׁיִּתְכַּחֵשׁ לְעַצְמוֹ וְיִקַּח אֶת צְלָבוֹ וְיֵלֵךְ אַחֲרַי
mi sherotzeh lavo acharai, sheyitkachesh le'atzmo veyikkach et tzelavo veyelech acharai
If any man would come after me, let him deny himself, and take up his cross, and follow me.

כִּי הֶחָפֵץ לְהַצִּיל אֶת נַפְשׁוֹ יְאַבֵּד אוֹתָהּ, אֲבָל הַמְאַבֵּד אֶת נַפְשׁוֹ לְמַעֲנִי יִמְצָאֶנָּה
ki hechafetz lehatzil et nafsho ye'abbed otah, aval ham'abbed et nafsho lema'ani yimtza'ennah
For whosoever would save his life shall lose it: and whosoever shall lose his life for my sake shall find it.

מַה תּוֹעֶלֶת תִּצְמַח לְאָדָם אִם יַרְוִיחַ אֶת כָּל הָעוֹלָם וְיַפְסִיד אֶת נַפְשׁוֹ
mah to'elet titzmach le'adam im yarviach et kol ha'olam veyafsid et nafsho
For what shall a man be profited, if he shall gain the whole world, and forfeit his life?

אוֹ מַה יִּתֵּן אָדָם כִּתְמוּרָה בְּעַד נַפְשׁוֹ
o mah yitten adam kitmurah be'ad nafsho
or what shall a man give in exchange for his life?

אָז הֵבִינוּ כִּי לֹא אָמַר לָהֶם לְהִזָּהֵר מִשְׂאוֹר הַלֶּחֶם
az hevinu ki lo amar lahem lehizzaher misho'or hallechem
Then understood they that he bade them not beware of the leaven of bread,

אֶלָּא מִתּוֹרַת הַפְּרוּשִׁים וְהַצְּדוֹקִים
ella mittorat happerushim vehatzedokim
but of the teaching of the Pharisees and Sadducees.

כְּשֶׁבָּא יֵשׁוּעַ אֶל סְבִיבוֹת קֵיסַרְיָה שֶׁל פִילִיפּוֹס שָׁאַל אֶת תַּלְמִידָיו
keshebba yeshua el sevivot keisaryah shel filipos sha'al et talmidav
Now when Jesus came into the parts of Cæsarea Philippi, he asked his disciples, saying,

מָה אוֹמְרִים הָאֲנָשִׁים עַל בֶּן־הָאָדָם, מִי הוּא
mah omerim ha'anashim al ben-ha'adam, mi hu
Who do men say that the Son of man is?

הֵשִׁיבוּ: יֵשׁ אוֹמְרִים, יוֹחָנָן הַמַּטְבִּיל; אֲחֵרִים אוֹמְרִים, אֵלִיָּהוּ; וַאֲחֵרִים - יִרְמְיָהוּ אוֹ אֶחָד מֵהַנְּבִיאִים
heshivu: yesh omerim, yochanan hammatbil; acherim omerim, eliyahu; va'acherim - yirmeyahu o echad mehannevi'im
And they said, Some say John the Baptist; some, Elijah; and others, Jeremiah, or one of the prophets.

שָׁאַל אוֹתָם: וְאַתֶּם מָה אוֹמְרִים, מִי אֲנִי
sha'al otam: ve'attem mah omerim, mi ani
He saith unto them, But who say ye that I am?

עָנָה שִׁמְעוֹן כֵּיפָא וְאָמַר: אַתָּה הַמָּשִׁיחַ, בֶּן־אֱלֹהִים חַיִּים
anah shim'on keifa ve'amar: attah hammashiach, ben-'elohim chayim
And Simon Peter answered and said, Thou art the Christ, the Son of the living God.

אָמַר לוֹ יֵשׁוּעַ: אַשְׁרֶיךָ שִׁמְעוֹן בַּר־יוֹנָה
amar lo yeshua: ashreicha shim'on bar-yonah
And Jesus answered and said unto him, Blessed art thou, Simon Bar-Jonah:

כִּי לֹא בָּשָׂר וָדָם גִּלָּה לְךָ, אֶלָּא אָבִי שֶׁבַּשָּׁמַיִם
ki lo bashar vadam gillah lecha, ella avi shebbashamayim
for flesh and blood hath not revealed it unto thee, but my Father who is in heaven.

וְגַם אֲנִי אוֹמֵר לְךָ כִּי אַתָּה כֵּיפָא וְעַל הַצּוּר הַזֶּה אֶבְנֶה אֶת קְהִלָּתִי
vegam ani omer lecha ki attah keifa ve'al hatzur hazzeh evneh et kehillati
And I also say unto thee, that thou art Peter, and upon this rock I will build my church;

וְשַׁעֲרֵי שְׁאוֹל לֹא יִגְבְּרוּ עָלֶיהָ
vesha'arei she'ol lo yigberu aleiha
and the gates of Hades shall not prevail against it.

אֶתֵּן לְךָ אֶת מַפְתְּחוֹת מַלְכוּת הַשָּׁמַיִם וְכָל מַה שֶּׁתֶּאֱסֹר עַל הָאָרֶץ יִהְיֶה אָסוּר בַּשָּׁמַיִם
etten lecha et maftechot malchut hashamayim vechol mah shette'esor al ha'aretz yihyeh asur bashamayim
I will give unto thee the keys of the kingdom of heaven: and whatsoever thou shalt bind on earth shall be bound in heaven;

וּבַבֹּקֶר, סַגְרִיר הַיּוֹם, כִּי אֲדֻמִּים וְקוֹדְרִים הַשָּׁמַיִם.
uvabboker, sagrir hayom, ki adummim vekoderim hashamayim
And in the morning, It will be foul weather to-day: for the heaven is red and lowering.

אֶת פְּנֵי הַשָּׁמַיִם אַתֶּם יוֹדְעִים לְפָרֵשׁ, אַךְ אֶת אוֹתוֹת הַזְּמַנִּים אֵינְכֶם יְכוֹלִים
Et penei hashamayim attem yode'im lefaresh, ach et otot hazzemannim einechem yecholim
Ye know how to discern the face of the heaven; but ye cannot discern the signs of the times.

דּוֹר רַע וּמְנָאֵף מְבַקֵּשׁ לוֹ אוֹת, וְאוֹת לֹא יִנָּתֵן לוֹ מִלְּבַד אוֹת יוֹנָה הַנָּבִיא
dor ra umena'ef mevakkesh lo ot, ve'ot lo yinnaten lo millevad ot yonah hannavi
An evil and adulterous generation seeketh after a sign; and there shall no sign be given unto it, but the sign of Jonah.

הוּא עָזַב אוֹתָם וְהָלַךְ
Hu azav otam vehalach
And he left them, and departed.

כְּשֶׁעָבְרוּ הַתַּלְמִידִים אֶל הַצַּד הַשֵּׁנִי שָׁכְחוּ לָקַחַת לֶחֶם. אָמַר לָהֶם יֵשׁוּעַ
keshe'avru hattalmidim el hatzad hasheni shachechu lakachat lechem. Amar lahem yeshua
And the disciples came to the other side and forgot to take bread.

שִׂימוּ לְבַבְכֶם וְהִזָּהֲרוּ מִשְּׂאוֹר הַפְּרוּשִׁים וְהַצְּדוֹקִים
simu levavchem vehizzaharu misho'or happerushim vehatzedokim
And Jesus said unto them, Take heed and beware of the leaven of the Pharisees and Sadducees.

אַךְ הֵם אָמְרוּ בִּלְבָבָם, לֶחֶם לֹא לָקַחְנוּ
ach hem ameru bilvavam, lechem lo lakachnu
And they reasoned among themselves, saying, We took no bread.

יֵשׁוּעַ הִבְחִין בָּזֶה וְאָמַר: קְטַנֵּי אֱמוּנָה, מַדּוּעַ אַתֶּם אוֹמְרִים בְּקִרְבְּכֶם שֶׁאֵין לָכֶם לֶחֶם
yeshua hivchin bazeh ve'amar. Ketannei emunah, maddua attem omerim bekirbechem she'ein lachem lechem
And Jesus perceiving it said, O ye of little faith, why reason ye among yourselves, because ye have no bread?

עֲדַיִן אֵינְכֶם מְבִינִים אַף לֹא זוֹכְרִים אֶת חָמֵשׁ כִּכְּרוֹת הַלֶּחֶם לַחֲמֵשֶׁת אֲלָפִים אִישׁ וְכַמָּה סַלִּים לְקַחְתֶּם
adayin einechem mevinim af lo zocherim et chamesh kikkerot hallechem lachameshet alafim ish vechammah sallim lekachtem
Do ye not yet perceive, neither remember the five loaves of the five thousand, and how many baskets ye took up?

גַּם לֹא אֶת שֶׁבַע כִּכְּרוֹת הַלֶּחֶם לְאַרְבַּעַת אֲלָפִים אִישׁ וְכַמָּה סַלִּים לְקַחְתֶּם
gam lo et sheva kikkerot hallechem le'arba'at alafim ish vechammah sallim lekachtem
Neither the seven loaves of the four thousand, and how many baskets ye took up?

אֵיךְ זֶה אֵינְכֶם מְבִינִים שֶׁלֹּא עַל כִּכְּרוֹת הַלֶּחֶם דִּבַּרְתִּי אֲלֵיכֶם?
eich zeh einechem mevinim shello al kikkerot hallechem dibbarti aleichem?
How is it that ye do not perceive that I spake not to you concerning bread?

הִזָּהֲרוּ מִשְּׂאוֹר הַפְּרוּשִׁים וְהַצְּדוֹקִים
hizzaharu misho'or happerushim vehatzedokim
But beware of the leaven of the Pharisees and Sadducees.

אֵינֶנִּי חָפֵץ לְשַׁלֵּחַ אוֹתָם רְעֵבִים פֶּן יִתְעַלְּפוּ בַּדֶּרֶךְ
einenni chafetz leshalleach otam re'evim pen yit'allefu badderech
and I would not send them away fasting, lest haply they faint on the way.

אָמְרוּ לוֹ תַּלְמִידָיו: מֵאַיִן לָנוּ בַּמִּדְבָּר דֵּי לֶחֶם לְהַשְׂבִּיעַ הָמוֹן רַב כָּזֶה
ameru lo talmidav: me'ayin lanu bammidbar dei lechem lehasbia hamon rav kazeh
And the disciples say unto him, Whence should we have so many loaves in a desert place as to fill so great a multitude?

אָמַר יֵשׁוּעַ: כַּמָּה כִּכְּרוֹת לֶחֶם יֵשׁ לָכֶם הֲשִׁיבוּ: שֶׁבַע, וּמְעַט דָּגִים קְטַנִּים
amar yeshua: kammah kikkerot lechem yesh lachem heshivu. Sheva', ume'at dagim ketannim
And Jesus said unto them, How many loaves have ye? And they said, Seven, and a few small fishes.

אָז צִוָּה אֶת הָעָם לָשֶׁבֶת עַל הָאָרֶץ
'az tzivvah et ha'am lashevet al ha'aretz
And he commanded the multitude to sit down on the ground;

לָקַח אֶת שֶׁבַע כִּכְּרוֹת הַלֶּחֶם וְאֶת הַדָּגִים וּלְאַחַר שֶׁבֵּרֵךְ, פָּרַס
lakach et sheva kikkerot hallechem ve'et haddagim ule'achar shebberech paras
and he took the seven loaves and the fishes; and he gave thanks and brake,

וְנָתַן לַתַּלְמִידִים וְהַתַּלְמִידִים נָתְנוּ לָעָם
venatan lattalmidim vehattalmidim natenu la'am
and gave to the disciples, and the disciples to the multitudes.

הַכֹּל אָכְלוּ וְשָׂבְעוּ, וּמִמַּה שֶׁנּוֹתַר אָסְפוּ שִׁבְעָה סַלִּים מְלֵאִים
hakkol achelu vesave'u, umimmah shennotar asefu shiv'ah sallim mele'im
And they all ate, and were filled: and they took up that which remained over of the broken pieces, seven baskets full.

מִסְפַּר הָאוֹכְלִים הָיָה אַרְבַּעַת אֲלָפִים אִישׁ מִלְּבַד הַנָּשִׁים וְהַטַּף
mispar ha'ochelim hayah arba'at alafim ish millevad hannashim vehattaf
And they that did eat were four thousand men, besides women and children.

לְאַחַר מִכֵּן שִׁלַּח אֶת הָעָם, יָרַד לַסִּירָה וְהִגִּיעַ אֶל אֵזוֹר מָגָדָן
le'achar mikken shillach et ha'am, yarad lassirah vehiggia el ezor magadan
And he sent away the multitudes, and entered into the boat, and came into the borders of Magadan.

טו

הַפְּרוּשִׁים וְהַצְּדוֹקִים נִגְּשׁוּ לְנַסּוֹת אוֹתוֹ וּבִקְשׁוּ מִמֶּנּוּ לְהַרְאוֹת לָהֶם אוֹת מִן הַשָּׁמַיִם
Happerushim vehatzedokim niggeshu lenassot oto uvikshu mimmennu lehar'ot lahem ot min hashamayim
And the Pharisees and Sadducees came, and trying him asked him to show them a sign from heaven.

הֵשִׁיב וְאָמַר לָהֶם: לְעֵת עֶרֶב אַתֶּם אוֹמְרִים, מֶזֶג אֲוִיר נָאֶה, כִּי הַשָּׁמַיִם אֲדֻמִּים
heshiv ve'amar lahem: le'et erev attem omerim, mezeg avir na'eh, ki hashamayim adummim
But he answered and said unto them, When it is evening, ye say, It will be fair weather: for the heaven is red.

הֵשִׁיב לָהּ בְּאָמְרוֹ: לֹא נָאֶה לָקַחַת אֶת הַלֶּחֶם שֶׁל הַבָּנִים וְלִזְרֹק אוֹתוֹ לַכְּלָבִים
heshiv lah be'amero. lo na'eh lakachat et hallechem shel habbanim velizrok oto lakkelavim
And he answered and said, It is not meet to take the children's bread and cast it to the dogs.

אָמְרָה לוֹ: כֵּן, אֲדוֹנִי, אֲבָל אֲפִלּוּ הַכְּלָבִים אוֹכְלִים מִן הַפְּרוּרִים הַנּוֹפְלִים מִשֻּׁלְחַן אֲדוֹנֵיהֶם
amerah lo: ken, adoni, aval afillu hakkelavim ochelim min happerurim hannofelim mishulchan adoneihem
But she said, Yea, Lord: for even the dogs eat of the crumbs which fall from their masters' table.

אָמַר לָהּ יֵשׁוּעַ: אִשָּׁה, גְּדוֹלָה אֱמוּנָתֵךְ. יְהִי לָךְ כִּרְצוֹנֵךְ
amar lah yeshua: ishah, gedolah emunatech. Yehi lach kirtzonech
Then Jesus answered and said unto her, O woman, great is thy faith: be it done unto thee even as thou wilt.

וּבְאוֹתָהּ שָׁעָה נִרְפְּאָה בִּתָּהּ
uve'otah sha'ah nirpe'ah bittah
And her daughter was healed from that hour.

יֵשׁוּעַ עָזַב אֶת הַמָּקוֹם, וּלְאַחַר שֶׁעָבַר לְיַד יָם הַגָּלִיל עָלָה לָהָר וְיָשַׁב שָׁם
yeshua azav et hammakom, ule'achar she'avar leyad yam haggalil alah lahar veyashav sham
And Jesus departed thence, and came nigh unto the sea of Galilee; and he went up into the mountain, and sat there.

בָּאוּ אֵלָיו הָמוֹן עַם רַב
ba'u elav hamon am rav
And there came unto him great multitudes,

וְאִתָּם פִּסְחִים, נָכִים, עִוְרִים, אִלְּמִים וְרַבִּים אֲחֵרִים שֶׁהֻנְּחוּ לְרַגְלָיו
ve'ittam pischim, nachim, ivrim, illemim verabbim acherim shehunnechu leraglav
having with them the lame, blind, dumb, maimed, and many others, and they cast them down at his feet;

וְהוּא רִפֵּא אוֹתָם
vehu rippei otam
and he healed them:

כִּרְאוֹת הָעָם אִלְּמִים מְדַבְּרִים, נָכִים בְּרִיאִים
kir'ot ha'am illemim medabberim, nachim beri'im
insomuch that the multitude wondered, when they saw the dumb speaking, the maimed whole,

פִּסְחִים מְהַלְּכִים וְעִוְרִים רוֹאִים, נִתְמַלְּאוּ פְּלִיאָה וְשִׁבְּחוּ אֶת אֱלֹהֵי יִשְׂרָאֵל
pischim mehallechim ve'ivrim ro'im, nitmalle'u peli'ah veshibbechu et elohei yisra'el
and the lame walking, and the blind seeing: and they glorified the God of Israel.

קָרָא יֵשׁוּעַ לְתַלְמִידָיו וְאָמַר: נִכְמְרוּ רַחֲמַי עַל הָעָם
kara yeshua letalmidav ve'amar: Nichmeru rachamai al ha'am
And Jesus called unto him his disciples, and said, I have compassion on the multitude,

זֶה שְׁלוֹשָׁה יָמִים הֵם נִמְצָאִים אִתִּי וְאֵין לָהֶם מַה לֶּאֱכֹל
zeh sheloshah yamim hem nimtza'im itti ve'ein lahem mah le'echol
because they continue with me now three days and have nothing to eat:

הֵגִיב כֵּיפָא וְאָמַר לוֹ: בָּאֵר נָא לָנוּ אֶת הַמָּשָׁל
hegiv keifa ve'amar lo. Ba'er na lanu et hammashal
And Peter answered and said unto him, Declare unto us the parable.

הֵשִׁיב יֵשׁוּעַ: גַּם אַתֶּם עוֹד חַסְרֵי בִּינָה
heshiv yeshua: gam attem od chasrei binah
And he said, Are ye also even yet without understanding?

הַאֵינְכֶם מְבִינִים שֶׁכֹּל מַה שֶּׁנִּכְנָס לַפֶּה יוֹרֵד אֶל הַבֶּטֶן וּמוּטָל לַמּוֹצָאוֹת
ha'einechem mevinim shekkol mah shennichnas lappeh yored el habbeten umutal lammotza'ot
Perceive ye not, that whatsoever goeth into the mouth passeth into the belly, and is cast out into the draught?

אֲבָל הַדְּבָרִים הַיּוֹצְאִים מִן הַפֶּה נוֹבְעִים מִן הַלֵּב וְאֵלֶּה מְטַמְּאִים אֶת הָאָדָם
aval haddevarim hayotze'im min happeh nove'im min hallev ve'elleh metamme'im et ha'adam
But the things which proceed out of the mouth come forth out of the heart; and they defile the man.

כִּי מִן הַלֵּב נוֹבְעוֹת מַחְשְׁבוֹת רֶשַׁע, רְצִיחוֹת, נִאוּפִים, זְנוּנִים, גְּנֵבוֹת, עֵדֻיּוֹת שֶׁקֶר וְגִדּוּפִים
ki min hallev nove'ot machshevot resha', retzichot, ni'ufim, znunim, genevot, ediyot sheker vegiddufim
For out of the heart come forth evil thoughts, murders, adulteries, fornications, thefts, false witness, railings:

אֵלֶּה הֵם הַמְטַמְּאִים אֶת הָאָדָם, אֲבָל אֲכִילָה בְּלֹא נְטִילַת יָדַיִם אֵינָה מְטַמֵּאת אֶת הָאָדָם
elleh hem hamtamme'im et ha'adam, aval achilah belo netilat yadayim einah metammet et ha'adam
these are the things which defile the man; but to eat with unwashen hands defileth not the man.

יֵשׁוּעַ יָצָא מִשָּׁם וּפָרַשׁ אֶל סְבִיבוֹת צוֹר וְצִידוֹן
yeshua yatza misham ufarash el sevivot tzor vetzidon
And Jesus went out thence, and withdrew into the parts of Tyre and Sidon.

וְהִנֵּה יָצְאָה מֵאוֹתוֹ הָאֵזוֹר אִשָּׁה כְּנַעֲנִית וְצָעֲקָה אֵלָיו
vehinneh yatze'ah me'oto ha'ezor ishah kena'anit vetza'akah elav
And behold, a Canaanitish woman came out from those borders, and cried, saying,

רַחֵם עָלַי, אֲדוֹנִי, בֶּן־דָּוִד. בִּתִּי מְעֻנָּה מְאֹד עַל־יְדֵי שֵׁד
Rachem alai, adoni, ben-david. Bitti me'unnah me'od al-yedei shed
Have mercy on me, O Lord, thou son of David; my daughter is grievously vexed with a demon.

אַךְ הוּא לֹא הֵשִׁיב לָהּ דָּבָר נִגְּשׁוּ תַּלְמִידָיו וּבִקְשׁוּ מִמֶּנּוּ: שְׁלַח אוֹתָהּ, כִּי הִיא צוֹעֶקֶת אַחֲרֵינוּ
ach hu lo heshiv lah davar niggeshu talmidav uvikshu mimmennu: shelach otah, ki hi tzo'eket achareinu
But he answered her not a word. And his disciples came and besought him, saying, Send her away; for she crieth after us.

עָנָה יֵשׁוּעַ וְאָמַר: לֹא נִשְׁלַחְתִּי אֶלָּא אֶל הַצֹּאן הָאוֹבְדוֹת אֲשֶׁר לְבֵית יִשְׂרָאֵל
anah yeshua ve'amar. lo nishlachti ella el hatzon ha'ovedot asher leveit yisra'el
But he answered and said, I was not sent but unto the lost sheep of the house of Israel.

הִיא הִתְקָרְבָה, הִשְׁתַּחֲוְתָה לוֹ וְאָמְרָה: אֲדוֹנִי, עֲזֹר לִי
hi hitkarevah, hishtachavtah lo ve'amrah: adoni, azor li
But she came and worshipped him, saying, Lord, help me.

כָּל דָּבָר מִשֶּׁלִּי שֶׁאַתָּה יָכוֹל לֵהָנוֹת מִמֶּנּוּ הֲרֵי הוּא הֶקְדֵּשׁ
kol davar misheli she'attah yachol lehanot mimmennu harei hu hekdesh
That wherewith thou mightest have been profited by me is given to God;

אֵינוֹ חַיָּב לְכַבֵּד אֶת אָבִיו וְאִמּוֹ; וַהֲפַרְתֶּם אֶת דְּבַר אֱלֹהִים לְמַעַן הַמָּסֹרֶת שֶׁלָּכֶם
eino chayav lechabbed et aviv ve'immo; vahafartem et devar elohim lema'an hammasoret shellachem
he shall not honor his father. And ye have made void the word of God because of your tradition.

צְבוּעִים! הֵיטֵב נִבָּא עֲלֵיכֶם יְשַׁעְיָהוּ בְּאָמְרוֹ
tzevu'im! heitev nibba aleichem yesha'yahu be'omero
Ye hypocrites, well did Isaiah prophesy of you, saying,

הָעָם הַזֶּה בִּשְׂפָתָיו כִּבְּדוּנִי וְלִבּוֹ רִחַק מִמֶּנִּי
ha'am hazzeh bisfatav kibbduni velibbo richak mimmenni
This people honoreth me with their lips; But their heart is far from me.

וַתְּהִי יִרְאָתָם אֹתִי מִצְוַת אֲנָשִׁים מְלֻמָּדָה
vattehi yir'atam oti mitzvat anashim melummadah
But in vain do they worship me, Teaching as their doctrines the precepts of men.

הוּא קָרָא לָעָם וְאָמַר לָהֶם: שִׁמְעוּ וְהָבִינוּ
hu kara la'am ve'amar lahem: shim'u vehavinu
And he called to him the multitude, and said unto them, Hear, and understand:

לֹא הַנִּכְנָס אֶל הַפֶּה מְטַמֵּא אֶת הָאָדָם
lo hannichnas el happeh metammei et ha'adam
Not that which entereth into the mouth defileth the man;

אֶלָּא הַיּוֹצֵא מִן הַפֶּה - זֶה מְטַמֵּא אֶת הָאָדָם
ella hayotzei min happeh - zeh metammei et ha'adam
but that which proceedeth out of the mouth, this defileth the man.

נִגְּשׁוּ תַּלְמִידָיו וְאָמְרוּ לוֹ
niggshu talmidav ve'ameru lo
Then came the disciples, and said unto him,

הַאִם אַתָּה יוֹדֵעַ שֶׁהַפְּרוּשִׁים בְּשָׁמְעָם אֶת הַדָּבָר הִזְדַּעְזְעוּ?
ha'im attah yodea shehapperushim beshome'am et haddavar hizda'ze'u?
Knowest thou that the Pharisees were offended, when they heard this saying?

הֵשִׁיב וְאָמַר: כָּל נֶטַע אֲשֶׁר לֹא נָטַע אָבִי שֶׁבַּשָּׁמַיִם עָקוֹר יֵעָקֵר
heshiv ve'amar: kol neta asher lo nata avi shebbashamayim akor ye'aker
But he answered and said, Every plant which my heavenly Father planted not, shall be rooted up.

הַנִּיחוּ לָהֶם. מוֹרֵי־דֶרֶךְ עִוְרִים הֵם לְעִוְרִים; וְאִם עִוֵּר מַדְרִיךְ אֶת הָעִוֵּר הֲרֵי שְׁנֵיהֶם יִפְּלוּ לַבּוֹר
hannichu lahem. morei-derech ivrim hem le'ivrim; ve'im ivver madrich et ha'ivver harei sheneihem yippelu labbor
Let them alone: they are blind guides. And if the blind guide the blind, both shall fall into a pit.

קְטַן אֱמוּנָה, מַדּוּעַ עָלָה סָפֵק בְּלִבְּךָ
ketan emunah, maddua alah safek belibbecha
O thou of little faith, wherefore didst thou doubt?

בַּעֲלוֹתָם לַסִּירָה פָּסְקָה הָרוּחַ
ba'alotam lassirah pasekah haruach
And when they were gone up into the boat, the wind ceased.

וְהָאֲנָשִׁים שֶׁהָיוּ בַּסִּירָה הִשְׁתַּחֲווּ לוֹ בְּאָמְרָם: בֶּאֱמֶת בֶּן־הָאֱלֹהִים אַתָּה
veha'anashim shehayu bassirah hishtachavu lo be'omram. be'emet ben-ha'elohim attah
And they that were in the boat worshipped him, saying, Of a truth thou art the Son of God.

הֵם עָבְרוּ אֶת הַיָּם וּבָאוּ לְחוֹף גִּנּוֹסַר
hem averu et hayam uva'u lechof ginnosar
And when they had crossed over, they came to the land, unto Gennesaret.

אַנְשֵׁי הַמָּקוֹם הִכִּירוּ אוֹתוֹ וְשָׁלְחוּ לְהוֹדִיעַ לְכָל הַסְּבִיבָה. הֵבִיאוּ אֵלָיו אֶת כָּל הַחוֹלִים
anshei hammakom hikkiru oto veshalechu lehodia lechol hassevivah. Hevi'u elav et kol hacholim
And when the men of that place knew him, they sent into all that region round about, and brought unto him all that were sick;

וּבִקְשׁוּ מִמֶּנּוּ רַק לִנְגֹּעַ בִּכְנַף בִּגְדוֹ; וְכָל הַנּוֹגְעִים נִרְפָּאוּ
uvikshu mimmennu rak lingoa bichnaf bigdo; vechol hannoge'im nirpe'u
and they besought him that they might only touch the border of his garment: and as many as touched were made whole.

טו

אַחֲרֵי כֵן נִגְּשׁוּ אֶל יֵשׁוּעַ סוֹפְרִים וּפְרוּשִׁים מִירוּשָׁלַיִם
acharei chen niggeshu el yeshua soferim uferushim mirushalayim
Then there come to Jesus from Jerusalem Pharisees and scribes, saying,

וְשָׁאֲלוּ אוֹתוֹ: מַדּוּעַ עוֹבְרִים תַּלְמִידֶיךָ עַל מָסֹרֶת הַזְּקֵנִים, שֶׁאֵין הֵם נוֹטְלִים יָדַיִם לַסְּעוּדָה
vesha'alu oto: maddua overim talmideicha al masoret hazzekenim, she'ein hem notelim yadayim lasse'udah
Why do thy disciples transgress the tradition of the elders? for they wash not their hands when they eat bread.

הֵשִׁיב וְאָמַר לָהֶם: מַדּוּעַ גַּם אַתֶּם עוֹבְרִים עַל מִצְוֹת אֱלֹהִים לְמַעַן הַמָּסֹרֶת שֶׁלָּכֶם
heshiv ve'amar lahema: maddua gam attem overim al mitzvat elohim lema'an hammasoret shellachem
And he answered and said unto them, Why do ye also transgress the commandment of God because of your tradition?

הֵן הָאֱלֹהִים צִוָּה, כַּבֵּד אֶת־אָבִיךָ וְאֶת־אִמֶּךָ וּמְקַלֵּל אָבִיו וְאִמּוֹ מוֹת יוּמָת
hen ha'elohim tzivvah, kabbed et-'avicha ve'et-'immecha umekallel aviv ve'immo mot yumat
For God said, Honor thy father and thy mother: and, He that speaketh evil of father or mother, let him die the death.

אֲבָל אַתֶּם אוֹמְרִים, כָּל הָאוֹמֵר לְאָבִיו אוֹ לְאִמּוֹ
aval attem omerim, kol ha'omer le'aviv o le'immo
But ye say, Whosoever shall say to his father or his mother,

מִיָּד הֵאִיץ בְּתַלְמִידָיו לְהִכָּנֵס לַסִּירָה
miyad he'itz betalmidav lehikkanes lassirah
And straightway he constrained the disciples to enter into the boat,

וּלְהַקְדִּים אוֹתוֹ בַּנְּסִיעָה אֶל עֵבֶר הַיָּם עַד שֶׁהוּא יְשַׁלַּח אֶת הֲמוֹן הָעָם
ulehakdim oto bannesi'ah el ever hayam ad shehu yeshalleach et hamon ha'am
and to go before him unto the other side, till he should send the multitudes away.

הוּא שִׁלַּח אֶת הָעָם וְעָלָה לָהָר לְבַדּוֹ כְּדֵי לְהִתְפַּלֵּל
hu shillach et ha'am ve'alah lahar levaddo kedei lehitpallel
And after he had sent the multitudes away, he went up into the mountain apart to pray:

לְעֵת עֶרֶב הָיָה שָׁם לְבַדּוֹ
le'et erev hayah sham levaddo
and when even was come, he was there alone.

בֵּינָתַיִם הִגִּיעָה הַסִּירָה לְמֶרְחָק כַּמָּה מִילִין מִן הַחוֹף כְּשֶׁהִיא מִטַּלְטֶלֶת עַל הַגַּלִּים וְהָרוּחַ נוֹשֶׁבֶת נֶגְדָּהּ
beinetayim higgi'ah hassirah lemerchak kammah milin min hachof keshehi mittaltelet al haggallim veharuach noshevet negdah
But the boat was now in the midst of the sea, distressed by the waves; for the wind was contrary.

וְהִנֵּה בְּאַשְׁמֹרֶת הַלַּיְלָה הָרְבִיעִית בָּא אֲלֵיהֶם יֵשׁוּעַ וְהוּא מְהַלֵּךְ עַל פְּנֵי הַיָּם
vehinneh be'ashmoret hallaylah harevi'it ba aleihem yeshua vehu mehallech al penei hayam
And in the fourth watch of the night he came unto them, walking upon the sea.

כְּשֶׁרָאוּהוּ הַתַּלְמִידִים מְהַלֵּךְ עַל פְּנֵי הַיָּם נִבְהֲלוּ. אָמְרוּ: רוּחַ רְפָאִים הִיא, וְהֵחֵלּוּ לִצְעֹק מִפַּחַד
keshera'uhu hattalmidim mehallech al penei hayam nivhalu. ameru: ruach refa'im hi, vehechellu litz'ok mippachad
And when the disciples saw him walking on the sea, they were troubled, saying, It is a ghost; and they cried out for fear.

מִיָּד דִּבֶּר אֲלֵיהֶם יֵשׁוּעַ וְאָמַר: חִזְקוּ, אֲנִי הוּא. אַל תִּפְחֲדוּ
miyad dibber aleihem yeshua ve'amar: chizku, ani hu. al tifchadu
But straightway Jesus spake unto them, saying, Be of good cheer; it is I; be not afraid.

הֵשִׁיב כֵּיפָא וְאָמַר אֵלָיו: אֲדוֹנִי, אִם אַתָּה הוּא, צַוֵּנִי לָבוֹא אֵלֶיךָ עַל פְּנֵי הַמַּיִם
heshiv keifa ve'amar elav: adoni, im attah hu, tzavveni lavo eleicha al penei hammayim
And Peter answered him and said, Lord, if it be thou, bid me come unto thee upon the waters.

בּוֹא אָמַר יֵשׁוּעַ: כֵּיפָא יָרַד מִן הַסִּירָה וְהָלַךְ עַל פְּנֵי הַמַּיִם לִקְרַאת יֵשׁוּעַ
bo! amar yeshua. keifa yarad min hassirah vehalach al penei hammayim likrat yeshua
And he said, Come. And Peter went down from the boat, and walked upon the waters to come to Jesus.

אוּלָם כְּשֶׁרָאָה אֶת הָרוּחַ הַסּוֹעֶרֶת פָּחַד וְהֵחֵל לִשְׁקֹעַ. הוּא צָעַק: אֲדוֹנִי, הַצֵּל אוֹתִי
ulam keshera'ah et haruach hasso'eret pachad vehechel lishkoa. hu tza'ak: adoni, hatzel oti
But when he saw the wind, he was afraid; and beginning to sink, he cried out, saying, Lord, save me.

מִיָּד הוֹשִׁיט יֵשׁוּעַ אֶת יָדוֹ, הֶחֱזִיק בּוֹ וְאָמַר לוֹ
miyad hoshit yeshua et yado, hechezik bo ve'amar lo
And immediately Jesus stretched forth his hand, and took hold of him, and saith unto him,

יֵשׁוּעַ שָׁמַע וְנָסַע מִשָּׁם בְּסִירָה אֶל מָקוֹם שׁוֹמֵם, הוּא לְבַדּוֹ
yeshua shama venasa misham besirah el makom shomem, hu levaddo
Now when Jesus heard it, he withdrew from thence in a boat, to a desert place apart:

כֵּיוָן שֶׁשָּׁמְעוּ הַהֲמוֹנִים הָלְכוּ אַחֲרָיו בָּרֶגֶל מִן הֶעָרִים
keivan sheshame'u hahamonim halechu acharav baregel min he'arim
and when the multitudes heard thereof, they followed him on foot from the cities.

כְּשֶׁיָּצָא רָאָה הֲמוֹן עַם רַב. הוּא נִתְמַלֵּא רַחֲמִים עֲלֵיהֶם וְרִפֵּא אֶת הַחוֹלִים שֶׁבֵּינֵיהֶם
kesheyatza ra'ah hamon am rav. hu nitmallei rachamim aleihem verippei et hacholim shebbeineihem
And he came forth, and saw a great multitude, and he had compassion on them, and healed their sick.

לְעֵת עֶרֶב נִגְּשׁוּ אֵלָיו תַּלְמִידָיו וְאָמְרוּ: הַמָּקוֹם שׁוֹמֵם וְהַשָּׁעָה כְּבָר מְאֻחֶרֶת
le'et erev niggeshu elav talmidav ve'ameru: hammakom shomem vehasha'ah kevar me'ucheret
And when even was come, the disciples came to him, saying, The place is desert, and the time is already past;

שְׁלַח אֶת הֲמוֹן הָעָם וְיֵלְכוּ אֶל הַכְּפָרִים לִקְנוֹת לָהֶם אֹכֶל
shelach et hamon ha'am veyelechu el hakkefarim liknot lahem ochel
send the multitudes away, that they may go into the villages, and buy themselves food.

אָמַר לָהֶם יֵשׁוּעַ: אֵין הֵם צְרִיכִים לָלֶכֶת. תְּנוּ לָהֶם אַתֶּם לֶאֱכֹל
amar lahem yeshua: ein hem tzerichim lalechet. Tenu lahem attem le'echol
But Jesus said unto them, They have no need to go away; give ye them to eat.

הֵשִׁיבוּ לוֹ: אֵין לָנוּ פֹּה אֶלָּא חָמֵשׁ כִּכְּרוֹת לֶחֶם וּשְׁנֵי דָגִים
heshivu lo: ein lanu poh ella chamesh kikkerot lechem ushenei dagim
And they say unto him, We have here but five loaves, and two fishes.

אָמַר: הָבִיאוּ אוֹתָם אֵלַי הֵנָּה
Amar: havi'u otam elai hennah
And he said, Bring them hither to me.

הוּא צִוָּה אֶת הָעָם לָשֶׁבֶת עַל הַדֶּשֶׁא, לָקַח אֶת חָמֵשׁ כִּכְּרוֹת הַלֶּחֶם וְאֶת שְׁנֵי הַדָּגִים
hu tzivvah et ha'am lashevet al haddeshe, lakach et chamesh kikkerot hallechem ve'et shenei haddagim
And he commanded the multitudes to sit down on the grass; and he took the five loaves, and the two fishes,

נָשָׂא עֵינָיו הַשָּׁמַיְמָה וּבֵרֵךְ. לְאַחַר מִכֵּן בָּצַע אֶת הַלֶּחֶם וְנָתַן לַתַּלְמִידִים וְהַתַּלְמִידִים נָתְנוּ לָעָם
nasa einav hashamaymah uverech. le'achar mikken batza et hallechem venatan lattalmidim vehattalmidim natenu la'am
and looking up to heaven, he blessed, and brake and gave the loaves to the disciples, and the disciples to the multitudes.

הַכֹּל אָכְלוּ וְשָׂבְעוּ, וּמִמַּה שֶׁנּוֹתַר אָסְפוּ שְׁנֵים־עָשָׂר סַלִּים מְלֵאִים
hakkol achelu vesave'u, umimmah shennotar asefu sheneim-'ashar sallim mele'im
And they all ate, and were filled: and they took up that which remained over of the broken pieces, twelve baskets full.

מִסְפַּר הָאוֹכְלִים הָיָה כַּחֲמֵשֶׁת אֲלָפִים אִישׁ מִלְּבַד הַנָּשִׁים וְהַטַּף
mispar ha'ochelim hayah kachameshet alafim ish millevad hannashim vehattaf
And they that did eat were about five thousand men, besides women and children.

אָמַר אֶל מְשָׁרְתָיו: זֶהוּ יוֹחָנָן הַמַּטְבִּיל. הוּא קָם מִן הַמֵּתִים וְלָכֵן פּוֹעֲלִים בּוֹ מַעֲשֵׂי הַנִּסִּים
amar el mesharetav. zehu yochanan hammatbil. hu kam min hammetim velachen po'alim bo ma'asei hannissim
and said unto his servants, This is John the Baptist; he is risen from the dead; and therefore do these powers work in him.

שֶׁכֵּן הוֹרְדוֹס תָּפַס אֶת יוֹחָנָן, כָּבַל אוֹתוֹ וְשָׂם אוֹתוֹ בְּבֵית הַסֹּהַר בִּגְלַל הוֹרוֹדְיָה אֵשֶׁת פִילִיפּוֹס אָחִיו
shekken horedos tafas et yochanan, kaval oto vesam oto beveit hassohar biglal horodeyah eshet filipos achiv
For Herod had laid hold on John, and bound him, and put him in prison for the sake of Herodias, his brother Philip's wife.

לְאַחַר שֶׁיּוֹחָנָן אָמַר לוֹ, אָסוּר לְךָ לָקַחַת אוֹתָהּ
le'achar sheyochanan amar lo, asur lecha lakachat otah
For John said unto him, It is not lawful for thee to have her.

הוֹרְדוֹס רָצָה לַהֲרֹג אוֹתוֹ, אוּלָם חָשַׁשׁ מִן הֶהָמוֹן מִפְּנֵי שֶׁחֲשָׁבוּהוּ לְנָבִיא
horedos ratzah laharog oto, ulam chashash min hehamon mippenei shechashavuhu lenavi
And when he would have put him to death, he feared the multitude, because they counted him as a prophet.

כְּשֶׁהוּחַג יוֹם הֻלַּדְתּוֹ שֶׁל הוֹרְדוֹס רָקְדָה בַּת־הוֹרוֹדְיָה בֵּין הַנּוֹכְחִים וּמָצְאָה חֵן בְּעֵינֵי הוֹרְדוֹס
keshehuchag yom hulladto shel horedos rakedah bat-horodeyah bein hannochechim umatze'ah chen be'einei horedos
But when Herod's birthday came, the daughter of Herodias danced in the midst, and pleased Herod.

לְפִיכָךְ הִבְטִיחַ לָהּ בִּשְׁבוּעָה לָתֵת לָהּ כָּל מַה שֶּׁתְּבַקֵּשׁ
lefichach hivtiach lah bishvu'ah latet lah kol mah shettevakkesh
Whereupon he promised with an oath to give her whatsoever she should ask.

עַל־פִּי הַדְרָכַת אִמָּהּ – אָמְרָה: תֵּן לִי פֹּה בִּקְעָרָה אֶת רֹאשׁ יוֹחָנָן הַמַּטְבִּיל
al-pi hadrachat immah – amerah: ten li poh bik'arah et rosh yochanan hammatbil
And she, being put forward by her mother, saith, Give me here on a platter the head of John the Baptist.

הִתְעַצֵּב הַמֶּלֶךְ
hit'atzev hammelech
And the king was grieved;

אֶלָּא שֶׁבִּגְלַל הַשְּׁבוּעָה וְהַמְסֻבִּים אִתּוֹ צִוָּה לָתֵת לָהּ
ella shebbiglal hashevu'ah vehamsubbim itto tzivvah latet lah
but for the sake of his oaths, and of them that sat at meat with him, he commanded it to be given;

הוּא שָׁלַח לִכְרֹת אֶת רֹאשׁ יוֹחָנָן בְּבֵית הַסֹּהַר
hu shalach lichrot et rosh yochanan beveit hassohar
and he sent and beheaded John in the prison.

וְכַאֲשֶׁר הוּבָא רֹאשׁוֹ בַּקְּעָרָה נְתָנוּהוּ לַנַּעֲרָה וְהִיא הֱבִיאָה אוֹתוֹ לְאִמָּהּ
vecha'asher huva rosho bakke'arah netanuhu lanna'arah vehi hevi'ah oto le'immah
And his head was brought on a platter, and given to the damsel: and she brought it to her mother.

בָּאוּ תַּלְמִידָיו, לָקְחוּ אֶת גּוּפָתוֹ וְקָבְרוּ אוֹתָהּ, וְהָלְכוּ וְהוֹדִיעוּ לְיֵשׁוּעַ
ba'u talmidav, lakechu et gufato vekaveru otah, vehalechu vehodi'u leyeshua'
And his disciples came, and took up the corpse, and buried him; and they went and told Jesus.

דּוֹמֶה לְבַעַל־בַּיִת הַמּוֹצִיא מֵאוֹצָרוֹ חֲדָשׁוֹת וְגַם יְשָׁנוֹת
domeh leva'al-bayit hammotzi me'otzaro chadashot vegam yeshanot
is like unto a man that is a householder, who bringeth forth out of his treasure things new and old.

כַּאֲשֶׁר סִיֵּם יֵשׁוּעַ אֶת הַמְּשָׁלִים הָאֵלֶּה הָלַךְ מִשָּׁם
ka'asher siyem yeshua et hammeshalim ha'elleh halach misham
And it came to pass, when Jesus had finished these parables, he departed thence.

הוּא בָּא אֶל עִירוֹ וְלִמֵּד אוֹתָם בְּבֵית הַכְּנֶסֶת עַד כִּי הִשְׁתּוֹמְמוּ וְאָמְרוּ
hu ba el iro velimmed otam beveit hakkneset ad ki hishtomemu ve'ameru
And coming into his own country he taught them in their synagogue, insomuch that they were astonished, and said,

מִנַּיִן לוֹ הַחָכְמָה הַזֹּאת וּמַעֲשֵׂי הַנִּסִּים
Minnayin lo hachachemah hazzot uma'asei hannissim
Whence hath this man this wisdom, and these mighty works?

הֲרֵי זֶה בְּנוֹ שֶׁל הַנַּגָּר. הֲלֹא שֵׁם אִמּוֹ מִרְיָם
harei zeh beno shel hannaggar. halo shem immo miryam
Is not this the carpenter's son? is not his mother called Mary?

וְאֶחָיו יַעֲקֹב וְיוֹסֵף וְשִׁמְעוֹן וִיהוּדָה
ve'echav ya'akov veyosef veshim'on viyehudah
and his brethren, James, and Joseph, and Simon, and Judas?

וְאַחְיוֹתָיו הֲרֵי כֻּלָּן פֹּה אִתָּנוּ. אִם כֵּן מִנַּיִן לוֹ כָּל הַדְּבָרִים הָאֵלֶּה
ve'achyotav harei kullan poh ittanu. im ken minnayin lo kol haddevarim ha'elleh
And his sisters, are they not all with us? Whence then hath this man all these things?

הוּא הָיָה לָהֶם לְמִכְשׁוֹל אָמַר לָהֶם יֵשׁוּעַ
hu hayah lahem lemichshol. amar lahem yeshua
And they were offended in him. But Jesus said unto them,

אֵין נָבִיא בְּעִירוֹ וּבְבֵיתוֹ
ein navi be'iro uveveito
A prophet is not without honor, save in his own country, and in his own house.

וְלֹא עָשָׂה שָׁם נִסִּים רַבִּים בִּגְלַל חֹסֶר אֱמוּנָתָם
velo asah sham nissim rabbim biglal choser emunatam
And he did not many mighty works there because of their unbelief.

יד

בָּעֵת הַהִיא שָׁמַע הוֹרְדוֹס שַׂר־רֹבַע הַמְּדִינָה אֶת שֵׁמַע יֵשׁוּעַ
ba'et hahi shama horedos sar-rova hammedinah et shema yeshua'
At that season Herod the tetrarch heard the report concerning Jesus,

דּוֹמָה מַלְכוּת הַשָּׁמַיִם לְאוֹצָר טָמוּן בַּשָּׂדֶה, וְהִנֵּה מְצָאוֹ אִישׁ. הוּא טוֹמֵן אוֹתוֹ שׁוּב
domah malchut hashamayim le'otzar tamun bassadeh, vehinneh metza'o ish. hu tomen oto shuv
The kingdom of heaven is like unto a treasure hidden in the field; which a man found, and hid;

וּבְשִׂמְחָתוֹ הוּא הוֹלֵךְ וּמוֹכֵר אֶת כָּל אֲשֶׁר לוֹ וְקוֹנֶה אֶת הַשָּׂדֶה הַהוּא
uvesimchato hu holech umocher et kol asher lo vekoneh et hassadeh hahu
and in his joy he goeth and selleth all that he hath, and buyeth that field.

עוֹד דּוֹמָה מַלְכוּת הַשָּׁמַיִם לְסוֹחֵר הַמְחַפֵּשׂ מַרְגָּלִיּוֹת יָפוֹת
od domah malchut hashamayim lesocher hamchappes margaliyot yafot
Again, the kingdom of heaven is like unto a man that is a merchant seeking goodly pearls:

כַּאֲשֶׁר מָצָא מַרְגָּלִית אַחַת יְקָרַת עֵרֶךְ הָלַךְ וּמָכַר אֶת כָּל אֲשֶׁר לוֹ וְקָנָה אוֹתָהּ
ka'asher matza margalit achat yikrat erech halach umachar et kol asher lo vekanah otah
and having found one pearl of great price, he went and sold all that he had, and bought it.

וְעוֹד דּוֹמָה מַלְכוּת הַשָּׁמַיִם לְרֶשֶׁת שֶׁהֻשְׁלְכָה לַיָּם וְאָסְפָה מִכָּל מִין
ve'od domah malchut hashamayim lereshet shehushlechah layam ve'asefah mikkol min
Again, the kingdom of heaven is like unto a net, that was cast into the sea, and gathered of every kind:

כַּאֲשֶׁר נִתְמַלְּאָה הֶעֱלוּ אוֹתָהּ לַחוֹף
ka'asher nitmalle'ah he'elu otah lachof
which, when it was filled, they drew up on the beach;

וְיָשְׁבוּ וְלִקְּטוּ אֶת הַטּוֹבִים לְתוֹךְ הַכֵּלִים וְאֶת הָרָעִים הִשְׁלִיכוּ
veyashevu velikketu et hattovim letoch hakkelim ve'et hara'im hishlichu
and they sat down, and gathered the good into vessels, but the bad they cast away.

כָּךְ יִהְיֶה בְּקֵץ הָעוֹלָם. הַמַּלְאָכִים יֵצְאוּ וְיַבְדִּילוּ אֶת הָרְשָׁעִים מִבֵּין הַצַּדִּיקִים
kach yihyeh beketz ha'olam. hammal'achim yetze'u veyavdilu et haresha'im mibbein hatzaddikim
So shall it be in the end of the world: the angels shall come forth, and sever the wicked from among the righteous,

וְיַשְׁלִיכוּ אוֹתָם אֶל תַּנּוּר הָאֵשׁ; שָׁם יִהְיוּ הַיְלָלָה וַחֲרוֹק הַשִּׁנַּיִם
veyashlichu otam el tanur ha'esh; sham yihyu haylalah vacharok hashinnayim
and shall cast them into the furnace of fire: there shall be the weeping and the gnashing of teeth.

הַאִם הֲבִינוֹתֶם אֶת כָּל זֶה? הֵשִׁיבוּ לוֹ: כֵּן
ha'im havinotem et kol zeh? heshivu lo: ken
Have ye understood all these things? They say unto him, Yea.

אָמַר לָהֶם
amar lahem
And he said unto them,

לָכֵן כָּל סוֹפֵר לִמּוּד מַלְכוּת שָׁמַיִם
lachen kol sofer lemud malchut shamayim
Therefore every scribe who hath been made a disciple to the kingdom of heaven

לְמַעַן יִתְקַיֵּם מַה שֶּׁנֶּאֱמַר בְּפִי הַנָּבִיא: אֶפְתְּחָה בְמָשָׁל פִּי
lema'an yitkayem mah shenne'emar befi hannavi: eftechah vemashal pi
that it might be fulfilled which was spoken through the prophet, saying, I will open my mouth in parables;

אַבִּיעָה חִידוֹת מִנִּי־קֶדֶם
abbi'ah chidot minni-kedem
I will utter things hidden from the foundation of the world.

אַחֲרֵי כֵן שִׁלַּח יֵשׁוּעַ אֶת הֲמוֹן הָעָם וְנִכְנַס הַבַּיְתָה. נִגְּשׁוּ אֵלָיו תַּלְמִידָיו וְאָמְרוּ
acharei chen shillach yeshua et hamon ha'am venichnas habbaytah. niggeshu elav talmidav ve'ameru
Then he left the multitudes, and went into the house: and his disciples came unto him, saying,

הַסְבֵּר נָא לָנוּ אֶת מְשַׁל הָעֲשָׂבִים הָרָעִים
hasber na lanu et meshal ha'asavim hara'im
Explain unto us the parable of the tares of the field.

הֵשִׁיב וְאָמַר: הַזּוֹרֵעַ אֶת הַזֶּרַע הַטּוֹב הוּא בֶּן־הָאָדָם
heshiv ve'amar.: hazzorea et hazzera hattov hu ben-ha'adam
And he answered and said, He that soweth the good seed is the Son of man;

הַשָּׂדֶה הוּא הַתֵּבֵל. הַזֶּרַע הַטּוֹב הוּא בְּנֵי הַמַּלְכוּת, וְהָעֲשָׂבִים הָרָעִים הֵם בְּנֵי הָרַע
hashodeh hu hattevel. hazzera hattov hu benei hammalchut, vha'asavim hara'im hem benei hara
and the field is the world; and the good seed, these are the sons of the kingdom; and the tares are the sons of the evil one;

הָאוֹיֵב הַזּוֹרֵעַ אוֹתָם הוּא הַשָּׂטָן. הַקָּצִיר הוּא קֵץ הָעוֹלָם, וְהַקּוֹצְרִים הֵם הַמַּלְאָכִים
ha'oyev hazzorea otam hu hassatan. hakkatzir hu ketz ha'olam, vehakkotzerim hem hammal'achim
and the enemy that sowed them is the devil: and the harvest is the end of the world; and the reapers are angels.

וּבְכֵן, כְּמוֹ שֶׁאוֹסְפִים אֶת הָעֲשָׂבִים הָרָעִים וְשׂוֹרְפִים אוֹתָם בָּאֵשׁ כָּךְ יִהְיֶה בְּקֵץ הָעוֹלָם
uvechen, kemo she'osefim et ha'asavim hara'im vesorefim otam be'esh kach yihyeh beketz ha'olam
As therefore the tares are gathered up and burned with fire; so shall it be in the end of the world.

בֶּן־הָאָדָם יִשְׁלַח אֶת מַלְאָכָיו
ben-ha'adam yishlach et mal'achav
The Son of man shall send forth his angels,

וִילַקְּטוּ מִמַּמְלַכְתּוֹ אֶת כָּל הַמַּכְשֵׁלוֹת וְאֶת כָּל עוֹשֵׂי הָרֶשַׁע
vilakketu mimmamlachto et kol hammachshelot ve'et kol osei haresha
and they shall gather out of his kingdom all things that cause stumbling, and them that do iniquity,

וְיַשְׁלִיכוּ אוֹתָם אֶל תַּנּוּר הָאֵשׁ; שָׁם יִהְיוּ הַיְלָלָה וַחֲרֹק הַשִּׁנַּיִם
veyashlichu otam el tanur ha'esh; sham yihyu haylalah vacharok hashinnayim
and shall cast them into the furnace of fire: there shall be the weeping and the gnashing of teeth.

אָז יַזְהִירוּ הַצַּדִּיקִים כַּשֶּׁמֶשׁ בְּמַמְלֶכֶת אֲבִיהֶם. מִי שֶׁאָזְנַיִם לוֹ, שֶׁיִּשְׁמַע
az yazhiru hatzaddikim kashemesh bemamlechet avihem. mi she'azenayim lo, sheyishma'
Then shall the righteous shine forth as the sun in the kingdom of their Father. He that hath ears, let him hear.

אָמַר לָהֶם, אִישׁ אוֹיֵב עָשָׂה זֹאת
amar lahem, ish oyev ashah zot
And he said unto them, An enemy hath done this.

שָׁאֲלוּ הָעֲבָדִים, הַאִם אַתָּה רוֹצֶה שֶׁנֵּלֵךְ וּנְלַקֵּט אוֹתָם
sha'alu ha'avadim, ha'im attah rotzeh shennelech unelakket otam?
And the servants say unto him, Wilt thou then that we go and gather them up?

הֵשִׁיב בַּעַל־הַבַּיִת, 'לֹא, שֶׁמָּא בְּלַקֶּטְכֶם אֶת הָעֲשָׂבִים הָרָעִים תַּעַקְרוּ אִתָּם גַּם אֶת הַחִטִּים
heshiv ba'al-habbayit, 'lo, shemma belakketchem et ha'asavim hara'im ta'akru ittam gam et hachittim
But he saith, Nay; lest haply while ye gather up the tares, ye root up the wheat with them.

הַנִּיחוּ לִשְׁנֵיהֶם לִגְדֹּל יַחַד עַד הַקָּצִיר. בְּעֵת הַקָּצִיר אֹמַר לַקּוֹצְרִים
hannichu lishneihem ligdol yachad ad hakkatzir. be'et hakkatzir omar lakkotzerim
Let both grow together until the harvest: and in the time of the harvest I will say to the reapers,

לִקְטוּ בָּרִאשׁוֹנָה אֶת הָעֲשָׂבִים הָרָעִים וְאִגְדוּ אוֹתָם לַאֲלֻמּוֹת כְּדֵי לְשָׂרְפָם, וְאֶת הַחִטִּים אִסְפוּ לַאֲסָם שֶׁלִּי
lakketu barishonah et ha'asavim hara'im ve'igdu otam la'alummot kedei lesorefam, ve'et hachittim isfu la'asam sheli
Gather up first the tares, and bind them in bundles to burn them; but gather the wheat into my barn.

הוֹסִיף וְסִפֵּר מָשָׁל אַחֵר
hosif vesipper mashal acher
Another parable set he before them, saying,

מַלְכוּת הַשָּׁמַיִם דּוֹמָה לְגַרְגִּיר חַרְדָּל אֲשֶׁר לְקָחוֹ אִישׁ וְזָרַע אוֹתוֹ בְּשָׂדֵהוּ
malchut hashamayim domah legargir chardal asher lekacho ish vezara oto besadehu
The kingdom of heaven is like unto a grain of mustard seed, which a man took, and sowed in his field:

אָמְנָם קָטֹן הוּא מִכָּל הַזְּרָעִים, אַךְ לְאַחַר צְמִיחָתוֹ גָּדוֹל הוּא מִן הַיְרָקוֹת
amenam katon hu mikkol hazzera'im, ach le'achar tzemichato gadol hu min hayerakot
which indeed is less than all seeds; but when it is grown, it is greater than the herbs,

וְהוֹפֵךְ לְעֵץ, כָּךְ שֶׁעוֹפוֹת הַשָּׁמַיִם בָּאִים וּמְקַנְּנִים בֵּין עֲנָפָיו
vehofech le'etz, kach she'ofot hashamayim ba'im umekannenim bein anafav
and becometh a tree, so that the birds of the heaven come and lodge in the branches thereof.

עוֹד מָשָׁל סִפֵּר לָהֶם: מַלְכוּת הַשָּׁמַיִם דּוֹמָה לִשְׂאוֹר
od mashal sipper lahem. malchut hashamayim domah lis'or
Another parable spake he unto them; The kingdom of heaven is like unto leaven,

אֲשֶׁר לְקָחָה אִשָּׁה וְטָמְנָה אוֹתוֹ בְּעֶשְׂרִים קִילוֹגְרַם קֶמַח עַד שֶׁהֶחְמִיץ כֻּלּוֹ
asher lakechah ishah vetamnah oto be'esrim kiloggeram kemach ad shehechmitz kullo
which a woman took, and hid in three measures of meal, till it was all leavened.

אֶת כָּל אֵלֶּה דִּבֶּר יֵשׁוּעַ לַהֲמוֹן הָעָם בִּמְשָׁלִים, וּבְלִי מָשָׁל לֹא דִּבֶּר אֲלֵיהֶם
et kol elleh dibber yeshua lahamon ha'am bimshalim, uveli mashal lo dibber aleihem
All these things spake Jesus in parables unto the multitudes; and without a parable spake he nothing unto them:

אַךְ אֵין לוֹ שֹׁרֶשׁ בְּתוֹכוֹ וְרַק לְשָׁעָה יַעֲמֹד
ach ein lo shoresh betocho verak lesha'ah ya'amod
yet hath he not root in himself, but endureth for a while;

וּבִהְיוֹת צָרָה אוֹ רְדִיפָה בִּגְלַל הַדָּבָר הוּא נִכְשָׁל מִיָּד
uvihyot tzarah o redifah biglal haddavar hu nichshal miyad
and when tribulation or persecution ariseth because of the word, straightway he stumbleth.

הַנִּזְרָע בֵּין הַקּוֹצִים הוּא הַשּׁוֹמֵעַ אֶת הַדָּבָר, אֶלָּא שֶׁדַּאֲגוֹת הָעוֹלָם הַזֶּה
hannizra bein hakkotzim hu hashomea et haddavar, ella shedda'agot ha'olam hazzeh
And he that was sown among the thorns, this is he that heareth the word; and the care of the world,

וּמַדּוּחֵי הָעֹשֶׁר מַחֲנִיקִים אֶת הַדָּבָר וְלֹא יַעֲשֶׂה פְּרִי
umadduchei ha'osher machanikim et haddavar velo ya'aseh peri
and the deceitfulness of riches, choke the word, and he becometh unfruitful.

הַנִּזְרָע עַל הָאֲדָמָה הַטּוֹבָה הוּא הַשּׁוֹמֵעַ אֶת הַדָּבָר
hannizra al ha'adamah hattovah hu hashomea et haddavar umevin
And he that was sown upon the good ground, this is he that heareth the word, and understandeth it;

וּמֵבִין וְגַם עוֹשֶׂה פְּרִי - זֶה עוֹשֶׂה פִּי מֵאָה, זֶה פִּי שִׁשִּׁים וְזֶה פִּי שְׁלוֹשִׁים
vegam oseh peri - zeh oseh pi me'ah, zeh pi shishim vezeh pi sheloshim
who verily beareth fruit, and bringeth forth, some a hundredfold, some sixty, some thirty.

הִמְשִׁיךְ וְסִפֵּר לָהֶם מָשָׁל אַחֵר
himshich vesipper lahem mashal acher
Another parable set he before them, saying,

מַלְכוּת הַשָּׁמַיִם דּוֹמָה לְאִישׁ הַזּוֹרֵעַ זֶרַע טוֹב בְּשָׂדֵהוּ
malchut hashamayim domah le'ish hazzorea zera tov besadehu
The kingdom of heaven is likened unto a man that sowed good seed in his field:

וְהִנֵּה כְּשֶׁיָּשְׁנוּ הָאֲנָשִׁים בָּא אוֹיֵב, זָרַע עֲשָׂבִים רָעִים בֵּין הַחִטִּים וְהָלַךְ לוֹ
vehinneh kesheyashenu ha'anashim ba oyev, zara asavim ra'im bein hachittim vehalach lo
but while men slept, his enemy came and sowed tares also among the wheat, and went away.

כַּאֲשֶׁר צָמְחוּ הַגִּבְעוֹלִים וְעָשׂוּ תְּבוּאָה נִרְאוּ גַּם הָעֲשָׂבִים הָרָעִים
ka'asher tzamechu haggiv'olim ve'asu tevu'ah nir'u gam ha'asavim hara'im
But when the blade sprang up and brought forth fruit, then appeared the tares also.

אָז נִגְּשׁוּ עַבְדֵי בַּעַל־הַבַּיִת וְאָמְרוּ אֵלָיו
az niggeshu avdei ba'al-habbayit ve'ameru elav
And the servants of the householder came and said unto him,

אֲדוֹנֵנוּ, הֲלֹא זֶרַע טוֹב זָרַעְתָּ בְּשָׂדְךָ; מִנַּיִן יֵשׁ בּוֹ עֲשָׂבִים רָעִים
adonenu, halo zera tov zara'ta besadcha; minnayin yesh bo asavim ra'im
Sir, didst thou not sow good seed in thy field? whence then hath it tares?

וּמִתְקַיֶּמֶת בָּהֶם נְבוּאַת יְשַׁעְיָהוּ לֵאמֹר: שִׁמְעוּ שָׁמוֹעַ וְאַל־תָּבִינוּ
umitkayemet bahem nevu'at yesha'yahu lemor: shim'u shamoa ve'al-tavinu
And unto them is fulfilled the prophecy of Isaiah, which saith, By hearing ye shall hear, and shall in no wise understand;

וּרְאוּ רָאוֹ וְאַל־תֵּדָעוּ
ure'u ra'o ve'al-teda'u
And seeing ye shall see, and shall in no wise perceive:

הַשְׁמֵן לֵב־הָעָם הַזֶּה וְאָזְנָיו הַכְבֵּד וְעֵינָיו הָשַׁע
hashmen lev-ha'am hazzeh ve'azenav hachbed ve'einav hasha'
For this people's heart is waxed gross, And their ears are dull of hearing, And their eyes they have closed;

פֶּן־יִרְאֶה בְעֵינָיו וּבְאָזְנָיו יִשְׁמָע וּלְבָבוֹ יָבִין
pen-yir'eh ve'einav uve'oznav yishma ulevavo yavin
Lest haply they should perceive with their eyes, And hear with their ears, And understand with their heart,

וָשָׁב וְרָפָא לוֹ
veshav verafa lo
And should turn again, And I should heal them.

אַשְׁרֵי עֵינֵיכֶם הָרוֹאוֹת וְאָזְנֵיכֶם הַשּׁוֹמְעוֹת
ashrei eineichem haro'ot ve'ozneichem hashome'ot
But blessed are your eyes, for they see; and your ears, for they hear.

אָמֵן. אוֹמֵר אֲנִי לָכֶם, נְבִיאִים וְצַדִּיקִים רַבִּים נִכְסְפוּ לִרְאוֹת אֶת אֲשֶׁר אַתֶּם רוֹאִים וְלֹא רָאוּ
amen. Omer ani lachem, nevi'im vetzaddikim rabbim nichsefu lir'ot et asher attem ro'im velo ra'u
For verily I say unto you, that many prophets and righteous men desired to see the things which ye see, and saw them not;

וְלִשְׁמֹעַ אֶת אֲשֶׁר אַתֶּם שׁוֹמְעִים וְלֹא שָׁמֵעוּ
velishmoa et asher attem shome'im velo shame'u
and to hear the things which ye hear, and heard them not.

וּבְכֵן שִׁמְעוּ אַתֶּם אֶת פֵּשֶׁר מְשַׁל הַזּוֹרֵעַ
uvechen shim'u attem et pesher meshal hazzorea
Hear then ye the parable of the sower.

כָּל הַשּׁוֹמֵעַ אֶת דְּבַר הַמַּלְכוּת וְאֵינֶנּוּ מֵבִין, בָּא הָרַע
kol hashomea et devar hammalchut ve'einennu mevin, ba hara
When any one heareth the word of the kingdom, and understandeth it not, then cometh the evil one,

וְחוֹטֵף אֶת מַה שֶּׁנִּזְרַע בִּלְבָבוֹ; זֶהוּ הַנִּזְרָע בְּשׁוּלֵי הַדֶּרֶךְ
vechotef et mah shennizra bilvavo; zehu hannizra beshulei hadderech
and snatcheth away that which hath been sown in his heart. This is he that was sown by the way side.

הַנִּזְרָע עַל אַדְמַת טְרָשִׁים הוּא הַשּׁוֹמֵעַ אֶת הַדָּבָר וּמִיָּד מְקַבֵּל אוֹתוֹ בְּשִׂמְחָה
hannizra al admat terashim hu hashomea et haddavar umiyad mekabbel oto besimchah
And he that was sown upon the rocky places, this is he that heareth the word, and straightway with joy receiveth it;

וּמִהֲרוּ לִצְמֹחַ מִפְּנֵי שֶׁלֹּא הָיְתָה לָהֶם אֲדָמָה עֲמֻקָּה
umiharu litzmoach mippenei shello hayetah lahem adamah amukkah
and straightway they sprang up, because they had no deepness of earth:

אוּלָם כְּשֶׁזָּרְחָה הַשֶּׁמֶשׁ נִצְרְבוּ וּבְאֵין שֹׁרֶשׁ הִתְיַבְּשׁוּ
ulam keshezzarechah hashemesh nitzrevu uve'ein shoresh hityabbeshu
and when the sun was risen, they were scorched; and because they had no root, they withered away.

אֲחֵרִים נָפְלוּ בֵּין קוֹצִים, אַךְ הַקּוֹצִים צָמְחוּ וְהֶחֱנִיקוּ אוֹתָם
acherim nafelu bein kotzim, ach hakkotzim tzamechu vehecheniku otam
And others fell upon the thorns; and the thorns grew up and choked them:

וַאֲחֵרִים נָפְלוּ עַל אֲדָמָה טוֹבָה וְעָשׂוּ פְּרִי - זֶה פִּי מֵאָה, זֶה פִּי שִׁשִּׁים וְזֶה פִּי שְׁלוֹשִׁים
va'acherim nafelu al adamah tovah ve'asu peri - zeh pi me'ah, zeh pi shishim vezeh pi sheloshim
and others fell upon the good ground, and yielded fruit, some a hundredfold, some sixty, some thirty.

מִי שֶׁאָזְנַיִם לוֹ, שֶׁיִּשְׁמַע
mi she'oznayim lo, sheyishma'
He that hath ears, let him hear.

נִגְּשׁוּ הַתַּלְמִידִים וְשָׁאֲלוּ: מַדּוּעַ אַתָּה מְדַבֵּר אֲלֵיהֶם בִּמְשָׁלִים
niggeshu hattalmidim vesha'alu: maddua attah medabber aleihem bimshalim
And the disciples came, and said unto him, Why speakest thou unto them in parables?

הֵשִׁיב וְאָמַר
heshiv ve'amar
And he answered and said unto them,

מִפְּנֵי שֶׁלָּכֶם נִתַּן לָדַעַת אֶת סוֹדוֹת מַלְכוּת הַשָּׁמַיִם, אַךְ לָהֶם לֹא נִתַּן
mippenei shellachem nittan lada'at et sodot malchut hashamayim, ach lahem lo nittan
Unto you it is given to know the mysteries of the kingdom of heaven, but to them it is not given.

כִּי מִי שֶׁיֵּשׁ לוֹ נָתוֹן יִנָּתֵן לוֹ וְשֶׁפַע יִהְיֶה לוֹ
ki mi sheyesh lo naton yinnaten lo veshefa yihyeh lo
For whosoever hath, to him shall be given, and he shall have abundance:

אַךְ מִי שֶׁאֵין לוֹ, גַּם מַה שֶׁיֵּשׁ לוֹ יִלָּקַח מִמֶּנּוּ
ach mi she'ein lo, gam mah sheyesh lo yillakach mimmennu
but whosoever hath not, from him shall be taken away even that which he hath.

לָכֵן בִּמְשָׁלִים אֲנִי מְדַבֵּר אֲלֵיהֶם
lachen bimshalim ani medabber aleihem
Therefore speak I to them in parables;

כִּי בִּרְאוֹתָם אֵינָם רוֹאִים וּבְשָׁמְעָם אֵינָם שׁוֹמְעִים אַף אֵינָם מְבִינִים
ki bir'otam einam ro'im uveshame'am einam shome'im af einam mevinim
because seeing they see not, and hearing they hear not, neither do they understand.

בְּשָׁעָה שֶׁדִּבֵּר אֶל הֲמוֹן הָעָם בָּאוּ אִמּוֹ וְאֶחָיו. הֵם עָמְדוּ בַּחוּץ וְרָצוּ לְדַבֵּר אִתּוֹ
besha'ah sheddibber el hamon ha'am ba'u immo ve'echav. hem amedu bachutz veratzu ledabber itto
While he was yet speaking to the multitudes, behold, his mother and his brethren stood without, seeking to speak to him.

אָמַר לוֹ מִישֶׁהוּ: הִנֵּה אִמְּךָ וְאַחֶיךָ עוֹמְדִים בַּחוּץ וּמְבַקְשִׁים לְדַבֵּר אִתְּךָ
amar lo mishehu: hinneh immech ve'acheicha omedim bachutz umevakshim ledabber ittcha
And one said unto him, Behold, thy mother and thy brethren stand without, seeking to speak to thee.

מִי הִיא אִמִּי וּמִי הֵם אַחַי? הֵשִׁיב וְאָמַר לָאִישׁ אֲשֶׁר הוֹדִיעַ לוֹ
mi hi immi umi hem achai? heshiv ve'amar la'ish asher hodia lo
But he answered and said unto him that told him, Who is my mother? and who are my brethren?

וּבְהוֹשִׁיטוֹ אֶת יָדוֹ אֶל תַּלְמִידָיו אָמַר: הִנֵּה אִמִּי וְאַחַי
uvehoshito et yado el talmidav amar: hinneh immi ve'achai
And he stretched forth his hand towards his disciples, and said, Behold, my mother and my brethren!

כִּי כָּל הָעוֹשֶׂה אֶת רְצוֹן אָבִי שֶׁבַּשָּׁמַיִם הוּא אָחִי וַאֲחוֹתִי וְאִמִּי
ki kol ha'oseh et retzon avi shebbashamayim hu achi va'achoti ve'immi
For whosoever shall do the will of my Father who is in heaven, he is my brother, and sister, and mother.

יג

בַּיּוֹם הַהוּא יָצָא יֵשׁוּעַ מִן הַבַּיִת וַיֵּשֶׁב עַל־יַד הַיָּם
Bayom hahu yatza yeshua min habbayit veyashav al-yad hayam
On that day went Jesus out of the house, and sat by the sea side.

כֵּיוָן שֶׁנִּקְהֲלוּ אֵלָיו הֲמוֹן עַם רַב יָרַד לַסִּירָה לָשֶׁבֶת בָּהּ
keivan shennik'halu elav hamon am rav yarad lassirah lashevet bah
And there were gathered unto him great multitudes, so that he entered into a boat, and sat;

וְכָל הֶהָמוֹן עָמַד עַל הַחוֹף
vechol hehamon amad al hachof
and all the multitude stood on the beach.

אָז דִּבֵּר אֲלֵיהֶם רַבּוֹת בִּמְשָׁלִים וְאָמַר: הִנֵּה הַזּוֹרֵעַ יָצָא לִזְרֹעַ
az dibber aleihem rabbot bimshalim ve'amar: hinneh hazzorea yatza lizroa'
And he spake to them many things in parables, saying, Behold, the sower went forth to sow;

כַּאֲשֶׁר זָרַע נָפְלוּ כַּמָּה זְרָעִים בְּשׁוּלֵי הַדֶּרֶךְ וּבָאוּ צִפֳּרִים וְאָכְלוּ אוֹתָם
ka'asher zara nafelu kammah zera'im beshulei hadderech uva'u tzipporim ve'achelu otam
and as he sowed, some seeds fell by the way side, and the birds came and devoured them:

אֲחֵרִים נָפְלוּ עַל אַדְמַת טְרָשִׁים, בְּמָקוֹם שֶׁלֹּא הָיְתָה לָהֶם הַרְבֵּה אֲדָמָה
acherim nafelu al admat terashim, bemakom shello hayetah lahem harbeh adamah
and others fell upon the rocky places, where they had not much earth:

הֵשִׁיב וְאָמַר לָהֶם: דּוֹר רַע וּמְנָאֵף מְבַקֵּשׁ אוֹת
heshiv ve'amar lahem: dor ra umena'ef mevakkesh ot
But he answered and said unto them, An evil and adulterous generation seeketh after a sign;

וְאוֹת לֹא יִנָּתֵן לוֹ מִלְּבַד אוֹת יוֹנָה הַנָּבִיא
ve'ot lo yinnaten lo millevad ot yonah hannavi
and there shall no sign be given to it but the sign of Jonah the prophet:

כְּמוֹ שֶׁהָיָה יוֹנָה בִּמְעֵי הַדָּג שְׁלֹשָׁה יָמִים וּשְׁלֹשָׁה לֵילוֹת
kemo shehayah yonah bim'ei haddag sheloshah yamim usheloshah leilot
for as Jonah was three days and three nights in the belly of the whale;

כָּךְ יִהְיֶה בֶּן־הָאָדָם בְּלֵב הָאֲדָמָה שְׁלוֹשָׁה יָמִים וּשְׁלוֹשָׁה לֵילוֹת
kach yihyeh ben-ha'adam belev ha'adamah sheloshah yamim usheloshah leilot
so shall the Son of man be three days and three nights in the heart of the earth.

אַנְשֵׁי נִינְוֵה יָקוּמוּ בַּמִּשְׁפָּט עִם הַדּוֹר הַזֶּה וְיַרְשִׁיעוּהוּ
anshei nineveh yakumu bammishpat im haddor hazzeh veyarshi'uhu
The men of Nineveh shall stand up in the judgment with this generation, and shall condemn it:

כִּי חָזְרוּ בִּתְשׁוּבָה בִּקְרִיאַת יוֹנָה; וְהִנֵּה גָּדוֹל מִיּוֹנָה כָּאן
ki chazeru bitshuvah bikri'at yonah; vehinneh gadol miyonah kan
for they repented at the preaching of Jonah; and behold, a greater than Jonah is here.

מַלְכַּת תֵּימָן תָּקוּם בַּמִּשְׁפָּט עִם הַדּוֹר הַזֶּה וְתַרְשִׁיעַ אוֹתוֹ
malkat teiman takum bammishpat im haddor hazzeh vetarshia oto
The queen of the south shall rise up in the judgment with this generation, and shall condemn it:

כִּי בָּאָה מִקְצֵה הָאָרֶץ לִשְׁמֹעַ אֶת חָכְמַת שְׁלֹמֹה; וְהִנֵּה גָּדוֹל מִשְּׁלֹמֹה כָּאן
ki ba'ah miktzeh ha'aretz lishmoa et chochmat shelomoh; vehinneh gadol mishelomoh kan
for she came from the ends of the earth to hear the wisdom of Solomon; and behold, a greater than Solomon is here.

הָרוּחַ הַטְּמֵאָה הַיּוֹצֵאת מִן הָאָדָם מְשׁוֹטֶטֶת בִּמְקוֹמוֹת צִיָּה וּמְבַקֶּשֶׁת לָהּ מָנוֹחַ וְאֵינָהּ מוֹצֵאת
haruach hatteme'ah hayotzet min ha'adam meshotetet bimkomot tziyah umevakkeshet lah manoach ve'einah motzet
But the unclean spirit, when he is gone out of the man, passeth through waterless places, seeking rest, and findeth it not.

אָז תֹּאמַר: 'אָשׁוּבָה אֶל בֵּיתִי שֶׁיָּצָאתִי מִמֶּנּוּ.' הִיא בָּאָה וּמוֹצֵאת אוֹתוֹ מְפֻנֶּה, מְטֻאטָא וּמְהֻדָּר
az tomar: ashuvah el beiti sheyatzati mimmennu. hi ba'ah umotzet oto mefunneh, metuta umehuddar
Then he saith, I will return into my house whence I came out; and when he is come, he findeth it empty, swept, and garnished.

מִיָּד הִיא הוֹלֶכֶת וְלוֹקַחַת אִתָּהּ שֶׁבַע רוּחוֹת אֲחֵרוֹת רָעוֹת מִמֶּנָּה וְכֻלָּן נִכְנָסוֹת לִשְׁכֹּן שָׁם
miyad hi holechet velokachat ittah sheva ruchot acherot ra'ot mimmennah vechullan nichnasot lishkon sham
Then goeth he, and taketh with himself seven other spirits more evil than himself, and they enter in and dwell there:

אָכֵן גְּרוּעָה אַחֲרִיתוֹ שֶׁל הָאִישׁ הַהוּא מֵרֵאשִׁיתוֹ. כֵּן גַּם יִהְיֶה לַדּוֹר הָרַע הַזֶּה
Achen geru'ah acharito shel ha'ish hahu mereshito. ken gam yihyeh laddor hara hazzeh
and the last state of that man becometh worse than the first. Even so shall it be also unto this evil generation.

עַל כֵּן אֲנִי אוֹמֵר לָכֶם
al ken ani omer lachem
Therefore I say unto you,

כָּל חֵטְא וְגִדּוּף יִסָּלַח לִבְנֵי אָדָם, אַךְ גִּדּוּף כְּלַפֵּי הָרוּחַ לֹא יִסָּלַח
kol chet vegidduf yissalach livnei adam, ach gidduf kelappei haruach lo yissalach
Every sin and blasphemy shall be forgiven unto men; but the blasphemy against the Spirit shall not be forgiven.

כָּל הַמְדַבֵּר דָּבָר נֶגֶד בֶּן־הָאָדָם יִסָּלַח לוֹ
kol hamedabber davar neged ben-ha'adam yissalach lo
And whosoever shall speak a word against the Son of man, it shall be forgiven him;

אֲבָל כָּל הַמְדַבֵּר נֶגֶד רוּחַ הַקֹּדֶשׁ לֹא יִסָּלַח לוֹ
aval kol hamedabber neged ruach hakkodesh lo yissalach lo
but whosoever shall speak against the Holy Spirit, it shall not be forgiven him,

לֹא בָּעוֹלָם הַזֶּה וְלֹא בָּעוֹלָם הַבָּא
lo ba'olam hazzeh velo ba'olam habba
neither in this world, nor in that which is to come.

אוֹ שֶׁהָעֵץ טוֹב וּפִרְיוֹ טוֹב, אוֹ שֶׁהָעֵץ רַע וּפִרְיוֹ רַע; שֶׁהֲרֵי בְּפִרְיוֹ נִכָּר הָעֵץ
'o sheha'etz tov ufiryo tov, o sheha'etz ra ufiryo ra'; sheharei befiryo nikkar ha'etz
Either make the tree good, and its fruit good; or make the tree corrupt, and its fruit corrupt: for the tree is known by its fruit.

יַלְדֵי צִפְעוֹנִים, אֵיךְ תּוּכְלוּ לְדַבֵּר טוֹבוֹת וְאַתֶּם רָעִים? הֵן מִתּוֹךְ הַשּׁוֹפֵעַ בַּלֵּב מְדַבֵּר הַפֶּה
yaldei tzif'onim, eich tuchelu ledabber tovot ve'attem ra'im? hen mittoch hashofea ballev medabber happeh
Ye offspring of vipers, how can ye, being evil, speak good things? for out of the abundance of the heart the mouth speaketh.

אִישׁ טוֹב מֵפִיק דְּבָרִים טוֹבִים מֵאוֹצָרוֹ הַטּוֹב
ish tov mefik devarim tovim me'otzaro hattov
The good man out of his good treasure bringeth forth good things:

אִישׁ רַע מֵפִיק דְּבָרִים רָעִים מֵאוֹצָרוֹ הָרָע
ish ra mefik devarim ra'im me'otzaro hara
and the evil man out of his evil treasure bringeth forth evil things.

וַאֲנִי אוֹמֵר לָכֶם, כָּל מִלָּה בְּטֵלָה שֶׁיְּדַבְּרוּ בְּנֵי אָדָם יִתְּנוּ עָלֶיהָ דִּין וְחֶשְׁבּוֹן בְּיוֹם הַדִּין
va'ani omer lachem, kol millah betelah sheyedabberu benei adam yittenu aleiha din vecheshbon beyom haddin
And I say unto you, that every idle word that men shall speak, they shall give account thereof in the day of judgment.

מִדְּבָרֶיךָ תִּצְדַּק וּמִדְּבָרֶיךָ תְּחֻיָּב
middevareicha titzadek umiddevareicha techuyav
For by thy words thou shalt be justified, and by thy words thou shalt be condemned.

אֲחָדִים מִן הַסּוֹפְרִים וְהַפְּרוּשִׁים פָּנוּ אֵלָיו וְאָמְרוּ: רַבִּי, רוֹצִים אָנוּ לִרְאוֹת מִמְּךָ אוֹת
achadim min hassoferim vehapperushim panu elav ve'ameru.: rabbi, rotzim anu lir'ot mimmecha ot
Then certain of the scribes and Pharisees answered him, saying, Teacher, we would see a sign from thee.

יֵשׁוּעַ רִפֵּא אוֹתוֹ וְהָאִלֵּם דִּבֶּר וְגַם רָאָה
yeshua rippei oto veha'illem dibber vegam ra'ah
and he healed him, insomuch that the dumb man spake and saw.

הִשְׁתּוֹמְמוּ כָּל הֲמוֹנֵי הָעָם וְאָמְרוּ: הַאִם לֹא זֶה בֶּן־דָּוִד
hishtomemu kol hamonei ha'am ve'ameru: ha'im lo zeh ben-david
And all the multitudes were amazed, and said, Can this be the son of David?

כְּשֶׁשָּׁמְעוּ זֹאת הַפְּרוּשִׁים אָמְרוּ: זֶה אֵינֶנּוּ מְגָרֵשׁ אֶת הַשֵּׁדִים אֶלָּא בְּעֶזְרַת בַּעַל־זְבוּל שַׂר הַשֵּׁדִים
kesheshame'u zot happerushim ameru: zeh einennu megaresh et hashedim ella be'ezrat ba'al-zvul sar hashedim
But when the Pharisees heard it, they said, This man doth not cast out demons, but by Beelzebub the prince of the demons.

הוֹאִיל וְיָדַע אֶת מַחְשְׁבוֹתֵיהֶם אָמַר לָהֶם: כָּל מַמְלָכָה הַמְפֻלֶּגֶת בְּתוֹךְ עַצְמָהּ סוֹפָהּ שֶׁהִיא נֶחֱרֶבֶת
ho'il veyada et machshevoteihem amar lahem: kol mamlachah hamfulleget betoch atzmah sofah shehi necherevet
And knowing their thoughts he said unto them, Every kingdom divided against itself is brought to desolation;

וְכָל עִיר אוֹ בַּיִת הַמְפֻלָּגִים בְּתוֹךְ עַצְמָם לֹא יַחֲזִיקוּ מַעֲמָד
vechol ir o bayit hamfullagim betoch atzmam lo yachaziku ma'amad
and every city or house divided against itself shall not stand:

אִם הַשָּׂטָן מְגָרֵשׁ אֶת הַשָּׂטָן, כִּי אָז הִתְפַּלֵּג בְּתוֹךְ עַצְמוֹ וְאֵיךְ תַּעֲמֹד מַמְלַכְתּוֹ
im hassatan megaresh et hassatan, ki az hitpalleg betoch atzmo ve'eich ta'amod mamlachto
and if Satan casteth out Satan, he is divided against himself; how then shall his kingdom stand?

וְאִם אֲנִי מְגָרֵשׁ אֶת הַשֵּׁדִים בְּעֶזְרַת בַּעַל־זְבוּל, בְּעֶזְרַת מִי מְגָרְשִׁים אוֹתָם בְּנֵיכֶם?
ve'im ani megaresh et hashedim be'ezrat ba'al-zevul, be'ezrat mi megareshim otam beneichem
And if I by Beelzebub cast out demons, by whom do your sons cast them out?

לָכֵן הֵם יִהְיוּ שׁוֹפְטֵיכֶם
lachen hem yihyu shofteichem
therefore shall they be your judges.

אַךְ אִם עַל־יְדֵי רוּחַ אֱלֹהִים אֲנִי מְגָרֵשׁ אֶת הַשֵּׁדִים, כִּי אָז הִגִּיעָה אֲלֵיכֶם מַלְכוּת הָאֱלֹהִים
ach im al-yedei ruach elohim ani megaresh et hashedim, ki az higgi'ah aleichem malchut ha'elohim
But if I by the Spirit of God cast out demons, then is the kingdom of God come upon you.

אוֹ אֵיךְ יוּכַל אִישׁ לְהִכָּנֵס לְבֵיתוֹ שֶׁל גִּבּוֹר וְלִטֹּל אֶת כֵּלָיו
o eich yuchal ish lehikkanes leveito shel gibbor velittol et kelav
Or how can one enter into the house of the strong man, and spoil his goods,

אִם לֹא יִכְפֹּת תְּחִלָּה אֶת הַגִּבּוֹר? רַק אַחֲרֵי כֵן יָבֹז אֶת בֵּיתוֹ
im lo yichpot techillah et haggibbor? rak acharei chen yavoz et beito
except he first bind the strong man? and then he will spoil his house.

מִי שֶׁאֵינֶנּוּ אִתִּי נֶגְדִּי הוּא, וּמִי שֶׁאֵינֶנּוּ אוֹסֵף אִתִּי - מְפַזֵּר
mi she'einenu itti negdi hu, umi she'einennu osef itti - mefazzer
He that is not with me is against me; and he that gathereth not with me scattereth.

וְכַמָּה חָשׁוּב הָאָדָם יוֹתֵר מִן הַכֶּבֶשׂ! לָכֵן מֻתָּר לַעֲשׂוֹת אֶת הַטּוֹב בְּשַׁבָּת
vechammah chashuv ha'adam yoter min hakkeves! lachen muttar la'asot et hattov beshabbat
How much then is a man of more value than a sheep! Wherefore it is lawful to do good on the sabbath day.

אָז אָמַר אֶל הָאִישׁ: הוֹשֵׁט יָדְךָ! הוּא הוֹשִׁיט אֶת יָדוֹ וְאָמְנָם שָׁבָה לְאֵיתָנָהּ וְהָיְתָה בְּרִיאָה כְּמוֹ הַשְּׁנִיָּה
az amar el ha'ish: hoshet yadecha! hu hoshit et yado ve'amenam shavah le'eitanah vehayetah beri'ah kemo hasheniyah
Then saith he to the man, Stretch forth thy hand. And he stretched it forth; and it was restored whole, as the other.

יָצְאוּ הַפְּרוּשִׁים וְטִכְּסוּ עֵצָה לְהַכְחִיד אֶת יֵשׁוּעַ
yatze'u happerushim vetikkesu etzah lehachchid et yeshua'
But the Pharisees went out, and took counsel against him, how they might destroy him.

יֵשׁוּעַ יָדַע אֶת זֹאת וְהִתְרַחֵק מִשָּׁם, אַךְ רַבִּים הָלְכוּ אַחֲרָיו. הוּא רִפֵּא אֶת כֻּלָּם
yeshua yada et zot vehitrachek misham, ach rabbim halechu acharav. hu rippei et kullam
And Jesus perceiving it withdrew from thence: and many followed him; and he healed them all,

וְהִזְהִיר אוֹתָם שֶׁלֹּא יְגַלּוּ אוֹתוֹ
vehizhir otam shello yegallu oto
and charged them that they should not make him known:

לְמַעַן יִתְקַיֵּם מַה שֶּׁנֶּאֱמַר בְּפִי יְשַׁעְיָהוּ הַנָּבִיא
lema'an yitkayem mah shenne'emar befi yesha'yahu hannavi
that it might be fulfilled which was spoken through Isaiah the prophet, saying,

הֵן עַבְדִּי אֶתְמָךְ־בּוֹ, בְּחִירִי רָצְתָה נַפְשִׁי
hen avdi etmach-bo, bechiri ratzetah nafshi
Behold, my servant whom I have chosen; My beloved in whom my soul is well pleased:

נָתַתִּי רוּחִי עָלָיו, מִשְׁפָּט לַגּוֹיִם יוֹצִיא
natatti ruchi alav, mishpat laggoyim yotzi
I will put my Spirit upon him, And he shall declare judgment to the Gentiles.

לֹא יִצְעַק וְלֹא יִשָּׂא וְלֹא־יַשְׁמִיעַ בַּחוּץ קוֹלוֹ
lo yitz'ak velo yisho velo-yashmia bachutz kolo
He shall not strive, nor cry aloud; Neither shall any one hear his voice in the streets.

קָנֶה רָצוּץ לֹא יִשְׁבּוֹר וּפִשְׁתָּה כֵהָה לֹא יְכַבֶּנָּה
kaneh ratzutz lo yishbor ufishtah kehah lo yechabbennah
A bruised reed shall he not break, And smoking flax shall he not quench, Till he send forth judgment unto victory.

עַד יוֹצִיא לָנֶצַח מִשְׁפָּט; וְלִשְׁמוֹ גּוֹיִם יְיַחֵלוּ
ad yotzi lenitzachon mishpat; velishmo goyim yeyachelu
And in his name shall the Gentiles hope.

אָז הוּבָא אֵלָיו אִישׁ אָחוּז שֵׁד וְהוּא עִוֵּר וְאִלֵּם
az huva elav ish achuz shed vehu ivver ve'illem
Then was brought unto him one possessed with a demon, blind and dumb:

הֵשִׁיב לָהֶם: הַאִם לֹא קְרָאתֶם מַה שֶּׁעָשָׂה דָּוִד כַּאֲשֶׁר רָעֵב הוּא וְהָאֲנָשִׁים אֲשֶׁר אִתּוֹ
heshiv lahem: ha'im lo keratem mah she'asah david ka'asher ra'av hu veha'anashim asher itto
But he said unto them, Have ye not read what David did, when he was hungry, and they that were with him;

הֲרֵי נִכְנַס לְבֵית הָאֱלֹהִים וְאָכַל אֶת לֶחֶם הַפָּנִים
harei nichnas leveit ha'elohim ve'achal et lechem happanim
how he entered into the house of God, and ate the showbread,

שֶׁלֹּא הָיָה מֻתָּר לוֹ וְלָאֲנָשָׁיו לֶאֱכֹל כִּי אִם לַכֹּהֲנִים בִּלְבַד
shello hayah muttar lo vela'anashav le'echol ki im lakkohanim bilvad
which it was not lawful for him to eat, neither for them that were with him, but only for the priests?

הַאִם לֹא קְרָאתֶם בַּתּוֹרָה כִּי בְּשַׁבָּתוֹת מְחַלְּלִים הַכֹּהֲנִים אֶת הַשַּׁבָּת בַּמִּקְדָּשׁ וְאֵין עֲלֵיהֶם אַשְׁמָה
ha'im lo keratem battorah ki beshabbatot mechallelim hakkohanim et hashabbat bammikdash ve'ein aleihem ashmah
Or have ye not read in the law, that on the sabbath day the priests in the temple profane the sabbath, and are guiltless?

וַאֲנִי אוֹמֵר לָכֶם שֶׁגָּדוֹל מִן הַמִּקְדָּשׁ נִמְצָא כָּאן
va'ani omer lachem sheggadol min hammikdash nimtza kan
But I say unto you, that one greater than the temple is here.

אַךְ אִלּוּ יְדַעְתֶּם מַה מַּשְׁמַע חֶסֶד חָפַצְתִּי וְלֹא־זֶבַח, לֹא הֱיִיתֶם מַרְשִׁיעִים אֶת הַנְּקִיִּים
ach illu yeda'tem mah mashma chesed chafatzti velo-zevach, lo heyitem marshi'im et hannekiyim
But if ye had known what this meaneth, I desire mercy, and not sacrifice, ye would not have condemned the guiltless.

שֶׁהֲרֵי בֶּן־הָאָדָם הוּא אֲדוֹן הַשַּׁבָּת
sheharei ben-ha'adam hu adon hashabbat
For the Son of man is lord of the sabbath.

הוּא הָלַךְ מִשָּׁם וְנִכְנַס לְבֵית הַכְּנֶסֶת
hu halach misham venichnas leveit hakkeneset
And he departed thence, and went into their synagogue:

הָיָה שָׁם אִישׁ שֶׁיָּדוֹ יְבֵשָׁה
hayah sham ish sheyado yeveshah
and behold, a man having a withered hand.

וְהֵם פָּנוּ אֵלָיו בִּשְׁאֵלָה: הַאִם מֻתָּר לְרַפֵּא בְּשַׁבָּת? וְזֹאת כְּדֵי שֶׁיּוּכְלוּ לְהַאֲשִׁים אוֹתוֹ
vehem panu elav bish'elah ha'im muttar lerappei beshabbat? vezot kedei sheyuchelu leha'ashim oto
And they asked him, saying, Is it lawful to heal on the sabbath day? That they might accuse him.

אָמַר לָהֶם: מִי מִכֶּם הָאִישׁ שֶׁכֶּבֶשׂ אֶחָד לוֹ
amar lahem: Mi mikkem ha'ish shekkeves echad lo
And he said unto them, What man shall there be of you, that shall have one sheep,

וְאִם יִפֹּל בְּשַׁבָּת לְתוֹךְ בּוֹר לֹא יַחֲזִיק בּוֹ וְיָרִים אוֹתוֹ
ve'im yippol beshabbat letoch bor lo yachazik bo veyarim oto
and if this fall into a pit on the sabbath day, will he not lay hold on it, and lift it out?

בָּעֵת הַהִיא אָמַר יֵשׁוּעַ: מוֹדֶה אֲנִי לְךָ, אָבִי, אֲדוֹן הַשָּׁמַיִם וְהָאָרֶץ
ba'et hahi amar yeshua: modeh ani lecha, avi, adon hashamayim veha'aretz
At that season Jesus answered and said, I thank thee, O Father, Lord of heaven and earth,

כִּי הִסְתַּרְתָּ אֶת הַדְּבָרִים הָאֵלֶּה מִן הַחֲכָמִים וְהַנְּבוֹנִים וְגִלִּיתָם לְעוֹלָלִים
ki histarta et haddevarim ha'elleh min hachachamim vehannevonim vegillitam le'olalim
that thou didst hide these things from the wise and understanding, and didst reveal them unto babes:

כֵּן, אָבִי, שֶׁהֲרֵי כָּךְ הָיָה רָצוֹן מִלְּפָנֶיךָ
ken, avi, sheharei kach hayah ratzon millefaneicha
yea, Father, for so it was well-pleasing in thy sight.

הַכֹּל נִמְסַר לִי מֵאֵת אָבִי וְאֵין אִישׁ מַכִּיר אֶת הַבֵּן, זוּלָתִי הָאָב
hakkol nimsar li me'et avi ve'ein ish makkir et habben, zulati ha'av
All things have been delivered unto me of my Father: and no one knoweth the Son, save the Father;

אַף אֵין אִישׁ מַכִּיר אֶת הָאָב, זוּלָתִי הַבֵּן וְכָל מִי שֶׁהַבֵּן רוֹצֶה לְגַלּוֹת לוֹ
af ein ish makkir et ha'av, zulati habben vechol mi shehabben rotzeh legallot lo
neither doth any know the Father, save the Son, and he to whomsoever the Son willeth to reveal him.

בּוֹאוּ אֵלַי כָּל הָעֲמֵלִים וְהָעֲמוּסִים וַאֲנִי אַמְצִיא לָכֶם מְנוּחָה
bo'u elai kol ha'amelim veha'amusim va'ani amtzi lachem menuchah
Come unto me, all ye that labor and are heavy laden, and I will give you rest.

קְחוּ עֲלֵיכֶם אֶת עֻלִּי וְלִמְדוּ מִמֶּנִּי, כִּי עָנָו אֲנִי וּנְמוּךְ רוּחַ; תִּמְצְאוּ מַרְגוֹעַ לְנַפְשׁוֹתֵיכֶם
kchu aleichem et ulli velimdu mimmenni, ki anav ani unmuch ruach; timtze'u margoa lenafshoteichem
Take my yoke upon you, and learn of me; for I am meek and lowly in heart: and ye shall find rest unto your souls.

כִּי עֻלִּי נָעִים וְקַל מַשָּׂאִי
ki ulli na'im vekal massaee
For my yoke is easy, and my burden is light.

יב

בְּאוֹתָהּ הָעֵת עָבַר יֵשׁוּעַ בְּשַׁבָּת בִּשְׂדֵה קָמָה
Be'otah ha'et avar yeshua beshabbat bisdeh kamah
At that season Jesus went on the sabbath day through the grainfields;

תַּלְמִידָיו הָיוּ רְעֵבִים וְהֵחֵלּוּ לִקְטֹף שִׁבֳּלִים וְלֶאֱכֹל
talmidav hayu re'evim vehechellu liktof shibbolim vele'echol
and his disciples were hungry and began to pluck ears and to eat.

רָאוּ זֹאת הַפְּרוּשִׁים וְאָמְרוּ לוֹ: הִנֵּה תַּלְמִידֶיךָ עוֹשִׂים מַה שֶּׁאָסוּר לַעֲשׂוֹת בְּשַׁבָּת
ra'u zot happerushim ve'ameru lo: hinneh talmideicha osim mah she'asur la'asot beshabbat
But the Pharisees, when they saw it, said unto him, Behold, thy disciples do that which it is not lawful to do upon the sabbath.

לְמִי אַשְׁוֶה אֶת הַדּוֹר הַזֶּה? דּוֹמֶה הוּא לִילָדִים הַיּוֹשְׁבִים בַּחֲצֵרוֹת הַשְּׁוָקִים וְקוֹרְאִים אֶל חַבְרֵיהֶם בְּקוֹל
lemi ashveh et haddor hazzeh? domeh hu liyladim hayoshevim bechatzrot hashevakim vekore'im el chavreihem bekol
But whereunto shall I liken this generation? It is like unto children sitting in the marketplaces, who call unto their fellows

חִלַּלְנוּ לָכֶם בַּחֲלִילִים וְלֹא רְקַדְתֶּם, קוֹנַנּוּ לָכֶם קִינָה וְלֹא בְכִיתֶם
chillalnu lachem bachalilim velo rekadtem, konannu lachem kinah velo bechitem
and say, We piped unto you, and ye did not dance; we wailed, and ye did not mourn.

כִּי בָא יוֹחָנָן, לֹא אָכַל וְלֹא שָׁתָה, וְאוֹמְרִים עָלָיו שֵׁד בּוֹ
ki ba yochanan, lo achal velo shatah, ve'omerim alav shed bo
For John came neither eating nor drinking, and they say, He hath a demon.

בָּא בֶן־הָאָדָם וְהוּא אוֹכֵל וְשׁוֹתֶה, וְאוֹמְרִים
ba ben-ha'adam vehu ochel veshoteh, ve'omerim
The Son of man came eating and drinking, and they say,

הִנֵּה אִישׁ זוֹלֵל וְסוֹבֵא, יְדִיד הַמּוֹכְסִים וְהַחוֹטְאִים. אָכֵן, צִדְקָתָהּ שֶׁל הַחָכְמָה הוּכְחָה בְּמַעֲשֶׂיהָ
hinneh ish zolel vesove, yedid hammochesim vehachote'im. achen, tzidkatah shel hachochmah huchechah bema'aseiha
Behold, a gluttonous man and a winebibber, a friend of publicans and sinners! And wisdom is justified by her works.

אָז הֵחֵל לִגְעֹר בֶּעָרִים שֶׁהִתְחוֹלְלוּ בָּהֶן נִסָּיו הָרַבִּים וְלֹא חָזְרוּ בִּתְשׁוּבָה
az hechel lig'or be'arim shehitcholelu bahen nissav harabbim velo chazeru bitshuvah
Then began he to upbraid the cities wherein most of his mighty works were done, because they repented not.

אוֹי לָךְ כּוֹרָזִין! אוֹי לָךְ בֵּית צַיְדָה! כִּי אִלּוּ נַעֲשׂוּ בְּצוֹר וּבְצִידוֹן הַפְּלָאוֹת
oy lach korazin! oy lach beit tzaydah! ki illu na'asu betzor uvetzidon happela'ot
Woe unto thee, Chorazin! woe unto thee, Bethsaida! for if the mighty works had been done in Tyre and Sidon

שֶׁנַּעֲשׂוּ בְּתוֹכְכֶן, הֲרֵי מִכְּבָר הָיוּ חוֹזְרוֹת בִּתְשׁוּבָה בְּשַׂק וָאֵפֶר
shenna'asu betochechen, harei mikkevar hayu chozerot bitshuvah besak va'efer
which were done in you, they would have repented long ago in sackcloth and ashes.

בְּרַם אוֹמֵר אֲנִי לָכֶן, קַל יוֹתֵר יִהְיֶה בְּיוֹם הַדִּין לְצוֹר וּלְצִידוֹן מֵאֲשֶׁר לָכֶן
beram omer ani lachen, kal yoter yihyeh beyom haddin letzor uletzidon me'asher lachen
But I say unto you, it shall be more tolerable for Tyre and Sidon in the day of judgment, than for you.

וְאַתְּ, כְּפַר נַחוּם, הַאִם לַשָּׁמַיִם תַּעֲלִי? אֶל שְׁאוֹל תֵּרְדִי
ve'at, kefar nachum, ha'im lashamayim ta'ali? el she'ol teredi
And thou, Capernaum, shalt thou be exalted unto heaven? thou shalt go down unto Hades:

כִּי אִלּוּ בִּסְדוֹם נַעֲשׂוּ הַנִּסִּים שֶׁהָיוּ בְּתוֹכֵךְ, עוֹמֶדֶת הָיְתָה עַל תִּלָּהּ עַד הַיּוֹם
ki illu bisdom na'asu hannissim shehayu betochech, omedet hayetah al tillah ad hayom
for if the mighty works had been done in Sodom which were done in thee, it would have remained until this day.

וְאוּלָם אֲנִי אוֹמֵר לָךְ, קַל יוֹתֵר יִהְיֶה בְּיוֹם הַדִּין לְאֶרֶץ סְדוֹם מֵאֲשֶׁר לָךְ
ve'ulam ani omer lach, kal yoter yihyeh beyom haddin le'eretz sedom me'asher lach
But I say unto you that it shall be more tolerable for the land of Sodom in the day of judgment, than for thee.

הֵם הָלְכוּ וְיֵשׁוּעַ הֵחֵל לְדַבֵּר אֶל הֲמוֹן הָעָם עַל־אוֹדוֹת יוֹחָנָן
hem halechu veyeshua hechel ledabber el hamon ha'am al-'odot yochanan
And as these went their way, Jesus began to say unto the multitudes concerning John,

מַה יְצָאתֶם לַמִּדְבָּר לִרְאוֹת? קָנֶה מִתְנוֹעֵעַ בָּרוּחַ
mah yetzatem lammidbar lir'ot? kaneh mitno'ea baruach
What went ye out into the wilderness to behold? a reed shaken with the wind?

וּבְכֵן מַה יְצָאתֶם לִרְאוֹת? אִישׁ לָבוּשׁ בְּגָדִים מְעֻדָּנִים? הֲרֵי הַלּוֹבְשִׁים לְבוּשׁ מְעֻדָּן בְּבָתֵּי מְלָכִים הֵם
uvechen mah yetzatem lir'ot? ish lavush begadim me'uddanim? harei halloveshim levush me'uddan bevattei melachim hem
But what went ye out to see? a man clothed in soft raiment? Behold, they that wear soft raiment are in kings' houses.

מַה בְּכָל זֹאת יְצָאתֶם לִרְאוֹת? נָבִיא? כֵּן, אֲנִי אוֹמֵר לָכֶם, אַף יוֹתֵר מִנָּבִיא
mah bechol zot yetzatem lir'ot? navi? ken, ani omer lachem, af yoter minnavi
But wherefore went ye out? to see a prophet? Yea, I say unto you, and much more than a prophet.

זֶה הוּא אֲשֶׁר כָּתוּב עָלָיו, הִנְנִי שׁוֹלֵחַ מַלְאָכִי לְפָנֶיךָ וּפִנָּה דַרְכְּךָ לְפָנֶיךָ
zeh hu asher katuv alav, hineni sholeach mal'achi lefaneicha ufinnah darkecha lefaneicha
This is he, of whom it is written, Behold, I send my messenger before thy face, Who shall prepare thy way before thee.

אָמֵן. אוֹמֵר אֲנִי לָכֶם, לֹא קָם בִּילוּדֵי אִשָּׁה גָּדוֹל מִיּוֹחָנָן הַמַּטְבִּיל
amen omer ani lachem, lo kam biludei ishah gadol miyochanan hammatbil
Verily I say unto you, Among them that are born of women there hath not arisen a greater than John the Baptist:

אַךְ הַקָּטֹן בְּמַלְכוּת הַשָּׁמַיִם גָּדוֹל מִמֶּנּוּ
ach hakkaton bemalchut hashamayim gadol mimmennu
yet he that is but little in the kingdom of heaven is greater than he.

וּמִימֵי יוֹחָנָן הַמַּטְבִּיל וְעַד עַתָּה מַלְכוּת הַשָּׁמַיִם פּוֹרֶצֶת
umimei yochanan hammatbil ve'ad attah malchut hashamayim poretzet
And from the days of John the Baptist until now the kingdom of heaven suffereth violence,

וְהַפּוֹרְצִים אוֹחֲזִים בָּהּ
vehapporetzim ochazim bah
and men of violence take it by force.

הֵן כָּל הַנְּבִיאִים וְהַתּוֹרָה עַד יוֹחָנָן נִבְּאוּ
hen kol hannevi'im vehattorah ad yochanan nibbe'u
For all the prophets and the law prophesied until John.

וְאִם תִּרְצוּ לְקַבֵּל הֲרֵי הוּא אֵלִיָּהוּ הֶעָתִיד לָבוֹא
ve'im tirtzu lekabbel harei hu eliyahu he'atid lavo
And if ye are willing to receive it, this is Elijah, that is to come.

מִי שֶׁאָזְנַיִם לוֹ, שֶׁיִּשְׁמַע
mi she'azenayim lo, sheyishma
He that hath ears to hear, let him hear.

וְהַמְקַבֵּל צַדִּיק מִשּׁוּם הֱיוֹתוֹ צַדִּיק שְׂכַר צַדִּיק יְקַבֵּל
vehamkabbel tzaddik mishum heyoto tzaddik sechar tzaddik yekabbel
and he that receiveth a righteous man in the name of a righteous man shall receive a righteous man's reward.

וְכָל הַמַּשְׁקֶה אֶת אַחַד הַקְּטַנִּים הָאֵלֶּה רַק כּוֹס מַיִם קָרִים מִשּׁוּם הֱיוֹתוֹ תַּלְמִיד
vechol hammashkeh et achad hakketannim ha'elleh rak kos mayim karim mishum heyoto talmid
And whosoever shall give to drink unto one of these little ones a cup of cold water only, in the name of a disciple,

אָמֵן אוֹמֵר אֲנִי לָכֶם, לֹא יֹאבַד שְׂכָרוֹ
amen omer ani lachem, lo yovad scharo
verily I say unto you he shall in no wise lose his reward.

יא

יֵשׁוּעַ סִיֵּם אֶת הוֹרָאוֹתָיו לִשְׁנֵים־עָשָׂר תַּלְמִידָיו
yeshua siyem et hora'otav lishneim-'asar talmidav
And it came to pass when Jesus had finished commanding his twelve disciples,

וְהָלַךְ מִשָּׁם לְלַמֵּד וּלְהַטִּיף בְּעָרֵיהֶם
vehalach misham lelammed ulehattif be'areihem
he departed thence to teach and preach in their cities.

כַּאֲשֶׁר שָׁמַע יוֹחָנָן בְּבֵית הַסֹּהַר עַל מַעֲשֵׂי הַמָּשִׁיחַ שָׁלַח בְּיַד תַּלְמִידָיו לִשְׁאֹל אוֹתוֹ
ka'asher shama yochanan beveit hassohar al ma'asei hammashiach shalach beyad talmidav lish'ol oto
Now when John heard in the prison the works of the Christ, he sent by his disciples

אַתָּה הוּא אֲשֶׁר נוֹעַד לָבוֹא, אוֹ נְחַכֶּה לְאַחֵר
attah hu asher no'ad lavo, o nechakkeh le'acher
and said unto him, Art thou he that cometh, or look we for another?

הֵשִׁיב יֵשׁוּעַ וְאָמַר לָהֶם: "לְכוּ הַגִּידוּ לְיוֹחָנָן אֶת אֲשֶׁר אַתֶּם שׁוֹמְעִים וְרוֹאִים
heshiv yeshua ve'amar lahem: lechu haggidu leyochanan et asher attem shome'im vero'im
And Jesus answered and said unto them, Go and tell John the things which ye hear and see:

עִוְרִים רֹאִים, פִּסְחִים מְהַלְּכִים, מְצֹרָעִים מְטֹהָרִים, חֵרְשִׁים שׁוֹמְעִים
ivrim ro'im, pischim mehallechim, metzora'im metoharim, chereshim shome'im
the blind receive their sight, and the lame walk, the lepers are cleansed, and the deaf hear,

מֵתִים קָמִים, עֲנִיִּים מִתְבַּשְּׂרִים
metim kamim, aniyim mitbassrim
and the dead are raised up, and the poor have good tidings preached to them.

וְאַשְׁרֵי מִי שֶׁלֹּא אֶהְיֶה לוֹ לְמִכְשׁוֹל
ve'ashrei mi shello ehyeh lo lemichshol
And blessed is he, whosoever shall find no occasion of stumbling in me.

כָּל מִי שֶׁיּוֹדֶה בִּי לִפְנֵי בְּנֵי אָדָם גַּם אֲנִי אוֹדֶה בּוֹ לִפְנֵי אָבִי שֶׁבַּשָּׁמַיִם
kol mi sheyodeh bi lifnei benei adam gam ani odeh bo lifnei avi shebbashamayim
Every one therefore who shall confess me before men, him will I also confess before my Father who is in heaven.

וְכָל הַמְכַחֵשׁ בִּי לִפְנֵי בְּנֵי אָדָם גַּם אֲנִי אֲכַחֵשׁ בּוֹ לִפְנֵי אָבִי שֶׁבַּשָּׁמַיִם
vechol hamchachesh bi lifnei benei adam gam ani achachesh bo lifnei avi shebbashamayim
But whosoever shall deny me before men, him will I also deny before my Father who is in heaven.

אַל תַּחְשְׁבוּ שֶׁבָּאתִי לְהָטִיל שָׁלוֹם עַל הָאָרֶץ. לֹא בָאתִי לְהָטִיל שָׁלוֹם אֶלָּא חֶרֶב
al tachshevu shebbati lehatil shalom al ha'aretz. lo bati lehatil shalom ella cherev
Think not that I came to send peace on the earth: I came not to send peace, but a sword.

שֶׁהֲרֵי בָּאתִי לִגְרֹם פִּלּוּג בֵּין אִישׁ לְאָבִיו, בֵּין בַּת לְאִמָּהּ
sheharei bati ligrom pillug bein ish le'aviv, bein bat le'immah
For I came to set a man at variance against his father, and the daughter against her mother,

וּבֵין כַּלָּה לַחֲמוֹתָהּ
uvein kallah lachamotah
and the daughter in law against her mother in law:

וְיִהְיוּ אֹיְבֵי אִישׁ אַנְשֵׁי בֵיתוֹ
veyihyu oyevei ish anshei veito
and a man's foes shall be they of his own household.

הָאוֹהֵב אֶת אָבִיו אוֹ אֶת אִמּוֹ יוֹתֵר מִמֶּנִּי אֵינוֹ כְּדַאי לִי
ha'ohev et aviv o et immo yoter mimmenni eino kedai li
He that loveth father or mother more than me is not worthy of me;

וְהָאוֹהֵב אֶת בְּנוֹ אוֹ אֶת בִּתּוֹ יוֹתֵר מִמֶּנִּי אֵינוֹ כְּדַאי לִי
veha'ohev et beno o et bitto yoter mimmenni eino kedai li
and he that loveth son or daughter more than me is not worthy of me.

וּמִי שֶׁאֵינוֹ לוֹקֵחַ אֶת צְלָבוֹ וְהוֹלֵךְ אַחֲרַי אֵינוֹ כְּדַאי לִי
umi she'eino lokeach et tzelavo veholech acharai eino kedai li
And he that doth not take his cross and follow after me, is not worthy of me.

הַמּוֹצֵא אֶת נַפְשׁוֹ יְאַבֵּד אוֹתָהּ, וְהַמְאַבֵּד אֶת נַפְשׁוֹ לְמַעֲנִי יִמְצָא אוֹתָהּ
hammotzei et nafsho ye'abbed otah, veham'abbed et nafsho lema'ani yimtza otah
He that findeth his life shall lose it; and he that loseth his life for my sake shall find it

הַמְקַבֵּל אֶתְכֶם מְקַבֵּל אוֹתִי, וְהַמְקַבֵּל אוֹתִי מְקַבֵּל אֶת אֲשֶׁר שְׁלָחַנִי
hamkabbel etchem mekabbel oti, vehamkabbel oti mekabbel et asher shelachani
He that receiveth you receiveth me, and he that receiveth me receiveth him that sent me.

הַמְקַבֵּל נָבִיא מִשּׁוּם הֱיוֹתוֹ נָבִיא שְׂכַר נָבִיא יְקַבֵּל
hamkabbel navi mishum heyoto navi sechar navi yekabbel
He that receiveth a prophet in the name of a prophet shall receive a prophet's reward:

כַּאֲשֶׁר יִרְדְּפוּ אֶתְכֶם בְּעִיר אַחַת נוּסוּ לְעִיר אַחֶרֶת
ka'asher yirdefu etchem be'ir achat nusu le'ir acheret
But when they persecute you in this city, flee into the next:

אָמֵן אוֹמֵר אֲנִי לָכֶם, לֹא תַסְפִּיקוּ לַעֲבֹר אֶת עָרֵי יִשְׂרָאֵל עַד שֶׁיָּבוֹא בֶּן־הָאָדָם
amen omer ani lachem, lo taspiku la'avor et arei yisra'el ad sheyavo ben-ha'adam
for verily I say unto you, Ye shall not have gone through the cities of Israel, till the Son of man be come.

תַּלְמִיד אֵינֶנּוּ גָּדוֹל מִן הַמּוֹרֶה אַף לֹא הָעֶבֶד גָּדוֹל מֵאֲדוֹנָיו
talmid einennu gadol min hammoreh af lo ha'eved gadol me'adonav
A disciple is not above his teacher, nor a servant above his lord.

דַּי לוֹ לַתַּלְמִיד שֶׁיִּהְיֶה כְּרַבּוֹ וְהָעֶבֶד כַּאֲדוֹנָיו
dai lo lattalmid sheyihyeh kerabbo veha'eved ka'adonav
It is enough for the disciple that he be as his teacher, and the servant as his lord.

אִם לְבַעַל הַבַּיִת קָרְאוּ בַּעַל־זְבוּל, כָּל שֶׁכֵּן לְאַנְשֵׁי בֵיתוֹ
im leva'al habbayit kare'u ba'al-zevul, kol shekken le'anshei beito
If they have called the master of the house Beelzebub, how much more them of his household!

לָכֵן אַל תִּפְחֲדוּ מִפְּנֵיהֶם, כִּי אֵין דָּבָר מְכֻסֶּה שֶׁלֹּא יִגָּלֶה וְאֵין נִסְתָּר שֶׁלֹּא יִוָּדַע
lachen al tifchadu mippeneihem, ki ein davar mechusseh shello yiggaleh ve'ein nistar shello yivvada
Fear them not therefore: for there is nothing covered, that shall not be revealed; and hid, that shall not be known.

אֶת מַה שֶׁאֲנִי אוֹמֵר לָכֶם בַּחֹשֶׁךְ אִמְרוּ בָאוֹר, וּמַה שֶׁנִּלְחַשׁ לְאָזְנֵיכֶם הַכְרִיזוּ מֵעַל הַגַּגּוֹת
et mah she'ani omer lachem bachoshech imru ba'or, umah shennilchash le'ozneichem hachrizu me'al haggaggot
What I tell you in the darkness, speak ye in the light; and what ye hear in the ear, proclaim upon the house-tops.

אַל תִּפְחֲדוּ מִן הַהוֹרְגִים אֶת הַגּוּף שֶׁאֵין בִּיכָלְתָּם לַהֲרֹג אֶת הַנֶּפֶשׁ
al tifchadu min hahoregim et hagguf she'ein biyecholetam laharog et hannefesh
And be not afraid of them that kill the body, but are not able to kill the soul:

אֶלָּא יִרְאוּ מִזֶּה אֲשֶׁר יָכוֹל לִגְרֹם הֵן לְאָבְדַן הַנֶּפֶשׁ וְהֵן לְאָבְדַן הַגּוּף בְּגֵיהִנֹּם
ella yir'u mizzeh asher yachol ligrom hen le'avedan hannefesh vehen le'avedan hagguf begeihinnom
but rather fear him who is able to destroy both soul and body in hell.

הַאִם לֹא נִמְכָּרוֹת שְׁתֵּי צִפֳּרִים בְּאִסָּר אֶחָד? גַּם אַחַת מֵהֶן לֹא תִּפֹּל אַרְצָה מִבְּלִי הַשְׁגָּחַת אֲבִיכֶם
ha'im lo nimkarot shetei tzipporim be'issar echad? gam achat mehen lo tippol artzah mibbeli hashgachat avichem
Are not two sparrows sold for a penny? and not one of them shall fall on the ground without your Father:

אַךְ אַתֶּם, אֲפִלּוּ שַׂעֲרוֹת רֹאשְׁכֶם נִמְנוּ כֻּלָּן
ach attem, afillu sa'arot roshechem nimnu kullan
but the very hairs of your head are all numbered.

לָכֵן אַל תִּפְחָדוּ; יְקָרִים אַתֶּם מִצִּפֳּרִים רַבּוֹת
lachen al tifchadu; yekarim attem mitzipporim rabbot
Fear not therefore: ye are of more value than many sparrows.

צְאוּ מִן הַבַּיִת הַהוּא וּמִן הָעִיר הַהִיא וְנַעֲרוּ אֶת הָאָבָק מֵעַל רַגְלֵיכֶם
tze'u min habbayit hahu umin ha'ir hahi vena'aru et ha'avak me'al ragleichem
as ye go forth out of that house or that city, shake off the dust of your feet.

אָמֵן אוֹמֵר אֲנִי לָכֶם
amen omer ani lachem
Verily I say unto you,

קַל יוֹתֵר יִהְיֶה בְּיוֹם הַדִּין לְאֶרֶץ סְדוֹם וַעֲמוֹרָה מֵאֲשֶׁר לְאוֹתָהּ עִיר
kal yoter yihyeh beyom haddin le'eretz sedom va'amorah me'asher le'otah ir
It shall be more tolerable for the land of Sodom and Gomorrah in the day of judgment, than for that city.

הִנֵּה אָנֹכִי שׁוֹלֵחַ אֶתְכֶם כִּכְבָשִׂים בֵּין זְאֵבִים. לָכֵן הֱיוּ עֲרוּמִים כַּנְּחָשִׁים וּתְמִימִים כַּיּוֹנִים
hinneh anochi sholeach etchem kichvasim bein ze'evim. lachen heyu arumim kinchashim utemimim keyonim
Behold, I send you forth as sheep in the midst of wolves: be ye therefore wise as serpents, and harmless as doves.

הִזָּהֲרוּ מִבְּנֵי אָדָם, כִּי יִמְסְרוּ אֶתְכֶם לְסַנְהֶדְרִיּוֹת וְיַלְקוּ אֶתְכֶם בְּבָתֵּי הַכְּנֶסֶת שֶׁלָּהֶם
hizzaharu mibbenei adam, ki yimseru etchem lesanhedriyot veyalku etchem bevattei hakkeneset shellahem
But beware of men: for they will deliver you up to councils, and in their synagogues they will scourge you;

לִפְנֵי מוֹשְׁלִים וּמְלָכִים תּוּבְאוּ בִּגְלָלִי, לְעֵדוּת לָהֶם וְלַגּוֹיִים
lifnei moshelim umelachim tuv'u biglali, le'edut lahem velaggoyim
yea and before governors and kings shall ye be brought for my sake, for a testimony to them and to the Gentiles.

אֲבָל כַּאֲשֶׁר יִמְסְרוּ אֶתְכֶם אַל תִּדְאֲגוּ אֵיךְ וּמָה תְּדַבְּרוּ
aval ka'asher yimseru etchem al tid'agu eich umah tedabberu
But when they deliver you up, be not anxious how or what ye shall speak:

כִּי בְּאוֹתָהּ שָׁעָה יִנָּתֵן לָכֶם מַה לּוֹמַר
ki be'otah sha'ah yinnaten lachem mah lomar
for it shall be given you in that hour what ye shall speak.

שֶׁכֵּן לֹא אַתֶּם תְּדַבְּרוּ, אֶלָּא רוּחַ אֲבִיכֶם הִיא אֲשֶׁר תְּדַבֵּר בָּכֶם
shekken lo attem tedabberu, ella ruach avichem hi asher tedabber bachem
For it is not ye that speak, but the Spirit of your Father that speaketh in you.

זֹאת וְעוֹד, אָח יִמְסֹר אֶת אָחִיו לַמָּוֶת וְאָב יִמְסֹר אֶת בְּנוֹ
zot ve'od, ach yimsor et achiv lammavet ve'av yimsor et beno
And brother shall deliver up brother to death, and the father his child:

בָּנִים יָקוּמוּ עַל הוֹרֵיהֶם וְיָמִיתוּ אוֹתָם
banim yakumu al horeihem veyamitu otam
and children shall rise up against parents, and cause them to be put to death.

וְתִהְיוּ שְׂנוּאִים עַל הַכֹּל לְמַעַן שְׁמִי, אַךְ הַמַּחֲזִיק מַעֲמָד עַד קֵץ הוּא יִוָּשַׁע
vetihyu senu'im al hakkol lema'an shemi, ach hammachazik ma'amad ad ketz hu yivvasha
And ye shall be hated of all men for my name's sake: but he that endureth to the end, the same shall be saved.

שִׁמְעוֹן הַקַּנָּאִי וִיהוּדָה אִישׁ קְרִיּוֹת ־הָאִישׁ שֶׁמָּסַר אוֹתוֹ
shim'on hakkanna viyehudah ish keriyot -ha'ish shemmasar oto
Simon the Cananæan, and Judas Iscariot, who also betrayed him.

אֶת שְׁנֵים־עָשָׂר אֵלֶּה שָׁלַח יֵשׁוּעַ בְּצַוּוֹתוֹ עֲלֵיהֶם אֶת הַדָּבָר הַזֶּה
et sheneim-'asar elleh shalach yeshua betzavvoto aleihem et haddavar hazzeh
These twelve Jesus sent forth, and charged them, saying,

אַל תֵּלְכוּ לְדֶרֶךְ הַגּוֹיִים וְאַל תִּכָּנְסוּ לְעִיר שֶׁל שׁוֹמְרוֹנִים
al telechu lederech haggoyim ve'al tikkanesu le'ir shel shomronim
Go not into any way of the Gentiles, and enter not into any city of the Samaritans:

אֶלָּא לְכוּ אֶל הַצֹּאן הָאוֹבְדוֹת אֲשֶׁר לְבֵית יִשְׂרָאֵל
ella lechu el hatzon ha'ovedot asher leveit yisra'el
but go rather to the lost sheep of the house of Israel.

וּבְלֶכְתְּכֶם הַכְרִיזוּ: קָרְבָה מַלְכוּת שָׁמַיִם!
uvelechtechem hachrizu: karevah malchut shamayim!
And as ye go, preach, saying, The kingdom of heaven is at hand.

רַפְּאוּ חוֹלִים, הָקִימוּ מֵתִים, טַהֲרוּ מְצֹרָעִים, גָּרְשׁוּ שֵׁדִים; חִנָּם קִבַּלְתֶּם, חִנָּם תִּתֵּנוּ
rappe'u cholim, hakimu metim, taharu metzora'im, gareshu shedim; chinnam kibbaltem, chinnam tittenu
Heal the sick, raise the dead, cleanse the lepers, cast out demons: freely ye received, freely give.

לֹא תִּקְחוּ זָהָב וְלֹא כֶּסֶף וְלֹא נְחֹשֶׁת בְּכִיסֵי חֲגוֹרוֹתֵיכֶם
lo tikchu zahav velo kesef velo nechoshet bechisei chagoroteichem
Get you no gold, nor silver, nor brass in your purses;

לֹא תַּרְמִיל לַדֶּרֶךְ, לֹא שְׁתֵּי כֻּתֳּנוֹת, לֹא נַעֲלַיִם וְלֹא מַקֵּל, כִּי רָאוּי הַפּוֹעֵל לְלַחְמוֹ
lo tarmil ladderech, lo shetei kuttanot, lo na'alayim velo makkel, ki ra'ui happo'el lelachmo
no wallet for your journey, neither two coats, nor shoes, nor staff: for the laborer is worthy of his food.

בְּכָל עִיר וּכְפָר שֶׁתִּכָּנְסוּ אֲלֵיהֶם בָּרְרוּ מִי רָאוּי בְּתוֹכָם וּשְׁבוּ שָׁם עַד צֵאתְכֶם
bechol ir uchfar shettikkanesu aleihem bareru mi ra'ui betocham ushevu sham ad tzetechem
And into whatsoever city or village ye shall enter, search out who in it is worthy; and there abide till ye go forth.

כְּשֶׁאַתֶּם נִכְנָסִים לְבַיִת בָּרְכוּהוּ בְּשָׁלוֹם
keshe'attem nichnasim levayit barechuhu beshalom
And as ye enter into the house, salute it.

אִם רָאוּי הַבַּיִת יָבוֹא עָלָיו הַ'שָּׁלוֹם' שֶׁלָּכֶם, אַךְ אִם אֵינֶנּוּ רָאוּי יָשׁוּב הַשָּׁלוֹם שֶׁלָּכֶם אֲלֵיכֶם.
im ra'ui habbayit yavo alav hashalom shellachem, ach im einennu ra'ui yashuv hashalom shellachem aleichem
And if the house be worthy, let your peace come upon it: but if it be not worthy, let your peace return to you.

כָּל מִי שֶׁלֹּא יְקַבֵּל אֶתְכֶם וְלֹא יִשְׁמַע לְדִבְרֵיכֶם
kol mi shello yekabbel etchem velo yishma ledivreichem
And whosoever shall not receive you, nor hear your words,

יֵשׁוּעַ עָבַר בְּכָל הֶעָרִים וְהַכְּפָרִים כְּשֶׁהוּא מְלַמֵּד בְּבָתֵּי הַכְּנֶסֶת
yeshua avar bechol he'arim vehakkefarim keshehu melammed bevattei hakkeneset
And Jesus went about all the cities and the villages, teaching in their synagogues,

מְבַשֵּׂר אֶת בְּשׂוֹרַת הַמַּלְכוּת וּמְרַפֵּא כָּל מַחֲלָה וְכָל מַדְוֶה בָּעָם
mevaser et besorat hammalchut umerappei kol machalah vechol madveh ba'am
and preaching the gospel of the kingdom, and healing all manner of disease and all manner of sickness.

כִּרְאוֹתוֹ אֶת הַהֲמוֹנִים נִתְמַלֵּא רַחֲמִים עֲלֵיהֶם
kir'oto et hahamonim nitmallei rachamim aleihem
But when he saw the multitudes, he was moved with compassion for them,

שֶׁכֵּן הָיוּ יְגֵעִים וְנִדָּחִים כַּצֹּאן אֲשֶׁר אֵין לָהֶם רוֹעֶה
shekken hayu yege'im veniddachim katzon asher ein lahem ro'eh
because they were distressed and scattered, as sheep not having a shepherd.

אָמַר אֶל תַּלְמִידָיו: הַקָּצִיר רַב, אֲבָל הַפּוֹעֲלִים מְעַטִּים
amar el talmidav: hakkatzir rav, aval happo'alim me'attim
Then saith he unto his disciples, The harvest indeed is plenteous, but the laborers are few.

לָכֵן הִתְפַּלְּלוּ אֶל אֲדוֹן הַקָּצִיר שֶׁיִּשְׁלַח פּוֹעֲלִים לִקְצִירוֹ
lachen hitpallelu el adon hakkatzir sheyishlach po'alim liktziro
Pray ye therefore the Lord of the harvest, that he send forth laborers into his harvest.

▪

הוּא קָרָא אֵלָיו אֶת שְׁנֵים־עָשָׂר תַּלְמִידָיו וְנָתַן לָהֶם סַמְכוּת עַל רוּחוֹת הַטֻּמְאָה
hu kara elav et sheneim-'asar talmidav venatan lahem samchut al ruchot hattum'ah
And he called unto him his twelve disciples, and gave them authority over unclean spirits,

לְגָרֵשׁ אוֹתָן וּלְרַפֵּא כָּל מַחֲלָה וְכָל מַדְוֶה
legaresh otan ulerappei kol machalah vechol madveh
to cast them out, and to heal all manner of disease and all manner of sickness.

וְאֵלֶּה שְׁמוֹת שְׁנֵים־עָשָׂר הַשְּׁלִיחִים
ve'elleh shemot sheneim-'asar hashelichim
Now the names of the twelve apostles are these:

הָרִאשׁוֹן שִׁמְעוֹן הַמְכֻנֶּה כֵּיפָא, אַנְדְּרֵי אָחִיו, יַעֲקֹב בֶּן זַבְדַּי וְיוֹחָנָן אָחִיו
harishon shim'on hamchunneh keifa, andrei achiv, ya'akov ben zavdai veyochanan achiv
The first, Simon, who is called Peter, and Andrew his brother; James the son of Zebedee, and John his brother;

פִילִיפּוֹס וּבַר־תַּלְמַי, תֹּאמָא וּמַתַּי הַמּוֹכֵס, יַעֲקֹב בֶּן חַלְפַי וְתַדַּי
filipos uvar-talmai, t'oma umattai hammoches, ya'akov ben chalfai vetaddai
Philip, and Bartholomew; Thomas, and Matthew the publican; James the son of Alphæus, and Thaddæus;

שָׁמַע הַדָּבָר הַזֶּה יָצָא בְּכָל אוֹתוֹ הָאֵזוֹר
shema haddavar hazzeh yatza bechol oto ha'ezor
And the fame hereof went forth into all that land.

כַּאֲשֶׁר יָצָא מִשָּׁם יֵשׁוּעַ הָלְכוּ אַחֲרָיו שְׁנֵי אֲנָשִׁים עִוְרִים כְּשֶׁהֵם צוֹעֲקִים
ka'asher yatza misham yeshua halechu acharav shenei anashim ivrim keshehem tzo'akim
And as Jesus passed by from thence, two blind men followed him, crying out, and saying,

בֶּן־דָּוִד, רַחֵם עָלֵינוּ
ben-david, rachem aleinu
Have mercy on us, thou son of David.

בְּהִכָּנְסוֹ הַבַּיְתָה נִגְּשׁוּ אֵלָיו הָעִוְרִים
behikkaneso habbaytah niggeshu elav ha'ivrim
And when he was come into the house, the blind men came to him:

אָמַר לָהֶם יֵשׁוּעַ: הַאִם מַאֲמִינִים אַתֶּם שֶׁאֲנִי יָכוֹל לַעֲשׂוֹת זֹאת? כֵּן, אֲדוֹנֵנוּ! הֵשִׁיבוּ
amar lahem yeshua: Ha'im ma'aminim attem she'ani yachol la'asot zot? ken, adonenu! heshivu
and Jesus saith unto them, Believe ye that I am able to do this? They say unto him, Yea, Lord.

נָגַע בְּעֵינֵיהֶם וְאָמַר: יְהֵא לָכֶם כֶּאֱמוּנַתְכֶם
naga be'eineihem ve'amar. טehei lachem ke'emunatchem
Then touched he their eyes, saying, According to your faith be it done unto you.

אָז נִפְקְחוּ עֵינֵיהֶם וְיֵשׁוּעַ הִזְהִיר אוֹתָם בְּאָמְרוֹ: שִׂימוּ לֵב שֶׁלֹּא יִוָּדַע לְאִישׁ
az nifkechu eineihem veyeshua hizhir otam be'amero. simu lev shello yivvada le'ish
And their eyes were opened. And Jesus strictly charged them, saying, See that no man know it.

אַךְ הֵם יָצְאוּ וְהִשְׁמִיעוּ אֶת שָׁמְעוֹ בְּכָל הָאֵזוֹר הַהוּא
ach hem yatze'u vehishmi'u et shim'o bechol ha'ezor hahu
But they went forth, and spread abroad his fame in all that land.

לְאַחַר שֶׁיָּצְאוּ הֵבִיאוּ אֵלָיו אִישׁ אִלֵּם אֲחוּז שֵׁד
le'achar sheyatze'u hevi'u elav ish illem achuz shed
And as they went forth, behold, there was brought to him a dumb man possessed with a demon.

הוּא גֵּרֵשׁ אֶת הַשֵּׁד, וְהָאִלֵּם הֵחֵל לְדַבֵּר. הִתְפַּלְּאוּ הֲהֲמוֹנִים וְאָמְרוּ
hu geresh et hashed, veha'illem hechel ledabber. hitpalle'u hahamonim ve'ameru
And when the demon was cast out, the dumb man spake: and the multitudes marvelled, saying,

מֵעוֹלָם לֹא נִרְאָה כַּדָּבָר הַזֶּה בְּיִשְׂרָאֵל
me'olam lo nir'ah kaddavar hazzeh beyisra'el
It was never so seen in Israel.

אַךְ הַפְּרוּשִׁים אָמְרוּ: בְּעֶזְרַת שַׂר הַשֵּׁדִים הוּא מְגָרֵשׁ אֶת הַשֵּׁדִים
ach happerushim ameru. Be'ezrat sar hashedim hu megaresh et hashedim
But the Pharisees said, By the prince of the demons casteth he out demons.

וְהַיַּיִן יִשָּׁפֵךְ וְהַנֹּאדוֹת לֹא יִצְלְחוּ עוֹד
vehayayin yishafech vehannodot lo yitzlechu od
and the wine is spilled, and the skins perish:

אֲבָל שָׂמִים אֶת הַיַּיִן הֶחָדָשׁ בְּנֹאדוֹת חֲדָשִׁים וּשְׁנֵיהֶם יַחְדָּו יִשָּׁמֵרוּ
aval samim et hayayin hechadash benodot chadashim ushneihem yachdav yishameru
but they put new wine into fresh wine-skins, and both are preserved

כַּאֲשֶׁר דִּבֶּר אֲלֵיהֶם אֶת הַדְּבָרִים הָאֵלֶּה בָּא אֶחָד הַנִּכְבָּדִים, הִשְׁתַּחֲוָה לוֹ וְאָמַר
ka'asher dibber aleihem et haddevarim ha'elleh ba achad hannichbadim, hishtachavah lo ve'amar
While he spake these things unto them, behold, there came a ruler, and worshipped him, saying,

זֶה עַתָּה מֵתָה בִּתִּי. בּוֹא נָא וְשִׂים אֶת יָדְךָ עָלֶיהָ וְתִחְיֶה
zeh attah metah bitti. bo na vesim et yadcha aleiha vetichyeh
My daughter is even now dead: but come and lay thy hand upon her, and she shall live.

יֵשׁוּעַ קָם וְהָלַךְ אַחֲרָיו הוּא וְתַלְמִידָיו
yeshua kam vehalach acharav hu vetalmidav
And Jesus arose, and followed him, and so did his disciples.

וְהִנֵּה אִשָּׁה שֶׁהָיְתָה זָבַת דָּם שְׁתֵּים־עֶשְׂרֵה שָׁנָה הִתְקָרְבָה מֵאָחוֹר וְנָגְעָה בִּכְנַף בִּגְדוֹ
vehinneh ishah shehayetah zavat dam sheteim-'esreh shanah hitkarevah me'achor venage'ah bichnaf bigdo
And behold, a woman, who had an issue of blood twelve years, came behind him, and touched the border of his garment:

כִּי אָמְרָה בְּלִבָּהּ 'אִם רַק אֶגַּע בְּבִגְדוֹ אֶתְרַפֵּא
ki amerah belibbah im rak egga bevigdo etrappe
for she said within herself, If I do but touch his garment, I shall be made whole.

פָּנָה יֵשׁוּעַ וְרָאָה אוֹתָהּ. אָמַר לָהּ: חִזְקִי, בִּתִּי, אֱמוּנָתֵךְ הוֹשִׁיעָה אוֹתָךְ
panah yeshua vera'ah otah. amar lah: Chizki, bitti, emunatech hoshi'ah otach
But Jesus turning and seeing her said, Daughter, be of good cheer; thy faith hath made thee whole.

מֵאוֹתָהּ שָׁעָה נִרְפְּאָה הָאִשָּׁה
me'otah sha'ah nirpe'ah ha'ishah
And the woman was made whole from that hour.

כְּשֶׁבָּא יֵשׁוּעַ אֶל בֵּית הַנִּכְבָּד וְרָאָה אֶת הַמְחַלְלִים בַּחֲלִילִים וְאֶת הָעָם הָרוֹגֵשׁ, אָמַר
keshebba yeshua el beit hannichbad vera'ah et hamchallelim bachalilim ve'et ha'am harogesh, amar
And when Jesus came into the ruler's house, and saw the flute-players, and the crowd making a tumult,

צְאוּ, כִּי הַיַּלְדָּה לֹא מֵתָה. הִיא רַק יְשֵׁנָה אַךְ הֵם צָחֲקוּ לוֹ
tze'u, ki hayaldah lo metah. Hi rak yeshenah ach hem tzachaku lo
he said, Give place: for the damsel is not dead, but sleepeth. And they laughed him to scorn.

לְאַחַר שֶׁהוּצְאוּ הָאֲנָשִׁים נִכְנַס, אָחַז בְּיָדָהּ וְהַנַּעֲרָה קָמָה
le'achar shehutze'u ha'anashim nichnas, achaz beyadah vehanna'arah kamah
But when the crowd was put forth, he entered in, and took her by the hand; and the damsel arose.

אָמַר אֵלָיו: לֵךְ אַחֲרַי. הוּא קָם וְהָלַךְ אַחֲרָיו
Amar elav: Lech acharai. hu kam vehalach acharav
and he saith unto him, Follow me. And he arose, and followed him.

כְּשֶׁהֵסֵב בַּבַּיִת
kshehesev babbayit
And it came to pass, as he sat at meat in the house,

בָּאוּ מוֹכְסִים וְחוֹטְאִים רַבִּים וְהֵסֵבּוּ עִם יֵשׁוּעַ וְתַלְמִידָיו
ba'u mochesim vechote'im rabbim vehesebbu im yeshua vetalmidav
behold, many publicans and sinners came and sat down with Jesus and his disciples.

רָאוּ הַפְּרוּשִׁים וְאָמְרוּ לְתַלְמִידָיו: מַדּוּעַ אוֹכֵל רַבְּכֶם עִם הַמּוֹכְסִים וְהַחוֹטְאִים
ra'u happerushim ve'ameru letalmidav: maddua ochel rabbechem im hammochesim vehachote'im
And when the Pharisees saw it, they said unto his disciples, Why eateth your Teacher with the publicans and sinners?

שָׁמַע יֵשׁוּעַ וְאָמַר לָהֶם: לֹא הַבְּרִיאִים צְרִיכִים לְרוֹפֵא, אֶלָּא הַחוֹלִים
shama yeshua ve'amar lahem: lo habberi'im tzerichim lerofe, ella hacholim
But when he heard it, he said, They that are whole have no need of a physician, but they that are sick.

וְאַתֶּם צְאוּ וְלִמְדוּ מַה מַּשְׁמַע 'חֶסֶד חָפַצְתִּי וְלֹא־זֶבַח', כִּי לֹא בָאתִי לִקְרֹא לַצַּדִּיקִים כִּי אִם לַחוֹטְאִים
ve'attem tze'u velimdu mah mashma 'chesed chafatzti velo-zevach', ki lo bati likro latzaddikim ki im lachote'im
But go ye and learn what this meaneth, I desire mercy, and not sacrifice: for I came not to call the righteous, but sinners.

אָז נִגְּשׁוּ אֵלָיו תַּלְמִידֵי יוֹחָנָן וְשָׁאֲלוּ: "מַדּוּעַ אֲנַחְנוּ וְהַפְּרוּשִׁים צָמִים הַרְבֵּה וְתַלְמִידֶיךָ אֵינָם צָמִים
az niggeshu elav talmidei yochanan vesha'alu: "maddua anachnu vehapperushim tzamim harbeh vetalmideicha einam tzamim
Then come to him the disciples of John, saying, Why do we and the Pharisees fast oft, but thy disciples fast not?

הֵשִׁיב לָהֶם יֵשׁוּעַ: הַאִם יְכוֹלִים בְּנֵי הַחֻפָּה לְהִתְאַבֵּל בְּעוֹד הֶחָתָן אִתָּם?
heshiv lahem yeshua: ha'im yecholim benei hachuppah lehit'abbel be'od hechatan ittam?
And Jesus said unto them, Can the sons of the bridechamber mourn, as long as the bridegroom is with them?

אַךְ יָמִים יָבוֹאוּ שֶׁהֶחָתָן יִלָּקַח מֵהֶם וְאָז יָצוּמוּ
ach yamim yavo'u shehechatan yillakach mehem ve'az yatzumu
but the days will come, when the bridegroom shall be taken away from them, and then will they fast.

אֵין אִישׁ שָׂם פִּסָּה שֶׁל בַּד חָדָשׁ עַל בֶּגֶד יָשָׁן
ein ish sam pissah shel bad chadash al beged yashan
And no man putteth a piece of undressed cloth upon an old garment;

שֶׁכֵּן הַטְּלַאי יִתָּלֵשׁ מִן הַבֶּגֶד וְהַקֶּרַע יִגְדַּל
shekken hattela yittalesh min habbeged vehakkera yigdal
for that which should fill it up taketh from the garment, and a worse rent is made.

וְאֵין שָׂמִים יַיִן חָדָשׁ בְּנֹאדוֹת יְשָׁנִים; אִם יַעֲשׂוּ כֵּן, יִתְבַּקְּעוּ הַנֹּאדוֹת
ve'ein samim yayin chadash benodot yeshanim; im ya'asu ken, yitbakke'u hannodot
Neither do men put new wine into old wine-skins: else the skins burst,

ט

הוּא יָרַד לַסִּירָה, עָבַר אֶת הַיָּם וּבָא אֶל עִירוֹ
hu yarad lassirah, avar et hayam uva el iro
And he entered into a boat, and crossed over, and came into his own city.

וְהִנֵּה הֵבִיאוּ אֵלָיו אִישׁ מְשֻׁתָּק שׁוֹכֵב עַל אֲלוּנְקָה
vehinneh hevi'u elav ish meshuttak shochev al alunekah
And behold, they brought to him a man sick of the palsy, lying on a bed:

כְּשֶׁרָאָה יֵשׁוּעַ אֶת אֱמוּנָתָם אָמַר אֶל הַמְשֻׁתָּק: הִתְחַזֵּק, בְּנִי, נִסְלְחוּ לְךָ חֲטָאֶיךָ
kesheraʼah yeshua et emunatam amar el hamshuttak. Hitchazzek, beni, nislechu lecha chataʼeicha
and Jesus seeing their faith said unto the sick of the palsy, Son, be of good cheer; thy sins are forgiven.

אֲחָדִים מִן הַסּוֹפְרִים אָמְרוּ בְּלִבָּם: זֶה מְגַדֵּף שֵׁם שָׁמַיִם
achadim min hassoferim ameru belibbam. Zeh megaddef shem shamayim
And behold, certain of the scribes said within themselves, This man blasphemeth.

יֵשׁוּעַ הִבְחִין בְּמַחְשְׁבוֹתֵיהֶם וְאָמַר: לָמָּה אַתֶּם חוֹשְׁבִים רָעוֹת בִּלְבַבְכֶם?
yeshua hivchin bemachshevoteihem veʼamar: lammah attem choshevim raʼot bilvavchem?
And Jesus knowing their thoughts said, Wherefore think ye evil in your hearts?

מַה יוֹתֵר קַל: לוֹמַר נִסְלְחוּ לְךָ חֲטָאֶיךָ, אוֹ לוֹמַר קוּם וְהִתְהַלֵּךְ?
mah yoter kal: lomar nislechu lecha chataʼeicha, o lomar kum vehitʼhallech?
For which is easier, to say, Thy sins are forgiven; or to say, Arise, and walk?

אַךְ לְמַעַן תֵּדְעוּ כִּי לְבֶן-הָאָדָם הַסַּמְכוּת עֲלֵי אֲדָמוֹת לִסְלֹחַ עַל חֲטָאִים, וְאָז פָּנָה וְאָמַר לַמְשֻׁתָּק
ach lemaʼan tedeʼu ki leven-haʼadam hassamchut alei adamot lisloach al chataʼim, veʼaz panah veʼamar lamshuttak
But that ye may know that the Son of man hath authority on earth to forgive sins (then saith he to the sick of the palsy),

קוּם, קַח אֶת הָאֲלוּנְקָה וְלֵךְ לְבֵיתְךָ
kum, kach et ha'alunekah velech leveitecha
Arise, and take up thy bed, and go unto thy house.

הוּא קָם וְהָלַךְ לְבֵיתוֹ
hu kam vehalach leveito
And he arose, and departed to his house.

כְּשֶׁרָאוּ זֹאת הֲמוֹן הָעָם נִתְמַלְּאוּ יִרְאָה וְשִׁבְּחוּ אֶת הָאֱלֹהִים שֶׁנָּתַן סַמְכוּת כָּזֹאת לִבְנֵי אָדָם
kesheraʼu zot hamon haʼam nitmalleʼu yirʼah veshibbchu et ha'elohim shennatan samchut kazot livnei adam
But when the multitudes saw it, they were afraid, and glorified God, who had given such authority unto men.

כַּאֲשֶׁר עָבַר מִשָּׁם רָאָה יֵשׁוּעַ אִישׁ יוֹשֵׁב בְּבֵית הַמֶּכֶס וּשְׁמוֹ מַתַּי
ka'asher avar misham ra'ah yeshua ish yoshev beveit hammeches ushemo mattai
And as Jesus passed by from thence, he saw a man, called Matthew, sitting at the place of toll:

בְּצֵאתָם מִמְּעָרוֹת הַקְּבָרִים. הֵם הָיוּ תּוֹקְפָנִיִּים כָּל כָּךְ, שֶׁאִישׁ לֹא הָיָה יָכוֹל לַעֲבֹר בְּאוֹתָהּ דֶּרֶךְ
betzetam mimme'arot hakkevarim. Hem hayu tokefaniyim kol kach, she'ish lo hayah yachol la'avor be'otah derech
coming forth out of the tombs, exceeding fierce, so that no man could pass by that way.

אָז הֵחֵלּוּ צוֹעֲקִים: מַה לָּנוּ וּלְךָ בֶּן־הָאֱלֹהִים
az hechellu tzo'akim. mah lanu ulecha ben-ha'elohim
And behold, they cried out, saying, What have we to do with thee, thou Son of God?

בָּאתָ הֵנָּה לְעַנּוֹת אוֹתָנוּ בְּטֶרֶם עֵת
bata hennah le'annot otanu beterem et
art thou come hither to torment us before the time?

בְּמֶרְחָק מֵהֶם רָעָה עֵדֶר חֲזִירִים גָּדוֹל
bemerchak mesyam mehem ra'ah eder chazirim gadolo
Now there was afar off from them a herd of many swine feeding.

הִפְצִירוּ בּוֹ הַשֵּׁדִים וְאָמְרוּ: אִם תְּגָרֵשׁ אוֹתָנוּ, שְׁלַח אוֹתָנוּ לְתוֹךְ עֵדֶר הַחֲזִירִים
hiftziru bo hashedim ve'ameru. Im tegaresh otanu, shelach otanu letoch eder hachazirim
And the demons besought him, saying, If thou cast us out, send us away into the herd of swine.

אָמַר לָהֶם: לְכוּ! הֵם יָצְאוּ וְנִכְנְסוּ לְתוֹךְ הַחֲזִירִים
amar lahem: lechu! hem yatze'u venichnesu letoch hachazirim
And he said unto them, Go. And they came out, and went into the swine:

וְהִנֵּה כָּל הָעֵדֶר הִסְתָּעֵר בַּמּוֹרָד אֶל הַיָּם וּמֵת בַּמַּיִם
vehinneh kol ha'eder hista'er bammorad el hayam umet bammayim
and behold, the whole herd rushed down the steep into the sea, and perished in the waters.

בָּרְחוּ הָרוֹעִים וּבָאוּ הָעִירָה
barchu haro'im uva'u ha'irah
And they that fed them fled, and went away into the city,

שָׁם סִפְּרוּ אֶת הַכֹּל וְאֶת מַה שֶּׁקָּרָה לַאֲחוּזֵי הַשֵּׁדִים
Sham sipperu et hakkol ve'et mah shekkarah la'achuzei hashedim
and told everything, and what was befallen to them that were possessed with demons.

וְכָל הָעִיר יָצְאָה לִקְרַאת יֵשׁוּעַ. כְּשֶׁרָאוּ אוֹתוֹ הַתּוֹשָׁבִים
vechol ha'ir yatze'ah likrat yeshua: keshera'u oto hattoshavim
And behold, all the city came out to meet Jesus: and when they saw him,

בִּקְשׁוּ מִמֶּנּוּ שֶׁיֵּלֵךְ מֵאֱזוֹרָם
bikshu mimmennu sheyelech me'ezoram
they besought him that he would depart from their borders.

נִגַּשׁ אֵלָיו אַחַד הַסּוֹפְרִים וְאָמַר לוֹ: רַבִּי, אֵלֵךְ אַחֲרֶיךָ אֶל כָּל מָקוֹם שֶׁתֵּלֵךְ
niggash elav achad hassoferim ve'amar lo: rabbi, elech achareicha el kol makom shettelech
And there came a scribe, and said unto him, Teacher, I will follow thee whithersoever thou goest.

עָנָה לוֹ יֵשׁוּעַ
anah lo yeshua
And Jesus saith unto him,

לַשּׁוּעָלִים יֵשׁ מְאוּרוֹת וּלְעוֹף הַשָּׁמַיִם קִנִּים, אַךְ בֶּן־הָאָדָם אֵין לוֹ מָקוֹם לְהַנִּיחַ אֶת רֹאשׁוֹ
Lashu'alim yesh me'urot ule'of hashamayim kinnim, ach ben-ha'adam ein lo makom lehanniach et rosho
The foxes have holes, and the birds of the heaven have nests; but the Son of man hath not where to lay his head.

אִישׁ אַחֵר מִן הַתַּלְמִידִים אָמַר אֵלָיו: אֲדוֹנִי, הַרְשֵׁה לִי תְּחִלָּה לָלֶכֶת לִקְבֹּר אֶת אָבִי
ish acher min hattalmidim amar elav: adoni, harsheh li techillah lalechet likbor et avi
And another of the disciples said unto him, Lord, suffer me first to go and bury my father.

אָמַר לוֹ יֵשׁוּעַ: לֵךְ אַחֲרַי וְהַנַּח לַמֵּתִים לִקְבֹּר אֶת מֵתֵיהֶם
amar lo yeshua: lech acharai vehannach lammetim likbor et meteihem
But Jesus saith unto him, Follow me; and leave the dead to bury their own dead.

הוּא נִכְנַס לַסִּירָה וְתַלְמִידָיו נִכְנְסוּ אַחֲרָיו
hu nichnas lassirah vetalmidav nichnesu acharav
And when he was entered into a boat, his disciples followed him.

וְהִנֵּה סְעָרָה גְּדוֹלָה הִתְחוֹלְלָה בַּיָּם עַד אֲשֶׁר כִּסּוּ הַגַּלִּים אֶת הַסִּירָה, אַךְ הוּא הָיָה יָשֵׁן
vehinneh se'arah gedolah hitcholelah bayam ad asher kissu haggallim et hassirah, ach hu hayah yashen
And behold, there arose a great tempest in the sea, insomuch that the boat was covered with the waves: but he was asleep.

נִגְּשׁוּ אֵלָיו וְהֵעִירוּ אוֹתוֹ בְּאָמְרָם: אֲדוֹנֵנוּ, הַצֵּל אוֹתָנוּ, אֲנַחְנוּ טוֹבְעִים
niggeshu elav vehe'iru oto be'omram: adonenu, hatzel otanu, anachnu tove'im
And they came to him, and awoke him, saying, Save, Lord; we perish.

אָמַר לָהֶם: לָמָה אַתֶּם פּוֹחֲדִים, קְטַנֵּי אֱמוּנָה
amar lahem: lamah attem pochadim, ketannei emunah
And he saith unto them, Why are ye fearful, O ye of little faith?

הוּא קָם וְגָעַר בָּרוּחוֹת וּבַיָּם וְנִשְׁתָּרְרָה דְּמָמָה עֲמֻקָּה
hu kam vega'ar baruchot uvayam venistarerah demamah amukkah
Then he arose, and rebuked the winds and the sea; and there was a great calm.

תָּמְהוּ הָאֲנָשִׁים וְאָמְרוּ: מִי הוּא זֶה שֶׁגַּם הָרוּחוֹת וְהַיָּם נִשְׁמָעִים לוֹ
tamehu ha'anashim ve'ameru: mi hu zeh sheggam haruchot vehayam nishma'im lo
And the men marvelled, saying, What manner of man is this, that even the winds and the sea obey him?

כַּאֲשֶׁר בָּא אֶל עֵבֶר הַיָּם, אֶל אֶרֶץ הַגַּדְרִיִּים, פְּגָשׁוּהוּ שְׁנֵי אֲנָשִׁים אֲחוּזֵי שֵׁדִים
ka'asher ba el ever hayam, el eretz haggadriyim, pegashuhu shenei anashim achuzei shedim
And when he was come to the other side into the country of the Gadarenes, there met him two possessed with demons,

וְיָסֵבּוּ עִם אַבְרָהָם וְיִצְחָק וְיַעֲקֹב בְּמַלְכוּת הַשָּׁמַיִם
veyasebbu im avraham veyitzchak veya'akov bemalchut hashamayim
and shall sit down with Abraham, and Isaac, and Jacob, in the kingdom of heaven:

אֲבָל בְּנֵי הַמַּלְכוּת יְגֹרְשׁוּ אֶל הַחֹשֶׁךְ הַחִיצוֹן
aval benei hammalchut yegorshu el hachoshech hachitzon
but the sons of the kingdom shall be cast forth into the outer darkness:

שָׁם יִהְיוּ הַיְלָלָה וַחֲרֹק הַשִּׁנַּיִם
sham yihyu haylalah vacharok hashinnayim
there shall be the weeping and the gnashing of teeth.

וּלְשַׂר־הַמֵּאָה אָמַר יֵשׁוּעַ׃ לֵךְ וּכְאֱמוּנָתְךָ כֵּן יִהְיֶה לָּךְ
ulesar-hamme'ah amar yeshua. lech uche'emunatecha ken yihyeh lecha
And Jesus said unto the centurion, Go thy way; as thou hast believed, so be it done unto thee.

אוֹתָהּ שָׁעָה נִרְפָּא נַעֲרוֹ
otah sha'ah nirpa na'aro
And the servant was healed in that hour.

כְּשֶׁנִּכְנַס יֵשׁוּעַ לְבֵיתוֹ שֶׁל כֵּיפָא רָאָה אֶת חֲמוֹתוֹ שׁוֹכֶבֶת וְהִיא סוֹבֶלֶת מֵחֹם
keshennichnas yeshua leveito shel keifa ra'ah et chamoto shochevet vehi sovelet mechom
And when Jesus was come into Peter's house, he saw his wife's mother lying sick of a fever.

הוּא נָגַע בְּיָדָהּ וְהַחֹם סָר מִמֶּנָּה׃ אָז קָמָה וְשֵׁרְתָה אוֹתָם
hu naga beyadah vehachom sar mimmennah. az kamah vesheretah otam
And he touched her hand, and the fever left her; and she arose, and ministered unto him.

לְעֵת עֶרֶב הֵבִיאוּ אֵלָיו רַבִּים שֶׁהָיוּ אֲחוּזֵי שֵׁדִים
le'et erev hevi'u elav rabbim shehayu achuzei shedim
And when even was come, they brought unto him many possessed with demons:

וְהוּא גֵּרֵשׁ אֶת הָרוּחוֹת בִּדְבַר פִּיו וְרִפֵּא אֶת כָּל הַחוֹלִים
vehu geresh et haruchot bidvar piv verippei et kol hacholim
and he cast out the spirits with a word, and healed all that were sick:

לְקַיֵּם אֶת אֲשֶׁר נֶאֱמַר בְּפִי יְשַׁעְיָהוּ הַנָּבִיא
lekayem et asher ne'emar befi yesha'yahu hannavi
that it might be fulfilled which was spoken through Isaiah the prophet, saying,

חֳלָיֵנוּ הוּא נָשָׂא וּמַכְאוֹבֵינוּ סְבָלָם
cholayenu hu nasa umach'oveinu sevalam
Himself took our infirmities, and bare our diseases.

כְּשֶׁרָאָה יֵשׁוּעַ הֲמוֹן עַם רַב מִסְּבִיבוֹ צִוָּה לַעֲבֹר אֶל עֵבֶר הַיָּם
keshera'ah yeshua hamon am rav missevivo tzivvah la'avor el ever hayam
Now when Jesus saw great multitudes about him, he gave commandment to depart unto the other side.

אָמַר לוֹ יֵשׁוּעַ
amar lo yeshua
And Jesus saith unto him,

רְאֵה, אַל תְּסַפֵּר לְאִישׁ, אֲבָל לֵךְ הֵרָאֵה אֶל הַכֹּהֵן וְהַקְרֵב אֶת הַקׇּרְבָּן אֲשֶׁר צִוָּה מֹשֶׁה לְעֵדוּת לָהֶם
Re'eh, al tesapper le'ish, aval lech hera'eh el hakkohen vehakrev et hakkorban asher tzivvah mosheh le'edut lahem
See thou tell no man; but go, show thyself to the priest, and offer the gift that Moses commanded, for a testimony unto them.

כַּאֲשֶׁר נִכְנַס לִכְפַר נַחוּם נִגַּשׁ אֵלָיו שַׂר־מֵאָה אֶחָד וְהִתְחַנֵּן לְפָנָיו
ka'asher nichnas lichfar nachum niggash elav sar-me'ah echad vehitchannen lefanav
And when he was entered into Capernaum, there came unto him a centurion, beseeching him,

אֲדוֹנִי, נַעֲרִי שׁוֹכֵב בַּבַּיִת וְהוּא מְשֻׁתָּק וְסוֹבֵל מְאֹד
adoni, na'ari shochev babbayit vehu meshuttak vesovel me'od
and saying, Lord, my servant lieth in the house sick of the palsy, grievously tormented.

אָמַר לוֹ יֵשׁוּעַ: אֲנִי אָבוֹא וַאֲרַפֵּא אוֹתוֹ
amar lo yeshua: ani avo va'arappei oto
And he saith unto him, I will come and heal him.

הֵשִׁיב שַׂר־הַמֵּאָה וְאָמַר: אֲדוֹנִי, אֵינֶנִּי רָאוּי לְכָךְ שֶׁתָּבוֹא בְּצֵל קוֹרָתִי
heshiv sar-hamme'ah ve'amar: adoni, einenni ra'ui lechach shettavo betzel korati
And the centurion answered and said, Lord, I am not worthy that thou shouldest come under my roof;

רַק דַּבֵּר דָּבָר וְיֵרָפֵא נַעֲרִי
Rak dabber davar vyerafei na'ari
but only say the word, and my servant shall be healed.

גַּם אֲנִי אִישׁ כָּפוּף לְמָרוּת וּכְפוּפִים לִי אַנְשֵׁי צָבָא, וְכַאֲשֶׁר אֲנִי אוֹמֵר לָזֶה
gam ani ish kafuf lemarut uchefufim li anshei tzava, vecha'asher ani omer lazeh
For I also am a man under authority, having under myself soldiers: and I say to this one,

לֵךְ!, הוּא הוֹלֵךְ; וּלְאַחֵר בּוֹא!, הוּא בָּא; וּלְעַבְדִּי, עֲשֵׂה זֹאת!, הוּא עוֹשֶׂה
lech!, hu holech; ule'acher bo!, hu ba; ule'avdi, aseh zot!, hu oseh
Go, and he goeth; and to another, Come, and he cometh; and to my servant, Do this, and he doeth it.

שָׁמַע יֵשׁוּעַ וְהִתְפַּלֵּא. אָמַר אֶל הַהוֹלְכִים אַחֲרָיו
shama yeshua vehitpale. amar el haholechim acharav
And when Jesus heard it, he marvelled, and said to them that followed,

אָמֵן אוֹמֵר אֲנִי לָכֶם, אֵצֶל שׁוּם אִישׁ בְּיִשְׂרָאֵל לֹא מָצָאתִי אֱמוּנָה כָּזֹאת
Amen omer ani lachem, etzel shum ish beyisra'el lo matzati emunah kazot
Verily I say unto you, I have not found so great faith, no, not in Israel.

וַאֲנִי אוֹמֵר לָכֶם, רַבִּים יָבוֹאוּ מִמִּזְרָח וּמִמַּעֲרָב
va'ani omer lachem, rabbim yavo'u mimmizrach umimma'arav
And I say unto you, that many shall come from the east and the west,

אַךְ הוּא לֹא נָפַל, כִּי יֻסַּד עַל הַסֶּלַע
ach hu lo nafal, ki yussad al hassela'
and it fell not: for it was founded upon the rock.

וְכָל הַשּׁוֹמֵעַ אֶת דְּבָרַי אֵלֶּה וְאֵינוֹ עוֹשֶׂה אֹתָם
vechol hashomea et devarai elleh ve'eino oseh otam
And every one that heareth these words of mine, and doeth them not,

יִדְמֶה לְאֱוִיל אֲשֶׁר בָּנָה אֶת בֵּיתוֹ עַל חוֹל
yidmeh le'evil asher banah et beito al chol
shall be likened unto a foolish man, who built his house upon the sand:

הַגֶּשֶׁם יָרַד, בָּאוּ הַשִּׁטְפוֹנוֹת וְנָשְׁבוּ הָרוּחוֹת וְהָלְמוּ בַּבַּיִת הַהוּא; נָפַל הַבַּיִת
haggeshem yarad, ba'u hashitfonot venashevu haruchot vehalemu babbayit hahu; nafal habbayit
and the rain descended, and the floods came, and the winds blew, and smote upon that house; and it fell:

וּגְדוֹלָה הָיְתָה מַפַּלְתּוֹ
ugedolah hayetah mappalto
and great was the fall thereof.

כְּשֶׁגָּמַר יֵשׁוּעַ אֶת דְּבָרָיו אֵלֶּה הִשְׁתּוֹמֵם הֲמוֹן הָעָם עַל תּוֹרָתוֹ
kesheggamar yeshua et devarav elleh hishtomem hamon ha'am al torato
And it came to pass, when Jesus had finished these words, the multitudes were astonished at his teaching:

כִּי לִמֵּד אוֹתָם כְּבַעַל סַמְכוּת וְלֹא כְּדֶרֶךְ שֶׁלִּמְּדוּ סוֹפְרֵיהֶם
ki limmed otam keva'al samchut velo kederech shellimmedu sofreihem
for he taught them as one having authority, and not as their scribes.

ח

הוּא יָרַד מִן הָהָר וַהֲמוֹן עַם רַב הָלְכוּ אַחֲרָיו
hu yarad min hahar vahamon am rav halechu acharav
And when he was come down from the mountain, great multitudes followed him.

אָז הִתְקָרֵב אִישׁ מְצֹרָע, הִשְׁתַּחֲוָה לוֹ וְאָמַר: אֲדוֹנִי, אִם תִּרְצֶה תּוּכַל לְטַהֵר אוֹתִי
az hitkarev ish metzora', hishtachavah lo ve'amar: adoni, im tirtzeh tuchal letaher oti
And behold, there came to him a leper and worshipped him, saying, Lord, if thou wilt, thou canst make me clean.

הוֹשִׁיט יֵשׁוּעַ אֶת יָדוֹ, נָגַע בּוֹ וְאָמַר: רוֹצֶה אֲנִי! הִטָּהֵר
hoshit yeshua et yado, naga bo ve'amar: rotzeh ani! hittaher!
And he stretched forth his hand, and touched him, saying, I will; be thou made clean.

וּמִיָּד נִרְפְּאָה צָרַעְתּוֹ
umiyad nirpe'ah tzara'to
And straightway his leprosy was cleansed.

כֵּן כָּל עֵץ טוֹב עוֹשֶׂה פְּרִי טוֹב וְהָעֵץ הַנִּשְׁחָת עוֹשֶׂה פְּרִי רַע
ken kol etz tov oseh peri tov veha'etz hannishchat oseh peri ra'
Even so every good tree bringeth forth good fruit; but the corrupt tree bringeth forth evil fruit.

עֵץ טוֹב אֵינֶנּוּ יָכוֹל לַעֲשׂוֹת פְּרִי רַע וְעֵץ נִשְׁחָת אֵינֶנּוּ יָכוֹל לַעֲשׂוֹת פְּרִי טוֹב
etz tov einennu yachol la'asot peri ra ve'etz nishchat einennu yachol la'asot peri tov
A good tree cannot bring forth evil fruit, neither can a corrupt tree bring forth good fruit.

כָּל עֵץ שֶׁאֵינוֹ עוֹשֶׂה פְּרִי טוֹב כּוֹרְתִים אוֹתוֹ וּמַשְׁלִיכִים אוֹתוֹ לְתוֹךְ הָאֵשׁ
kol etz she'eino oseh peri tov koretim oto umashlichim oto letoch ha'esh
Every tree that bringeth not forth good fruit is hewn down, and cast into the fire.

לָכֵן בְּפֵרוֹתֵיהֶם תַּכִּירוּ אוֹתָם
lachen veferoteihem takkiru otam
Therefore by their fruits ye shall know them.

לֹא כָּל הָאוֹמֵר לִי 'אֲדוֹנִי, אֲדוֹנִי' יִכָּנֵס לְמַלְכוּת הַשָּׁמַיִם
lo kol ha'omer li adoni, adoni yikkanes lemalchut hashamayim
Not every one that saith unto me, Lord, Lord, shall enter into the kingdom of heaven;

אֶלָּא הָעוֹשֶׂה אֶת רְצוֹן אָבִי שֶׁבַּשָּׁמַיִם
ella ha'oseh et retzon avi shebbashamayim
but he that doeth the will of my Father who is in heaven.

רַבִּים יֹאמְרוּ אֵלַי בַּיּוֹם הַהוּא: 'אֲדוֹנִי, אֲדוֹנִי, הֲלֹא בְּשִׁמְךָ נִבֵּאנוּ
rabbim yomeru elai bayom hahu: adoni, adoni, halo beshimcha nibbenu
Many will say to me in that day, Lord, Lord, did we not prophesy by thy name,

וּבְשִׁמְךָ גֵּרַשְׁנוּ שֵׁדִים וּבְשִׁמְךָ עָשִׂינוּ נִפְלָאוֹת רַבּוֹת
uveshimcha gerashnu shedim uveshimcha asinu nifla'ot rabbot
and by thy name cast out demons, and by thy name do many mighty works?

אָז אוֹדִיעַ לָהֶם: 'מֵעוֹלָם לֹא הִכַּרְתִּי אֶתְכֶם, סוּרוּ מִמֶּנִּי עוֹשֵׂי רֶשַׁע
az odia lahem: me'olam lo hikkarti etchem, suru mimmenni osei resha
And then will I profess unto them, I never knew you: depart from me, ye that work iniquity.

לָכֵן כָּל הַשּׁוֹמֵעַ אֶת דְּבָרַי אֵלֶּה וְעוֹשֶׂה אוֹתָם
lachen kol hashomea et devarai elleh ve'oseh otam
Every one therefore that heareth these words of mine, and doeth them,

יִהְיֶה דּוֹמֶה לְאִישׁ נָבוֹן אֲשֶׁר בָּנָה אֶת בֵּיתוֹ עַל הַסֶּלַע
yihyeh domeh le'ish navon asher banah et beito al hassela
shall be likened unto a wise man, who built his house upon the rock:

הַגֶּשֶׁם יָרַד, בָּאוּ הַשִּׁטְפוֹנוֹת וְנָשְׁבוּ הָרוּחוֹת וְהָלְמוּ בַּבַּיִת הַהוּא
haggeshem yarad, ba'u hashitfonot venashevu haruchot vehalemu babbayit hahu
and the rain descended, and the floods came, and the winds blew, and beat upon that house;

כִּי כָּל הַמְבַקֵּשׁ מְקַבֵּל, וְהַמְחַפֵּשׂ מוֹצֵא, וְהַמִּתְדַּפֵּק יִפָּתַח לוֹ
ki kol hamvakkesh mekabbel, vehamchappes motze, vehammitdappek yippatach lo
for every one that asketh receiveth; and he that seeketh findeth; and to him that knocketh it shall be opened.

מִי מִכֶּם הָאִישׁ אֲשֶׁר בְּנוֹ יְבַקֵּשׁ לֶחֶם וְהוּא יִתֶּן לוֹ אֶבֶן
mi mikkem ha'ish asher beno yevakkesh lechem vehu yitten lo even
Or what man is there of you, who, if his son shall ask him for a loaf, will give him a stone;

אוֹ אִם יְבַקֵּשׁ דָּג הֲיִתֶּן לוֹ נָחָשׁ
o im yevakkesh dag hayitten lo nachash
or if he shall ask for a fish, will give him a serpent?

הֵן אִם אַתֶּם הָרָעִים יוֹדְעִים לָתֵת מַתָּנוֹת טוֹבוֹת לִבְנֵיכֶם
hen im attem hara'im yode'im latet mattanot tovot livneichem
If ye then, being evil, know how to give good gifts unto your children,

כָּל שֶׁכֵּן אֲבִיכֶם שֶׁבַּשָּׁמַיִם יִתֵּן אַךְ טוֹב לַמְבַקְשִׁים מִמֶּנּוּ
kol shekken avichem shebbashamayim yitten ach tov lamvakshim mimmennu
how much more shall your Father who is in heaven give good things to them that ask him?

לָכֵן כָּל מַה שֶׁתִּרְצוּ שֶׁיַּעֲשׂוּ לָכֶם בְּנֵי הָאָדָם
lachen kol mah shettirtzu sheya'asu lachem benei ha'adam
All things therefore whatsoever ye would that men should do unto you,

כֵּן גַּם אַתֶּם עֲשׂוּ לָהֶם, כִּי זֹאת הַתּוֹרָה וְהַנְּבִיאִים
ken gam attem asu lahem, ki zot hattorah vehannevi'im
even so do ye also unto them: for this is the law and the prophets.

הִכָּנְסוּ דֶּרֶךְ הַפֶּתַח הַצַּר, כִּי רָחָב הַפֶּתַח וּמְרֻוַּחַת הַדֶּרֶךְ הַמּוֹלִיכָה לָאֲבַדּוֹן
hikkansu derech happetach hatzar, ki rachav happetach umeruvvachat hadderech hammolichah la'avaddon
Enter ye in by the narrow gate: for wide is the gate, and broad is the way, that leadeth to destruction,

וְרַבִּים הַהוֹלְכִים בָּהּ
verabbim haholechim bah
and many are they that enter in thereby.

אַךְ צַר הַפֶּתַח וְצָרָה הַדֶּרֶךְ הַמּוֹלִיכָה לַחַיִּים וּמְעַטִּים הַמּוֹצְאִים אוֹתָהּ
ach tzar happetach vetzarah hadderech hammolichah lachayim ume'attim hammotze'im otah
For narrow is the gate, and straitened the way, that leadeth unto life, and few are they that find it.

הִזָּהֲרוּ מִנְּבִיאֵי הַשֶּׁקֶר הַבָּאִים אֲלֵיכֶם בִּלְבוּשׁ כְּבָשִׂים וּבְתוֹךְ תּוֹכָם זְאֵבִים טוֹרְפִים הֵם
hizzaharu minnevi'ei hasheker habba'im aleichem bilvush kevasim uvetoch tocham ze'evim torefim hem
Beware of false prophets, who come to you in sheep's clothing, but inwardly are ravening wolves.

בְּפֵרוֹתֵיהֶם תַּכִּירוּ אוֹתָם. הַאִם אוֹסְפִים עֲנָבִים מִן הַקּוֹצִים אוֹ תְּאֵנִים מִן הַבַּרְקָנִים
beferoteihem takkiru otam. Ha'im osefim anavim min hakkotzim o te'enim min habbarkanim
By their fruits ye shall know them. Do men gather grapes of thorns, or figs of thistles?

אַתֶּם בַּקְּשׁוּ תְּחִלָּה אֶת מַלְכוּתוֹ וְאֶת צִדְקָתוֹ, וְכָל אֵלֶּה יִוָּסְפוּ לָכֶם
attem bakkeshu techillah et malchuto ve'et tzidkato, vechol elleh yivvasfu lachem
But seek ye first his kingdom, and his righteousness; and all these things shall be added unto you.

לָכֵן אַל תִּדְאֲגוּ לְיוֹם מָחָר, כִּי הַמָּחָר יִדְאַג לְעַצְמוֹ; דַּי לוֹ לַיּוֹם צָרָתוֹ
lachen al tid'agu leyom machar, ki hammachar yid'ag le'atzmo; dai lo layom tzarato
Be not therefore anxious for the morrow: for the morrow will be anxious for itself. Sufficient unto the day is the evil thereof.

ז

אַל תִּשְׁפְּטוּ לְמַעַן לֹא תִּשָּׁפֵטוּ
al tishpetu lema'an lo tishafetu
Judge not, that ye be not judged.

כִּי בַּמִּשְׁפָּט אֲשֶׁר אַתֶּם שׁוֹפְטִים תִּשָּׁפְטוּ וּבַמִּדָּה אֲשֶׁר אַתֶּם מוֹדְדִים יִמַּדֵד לָכֶם
ki bammishpat asher attem shofetim tishafetu uvammiddah asher attem modedim yimmaded lachem
For with what judgment ye judge, ye shall be judged: and with what measure ye mete, it shall be measured unto you.

מַדּוּעַ אַתָּה רוֹאֶה אֶת הַקֵּיסָם אֲשֶׁר בְּעֵין אָחִיךָ וְאֵינְךָ שָׂם לֵב לַקּוֹרָה אֲשֶׁר בְּעֵינֶךָ
maddua attah ro'eh et hakkeisam asher be'ein achicha ve'einecha sam lev lakkorah asher be'einecha?
And why beholdest thou the mote that is in thy brother's eye, but considerest not the beam that is in thine own eye?

אֵיךְ תֹּאמַר לְאָחִיךָ: 'הַנַּח לִי לְהוֹצִיא אֶת הַקֵּיסָם מֵעֵינֶךָ', וְהִנֵּה הַקּוֹרָה בְּעֵינֶךָ
eich tomar le'achicha: 'hannach li lehotzi et hakkeisam me'einecha', vehinneh hakkorah be'einecha
Or how wilt thou say to thy brother, Let me cast out the mote out of thine eye; and lo, the beam is in thine own eye?

צָבוּעַ! הוֹצֵא תְּחִלָּה אֶת הַקּוֹרָה מֵעֵינֶךָ
tzavua'! hotzei techillah et hakkorah me'einecha
Thou hypocrite, cast out first the beam out of thine own eye;

אַחֲרֵי כֵן תִּרְאֶה הֵיטֵב וְתוּכַל לְהוֹצִיא אֶת הַקֵּיסָם מֵעֵינוֹ שֶׁל אָחִיךָ
acharei chen tir'eh heitev vetuchal lehotzi et hakkeisam me'eino shel achicha
and then shalt thou see clearly to cast out the mote out of thy brother's eye.

אַל תִּתְּנוּ אֶת הַקֹּדֶשׁ לַכְּלָבִים וְאַל תַּשְׁלִיכוּ פְּנִינֵיכֶם לִפְנֵי הַחֲזִירִים
al tittenu et hakkodesh lakkelavim ve'al tashlichu penineichem lifnei hachazirim,
Give not that which is holy unto the dogs, neither cast your pearls before the swine,

פֶּן יִרְמְסוּ אוֹתָם בְּרַגְלֵיהֶם וְיִפְנוּ וְיִטְרְפוּ אֶתְכֶם
pen yirmesu otam beragleihem veyifnu veyitrefu etchem
lest haply they trample them under their feet, and turn and rend you.

בַּקְּשׁוּ וְיִנָּתֵן לָכֶם. חַפְּשׂוּ וְתִמְצָאוּ. דִּפְקוּ וְיִפָּתַח לָכֶם
bakkshu veyinnaten lachem. chapsu vetimtze'u. difku veyippatach lachem
Ask, and it shall be given you; seek, and ye shall find; knock, and it shall be opened unto you:

לָכֵן אוֹמֵר אֲנִי לָכֶם: אַל תִּדְאֲגוּ לְנַפְשְׁכֶם - מַה תֹּאכְלוּ אוֹ מַה תִּשְׁתּוּ
lachen omer ani lachem: al tid'agu lenafshechem - mah tochelu o mah tishtu
Therefore I say unto you, Be not anxious for your life, what ye shall eat, or what ye shall drink;

וּלְגוּפְכֶם - מַה תִּלְבָּשׁוּ. הֲלֹא הַנֶּפֶשׁ חֲשׁוּבָה מִן הַמָּזוֹן, וְהַגּוּף חָשׁוּב מִן הַלְּבוּשׁ
ulegufechem - mah tilbeshu. Halo hannefesh chashuvah min hammazon, vehagguf chashuv min hallevush
nor yet for your body, what ye shall put on. Is not the life more than the food, and the body than the raiment?

הַבִּיטוּ אֶל עוֹף הַשָּׁמַיִם: אֵינָם זוֹרְעִים וְאֵינָם קוֹצְרִים
habbitu el of hashamayim. einam zore'im ve'einam kotzerim
Behold the birds of the heaven, that they sow not, neither do they reap,

אַף אֵינָם אוֹסְפִים אֶל אֲסָמִים, וַאֲבִיכֶם שֶׁבַּשָּׁמַיִם מְכַלְכֵּל אוֹתָם. הֲלֹא אַתֶּם חֲשׁוּבִים יוֹתֵר מֵהֶם
af einam osefim el asamim, va'avichem shebbashamayim mechalkel otam. halo attem chashuvim yoter mehem
nor gather into barns; and your heavenly Father feedeth them. Are not ye of much more value than they?

וּמִי מִכֶּם בְּדַאֲגָתוֹ יָכוֹל לְהוֹסִיף טֶפַח אֶחָד עַל שְׁנוֹת חַיָּיו
umi mikkem beda'agato yachol lehosif tefach echad al shenot chayav
And which of you by being anxious can add one cubit unto the measure of his life?

וְלָמָּה אַתֶּם דּוֹאֲגִים לַלְּבוּשׁ
velammah attem do'agim lallevush
And why are ye anxious concerning raiment?

הִתְבּוֹנְנוּ אֶל שׁוֹשַׁנֵּי הַשָּׂדֶה וּרְאוּ אֵיךְ הֵם גְּדֵלִים: אֵינָם עֲמֵלִים וְאֵינָם טוֹוִים
hitbonenu el shoshannei hashodeh ure'u eich hem gedelim. einam amelim ve'einam tovim
Consider the lilies of the field, how they grow; they toil not, neither do they spin:

אוֹמֵר אֲנִי לָכֶם שֶׁגַּם שְׁלֹמֹה בְּכָל הֲדָרוֹ לֹא הָיָה לָבוּשׁ כְּאַחַד מֵהֶם
omer ani lachem sheggam shelomoh bechol hadaro lo hayah lavush ke'echad mehem
yet I say unto you, that even Solomon in all his glory was not arrayed like one of these.

וְאִם כָּכָה מַלְבִּישׁ אֱלֹהִים אֶת חֲצִיר הַשָּׂדֶה אֲשֶׁר הַיּוֹם יֶשְׁנוֹ וּמָחָר יֻשְׁלַךְ לְתוֹךְ הַתַּנּוּר
ve'im kachah malbish elohim et chatzir hassadeh asher hayom yeshno umachar yushlach letoch hattannur
But if God doth so clothe the grass of the field, which to-day is, and to-morrow is cast into the oven,

עַל אַחַת כַּמָּה וְכַמָּה אֶתְכֶם, קְטַנֵּי אֱמוּנָה
al achat kamah vechammah etchem, ketannei emunah
shall he not much more clothe you, O ye of little faith?

לָכֵן אַל תִּדְאֲגוּ לֵאמֹר: מַה נֹּאכַל? מַה נִּשְׁתֶּה? וּמַה נִּלְבַּשׁ
lachen al tid'agu lemor. Mah nochal? mah nishteh? umah nilbash
Be not therefore anxious, saying, What shall we eat? or, What shall we drink? or, Wherewithal shall we be clothed?

הֵן אֶת כָּל אֵלֶּה מְבַקְשִׁים הַגּוֹיִים, וַהֲרֵי אֲבִיכֶם שֶׁבַּשָּׁמַיִם יוֹדֵעַ שֶׁצְּרִיכִים אַתֶּם לְכָל אֵלֶּה
hen et kol elleh mevakshim haggoyim, vaharei avichem shebbashamayim yodea shetzerichim attem lechol elleh
For after all these things do the Gentiles seek; for your heavenly Father knoweth that ye have need of all these things.

כְּדֵי שֶׁלֹּא תֵרָאֶה צָם לִבְנֵי אָדָם כִּי אִם לְאָבִיךָ אֲשֶׁר בַּסֵּתֶר
kedei shello tera'eh tzam livnei adam ki im le'avicha asher basseter
that thou be not seen of men to fast, but of thy Father who is in secret:

וְאָבִיךָ הָרוֹאֶה בַּמִּסְתָּרִים הוּא יִגְמֹל לְךָ
ve'avicha haro'eh bammistarim hu yigmol lecha
and thy Father, who seeth in secret, shall recompense thee.

אַל תַּאַצְרוּ לָכֶם אוֹצָרוֹת עֲלֵי אֲדָמוֹת
al ta'atzru lachem otzarot alei adamot
Lay not up for yourselves treasures upon the earth,

בְּמָקוֹם שֶׁהָעָשׁ וְהֶחָלוּדָה מַשְׁחִיתִים וְהַגַּנָּבִים חוֹפְרִים וְגוֹנְבִים
bemakom sheha'ash vehachaludah mashchitim vehaggannavim choferim vegonevim
where moth and rust consume, and where thieves break through and steal:

אִצְרוּ לָכֶם אוֹצָרוֹת בַּשָּׁמַיִם
itzru lachem otzarot bashamayim
but lay up for yourselves treasures in heaven,

בְּמָקוֹם אֲשֶׁר עָשׁ וַחֲלוּדָה לֹא יַשְׁחִיתוּ וְגַנָּבִים לֹא יַחְפְּרוּ וְלֹא יִגְנְבוּ
bemakom asher ash vachaludah lo yashchitu vegannavim lo yachperu velo yignevu
where neither moth nor rust doth consume, and where thieves do not break through nor steal:

כִּי בַּמָּקוֹם שֶׁאוֹצָרְךָ נִמְצָא, שָׁם יִהְיֶה גַּם לְבָבְךָ
ki bammakom she'otzarecha nimtza, sham yihyeh gam levavecha
for where thy treasure is, there will thy heart be also.

מְנוֹרַת הַגּוּף הִיא הָעַיִן. לְפִיכָךְ אִם עֵינְךָ טוֹבָה כָּל גּוּפְךָ יֵאוֹר
menorat hagguf hi ha'ayin. lefichach im einecha tovah kol gufcha ye'or
The lamp of the body is the eye: if therefore thine eye be single, thy whole body shall be full of light.

אַךְ אִם עֵינְךָ רָעָה כָּל גּוּפְךָ יֶחְשַׁךְ
ach im einecha ra'ah kol gufcha yechshach
But if thine eye be evil, thy whole body shall be full of darkness.

וְאִם יֶחְשַׁךְ הָאוֹר אֲשֶׁר בְּקִרְבְּךָ, מַה רַב הַחֹשֶׁךְ
ve'im yechshach ha'or asher bekirbecha, mah rav hachoshech
If therefore the light that is in thee be darkness, how great is the darkness!

אֵין אִישׁ יָכוֹל לַעֲבֹד שְׁנֵי אֲדוֹנִים, שֶׁכֵּן אוֹ יִשְׂנָא אֶחָד וְיֹאהַב אֶת הַשֵּׁנִי
ein ish yachol la'avod shenei adonim, shekken o yisna echad veyohav et hasheni
No man can serve two masters: for either he will hate the one, and love the other;

אוֹ יִהְיֶה מָסוּר לְאֶחָד וִיזַלְזֵל בַּשֵּׁנִי. אֵינְכֶם יְכוֹלִים לַעֲבֹד אֶת הָאֱלֹהִים וְאֶת הַמָּמוֹן
o yihyeh masur le'echad vizalzel basheni. einechem yecholim la'avod et ha'elohim ve'et hammamon
or else he will hold to one, and despise the other. Ye cannot serve God and mammon.

כַּאֲשֶׁר אַתֶּם מִתְפַּלְלִים הִמָּנְעוּ מִלְּגַבֵּב מִלִּים כַּגּוֹיִים, הַחוֹשְׁבִים שֶׁבְּרֹב דִּבּוּרָם יִשָּׁמֵעוּ
ka'asher attem mitpallelim himmane'u millegabbev millim kaggoyim, hachoshevim shebberov dibburam yishame'u
And in praying use not vain repetitions, as the Gentiles do: for they think that they shall be heard for their much speaking.

אַל תִּהְיוּ דּוֹמִים לָהֶם, כִּי יוֹדֵעַ אֲבִיכֶם אֶת צָרְכֵיכֶם בְּטֶרֶם תְּבַקְשׁוּ מִמֶּנּוּ
al tihyu domim lahem, ki yodea avichem et tzorcheichem beterem tevakshu mimmennu
Be not therefore like unto them: for your Father knoweth what things ye have need of, before ye ask him.

לָכֵן כָּךְ הִתְפַּלְלוּ אַתֶּם אָבִינוּ שֶׁבַּשָּׁמַיִם, יִתְקַדֵּשׁ שִׁמְךָ
lachen kach hitpallelu attem avinu shebbashamayim, yitkaddesh shimcha
After this manner therefore pray ye: Our Father who art in heaven, Hallowed be thy name.

תָּבוֹא מַלְכוּתְךָ, יֵעָשֶׂה רְצוֹנְךָ כְּבַשָּׁמַיִם כֵּן בָּאָרֶץ
tavo malchutcha, ye'aseh retzonecha kevashamayim ken ba'aretz
Thy kingdom come. Thy will be done, as in heaven, so on earth.

אֶת לֶחֶם חֻקֵּנוּ תֶּן לָנוּ הַיּוֹם
et lechem chukkenu ten lanu hayom
Give us this day our daily bread.

וּסְלַח לָנוּ עַל חֲטָאֵינוּ כְּפִי שֶׁסּוֹלְחִים גַּם אֲנַחְנוּ לַחוֹטְאִים לָנוּ
uselach lanu al chata'einu kefi shessolechim gam anachnu lachote'im lanu
And forgive us our debts, as we also have forgiven our debtors.

וְאַל תְּבִיאֵנוּ לִידֵי נִסָּיוֹן, כִּי אִם חַלְּצֵנוּ מִן הָרַע
ve'al tevi'enu liydei nissayon, ki im challetzenu min hara'
And bring us not into temptation, but deliver us from the evil one.

כִּי אִם תִּסְלְחוּ לִבְנֵי אָדָם עַל חַטֹּאתֵיהֶם, גַּם אֲבִיכֶם שֶׁבַּשָּׁמַיִם יִסְלַח לָכֶם
ki im tislechu livnei adam al chattoteihem, gam avichem shebbashamayim yislach lachem
For if ye forgive men their trespasses, your heavenly Father will also forgive you.

וְאִם לֹא תִּסְלְחוּ לִבְנֵי אָדָם, גַּם אֲבִיכֶם לֹא יִסְלַח לָכֶם עַל חַטֹּאתֵיכֶם
ve'im lo tislechu livnei adam, gam avichem lo yislach lachem al chattoteichem
But if ye forgive not men their trespasses, neither will your Father forgive your trespasses.

כַּאֲשֶׁר אַתֶּם צָמִים אַל תְּהַלְּכוּ קוֹדְרִים כְּמוֹ הַצְּבוּעִים, הַמְשַׁנִּים אֶת פְּנֵיהֶם
ka'asher attem tzamim al tehallchu koderim kemo hatzevu'im, hamshannim et peneihem
Moreover when ye fast, be not, as the hypocrites, of a sad countenance: for they disfigure their faces,

כְּדֵי לְהֵרָאוֹת צָמִים לִבְנֵי אָדָם. אָמֵן אוֹמֵר אֲנִי לָכֶם, שְׂכָרָם אִתָּם
kedei lehera'ot tzamim livnei adam. amen omer ani lachem, scharam ittam
that they may be seen of men to fast. Verily I say unto you, They have received their reward.

וְאַתָּה כַּאֲשֶׁר תָּצוּם מְשַׁח אֶת רֹאשְׁךָ בְּשֶׁמֶן וּרְחַץ אֶת פָּנֶיךָ
ve'attah ka'asher tatzum meshach et roshecha beshemen urechatz et paneicha
But thou, when thou fastest, anoint thy head, and wash thy face;

I

הִשָּׁמְרוּ מִלַּעֲשׂוֹת אֶת צִדְקַתְכֶם לִפְנֵי בְּנֵי אָדָם מִתּוֹךְ כַּוָּנָה שֶׁיִּרְאוּ אֶתְכֶם
Hishameru milla'asot et tzidkatchem lifnei bnei adam mittoch kavvanah sheyir'u etchem
Take heed that ye do not your righteousness before men, to be seen of them:

אִם תַּעֲשׂוּ כֵן, אֵין לָכֶם שָׂכָר אֵצֶל אֲבִיכֶם שֶׁבַּשָּׁמַיִם
im ta'asu chen, ein lachem sachar etzel avichem shebbashamayim
else ye have no reward with your Father who is in heaven.

לָכֵן בַּעֲשׂוֹתְךָ מַעֲשֵׂי חֶסֶד אַל תַּשְׁמִיעַ קוֹל תְּרוּעָה לְפָנֶיךָ כְּמוֹ שֶׁעוֹשִׂים הַצְּבוּעִים
lachen ba'asotecha ma'asei chesed al tashmia kol teru'ah lefaneicha kemo she'osim hatzevu'im
When therefore thou doest alms, sound not a trumpet before thee, as the hypocrites do

בְּבָתֵּי הַכְּנֶסֶת וּבָרְחוֹבוֹת כְּדֵי שֶׁיְּכַבְּדוּ אוֹתָם הַבְּרִיּוֹת. אָמֵן אוֹמֵר אֲנִי לָכֶם, שְׂכָרָם אִתָּם
bevattei hakkeneset uvarechovot kedei sheyechabbedu otam habberiyot. amen omer ani lachem, secharam ittam
in the synagogues and in the streets, that they may have glory of men. Verily I say unto you, They have received their reward.

וְאַתָּה בַּעֲשׂוֹתְךָ מַעֲשֵׂה חֶסֶד אַל תֵּדַע שְׂמֹאלְךָ אֶת אֲשֶׁר עוֹשָׂה יְמִינֶךָ
ve'attah ba'asotecha ma'aseh chesed al teda semolcha et asher osah yeminecha
But when thou doest alms, let not thy left hand know what thy right hand doeth:

לְמַעַן יִהְיוּ חֲסָדֶיךָ בַּסֵּתֶר וְאָבִיךָ הָרוֹאֶה בַּמִּסְתָּרִים יִגְמֹל לָךְ
lema'an yihyu chasadeicha basseter ve'avicha haro'eh bammistarim yigmol lecha
that thine alms may be in secret: and thy Father who seeth in secret shall recompense thee.

כַּאֲשֶׁר אַתֶּם מִתְפַּלְּלִים אַל תִּהְיוּ כַּצְּבוּעִים
ka'asher attem mitpallelim al tihyu katzevu'im
And when ye pray, ye shall not be as the hypocrites:

הָאוֹהֲבִים לְהִתְפַּלֵּל בְּעָמְדָם בְּבָתֵּי כְּנֶסֶת וּבִפְנוֹת שֶׁל רְחוֹבוֹת לְמַעַן יֵרָאוּ לִבְנֵי אָדָם
ha'ohavim lehitpallel be'amedam bevattei keneset uvefinnot shel rechovot lema'an yera'u livnei adam
for they love to stand and pray in the synagogues and in the corners of the streets, that they may be seen of men.

אָמֵן אוֹמֵר אֲנִי לָכֶם, שְׂכָרָם אִתָּם
amen omer ani lachem, secharam ittam
Verily I say unto you, They have received their reward.

וְאַתָּה כַּאֲשֶׁר תִּתְפַּלֵּל הִכָּנֵס לְחַדְרְךָ, סְגֹר אֶת הַדֶּלֶת בַּעֲדְךָ וְהִתְפַּלֵּל לְאָבִיךָ אֲשֶׁר בַּסֵּתֶר
ve'attah ka'asher titpallel hikkanes lechadrecha, sgor et haddelet ba'adcha vehitpallel le'avicha asher basseter
But thou, when thou prayest, enter into thine inner chamber, and having shut thy door, pray to thy Father who is in secret,

וְאָבִיךָ הָרוֹאֶה בַּמִּסְתָּרִים יִגְמֹל לָךְ
v'avicha haro'eh bammistarim yigmol lecha
and thy Father who seeth in secret shall recompense thee.

וַאֲנִי אוֹמֵר לָכֶם שֶׁלֹּא לְהִתְקוֹמֵם עַל עוֹשֵׂה הָרַע
va'ani omer lachem shello lehitkomem al oseh hara
but I say unto you, Resist not him that is evil:

אַדְרַבָּא, הַסּוֹטֵר לְךָ עַל הַלְּחִי הַיְמָנִית, הַפְנֵה אֵלָיו גַּם אֶת הָאַחֶרֶת
Adderabba, hassoter lecha al hallechi haymanit, hafneh elav gam et ha'acheret
but whosoever smiteth thee on thy right cheek, turn to him the other also.

מִי שֶׁרוֹצֶה לִתְבֹּעַ אוֹתְךָ לְדִין כְּדֵי לָקַחַת אֶת כֻּתָּנְתְּךָ, הַנַּח לוֹ גַּם אֶת מְעִילְךָ
mi sherotzeh litboa otecha ledin kedei lakachat et kuttanetecha, hannach lo gam et me'ilecha
And if any man would go to law with thee, and take away thy coat, let him have thy cloak also.

וּמִי שֶׁמְּאַלֵּץ אוֹתְךָ לָלֶכֶת אִתּוֹ מֶרְחָק שֶׁל מִיל אֶחָד, לֵךְ אִתּוֹ שְׁנַיִם
umi shemme'alletz otecha lalechet itto merchak shel mil echad, lech itto shnayim
And whosoever shall compel thee to go one mile, go with him two.

תֵּן לַמְבַקֵּשׁ מִמְּךָ וְאַל תִּפְנֶה מִן הָרוֹצֶה לִלְווֹת מִמְּךָ
ten lamvakkesh mimmecha ve'al tifneh min harotzeh lilvot mimmecha
Give to him that asketh thee, and from him that would borrow of thee turn not thou away.

'שְׁמַעְתֶּם כִּי נֶאֱמַר 'אֱהַב אֶת רֵעֲךָ וּשְׂנָא אֶת אוֹיִבְךָ
shema'tem ki ne'emar ehav et re'acha usna et oyivcha
Ye have heard that it was said, Thou shalt love thy neighbor, and hate thine enemy:

וַאֲנִי אוֹמֵר לָכֶם, אֶהֱבוּ אֶת אוֹיְבֵיכֶם וְהִתְפַּלְּלוּ בְּעַד רוֹדְפֵיכֶם
va'ani omer lachem, ehevu et oyeveichem vehitpallelu be'ad rodfeichem
but I say unto you, Love your enemies, and pray for them that persecute you;

לְמַעַן תִּהְיוּ בָּנִים לַאֲבִיכֶם שֶׁבַּשָּׁמַיִם
lema'an tihyu banim la'avichem shebbashamayim
that ye may be sons of your Father who is in heaven:

כִּי הוּא מַזְרִיחַ שִׁמְשׁוֹ עַל רָעִים וְעַל טוֹבִים וּמַמְטִיר גֶּשֶׁם עַל צַדִּיקִים וְעַל רְשָׁעִים
ki hu mazriach shimsho al ra'im ve'al tovim umamtir geshem al tzaddikim ve'al resha'im
for he maketh his sun to rise on the evil and the good, and sendeth rain on the just and the unjust.

הֵן אִם תֹּאהֲבוּ אֶת אוֹהֲבֵיכֶם מַה שְּׂכַרְכֶם? הֲלֹא גַּם הַמּוֹכְסִים עוֹשִׂים זֹאת
hen im tohavu et ohaveichem mah shocharchem? halo gam hammochesim osim zot
For if ye love them that love you, what reward have ye? do not even the publicans the same?

וְאִם תִּשְׁאֲלוּ בִּשְׁלוֹם אֲחֵיכֶם בִּלְבַד, מַהוּ הַמְיֻחָד שֶׁאַתֶּם עוֹשִׂים? הֲלֹא גַּם הַגּוֹיִים עוֹשִׂים זֹאת
ve'im tish'alu bishlom acheichem bilvad, mahu hameyuchad she'attem osim? halo gam haggoyim osim zot
And if ye salute your brethren only, what do ye more than others? do not even the Gentiles the same?

לָכֵן הֱיוּ שְׁלֵמִים, כְּמוֹ שֶׁאֲבִיכֶם שֶׁבַּשָּׁמַיִם שָׁלֵם הוּא
lachen heyu shelemim, kemo she'avichem shebbashamayim shalem hu
Ye therefore shall be perfect, as your heavenly Father is perfect.

וְאִם יָדְךָ הַיְמָנִית תַּכְשִׁיל אוֹתְךָ, קַצֵּץ אוֹתָהּ וְהַשְׁלֵךְ אוֹתָהּ מִמֶּךָ
ve'im yadecha haymanit tachshil otecha, katzetz otah vehashlech otah mimmecha
And if thy right hand causeth thee to stumble, cut it off, and cast it from thee:

כִּי מוּטָב לְךָ שֶׁיֹּאבַד אֶחָד מֵאֲבָרֶיךָ מֵרֶדֶת כָּל גּוּפְךָ לְגֵיהִנֹּם
ki mutav lecha sheyovad echad me'evareicha meredet kol gufecha legeihinnom
for it is profitable for thee that one of thy members should perish, and not thy whole body go into hell.

נֶאֱמַר, אִישׁ כִּי יְשַׁלַּח אֶת אִשְׁתּוֹ יִתֵּן לָהּ סֵפֶר כְּרִיתֻת
ne'emar, ish ki yeshallach et ishto yitten lah sefer keritut
It was said also, Whosoever shall put away his wife, let him give her a writing of divorcement:

וַאֲנִי אוֹמֵר לָכֶם: כָּל הַמְגָרֵשׁ אֶת אִשְׁתּוֹ חוּץ מֵאֲשֶׁר עַל־דְּבַר זְנוּת, עוֹשֶׂה אוֹתָהּ לְנוֹאֶפֶת
va'ani omer lachem: kol hamgaresh et ishto chutz me'asher al-devar zenut, oseh otah leno'efet
but I say unto you, that every one that putteth away his wife, saving for the cause of fornication, maketh her an adulteress:

וְהַלּוֹקֵחַ אֶת הַגְּרוּשָׁה לְאִשָּׁה נוֹאֵף הוּא
vehallokeach et haggerushah le'ishah no'ef hu
and whosoever shall marry her when she is put away committeth adultery.

עוֹד שְׁמַעְתֶּם כִּי נֶאֱמַר לָרִאשׁוֹנִים
od shema'tem ki ne'emar larishonim
Again, ye have heard that it was said to them of old time,

'לֹא תִשָּׁבַע לַשֶּׁקֶר וְשַׁלֵּם לַאדֹנָי נְדָרֶיךָ'
lo tishava lasheker veshallem la'adonai nedareicha
Thou shalt not forswear thyself, but shalt perform unto the Lord thine oaths:

וַאֲנִי אוֹמֵר לָכֶם שֶׁלֹּא לְהִשָּׁבַע בִּכְלָל: לֹא בַּשָּׁמַיִם, כִּי כִסֵּא אֱלֹהִים הֵם
va'ani omer lachem shello lehishava bichlal. lo bashamayim, ki kissei elohim hem
but I say unto you, Swear not at all; neither by the heaven, for it is the throne of God;

אַף לֹא בָּאָרֶץ, כִּי הֲדֹם רַגְלָיו הִיא; וְלֹא בִּירוּשָׁלַיִם, שֶׁהֲרֵי קִרְיַת מֶלֶךְ רַב הִיא
af lo ba'aretz, ki hadom raglav hi; velo biyerushalayim, sheharei kiryat melech rav hi
nor by the earth, for it is the footstool of his feet; nor by Jerusalem, for it is the city of the great King.

גַּם בְּרֹאשְׁךָ אַל תִּשָּׁבַע, כִּי אֵינְךָ יָכוֹל לַהֲפֹךְ שַׂעֲרָה אַחַת לְלִבְנָה אוֹ לִשְׁחוֹרָה
gam beroshecha al tishava', ki einecha yachol lahafoch sa'arah achat lilvanah o lishchorah
Neither shalt thou swear by thy head, for thou canst not make one hair white or black.

אַךְ תְּהֵא מִלַּתְכֶם 'כֵּן', כֵּן; 'לֹא', לֹא. יוֹתֵר מִזֶּה מִן הָרָע הוּא
ach tehei millatchem ken, ken; lo, lo. Yoter mizzeh min hara hu
But let your speech be, Yea, yea; Nay, nay: and whatsoever is more than these is of the evil one.

'שְׁמַעְתֶּם כִּי נֶאֱמַר עַיִן תַּחַת עַיִן, שֵׁן תַּחַת שֵׁן
shema'tem ki ne'emar ayin tachat ayin, shen tachat shen
Ye have heard that it was said, An eye for an eye, and a tooth for a tooth:

לָכֵן אִם תָּבִיא אֶת קָרְבָּנְךָ אֶל הַמִּזְבֵּחַ
lachen im tavi et korbancha el hammizbeach
If therefore thou art offering thy gift at the altar,

וְשָׁם תִּזְכַּר כִּי לְאָחִיךָ דָּבָר נֶגְדֶּךָ
vesham tizzacher ki le'achicha davar negdecha
and there rememberest that thy brother hath aught against thee,

עֲזֹב אֶת קָרְבָּנְךָ שָׁם לִפְנֵי הַמִּזְבֵּחַ
azov et korbancha sham lifnei hammizbeach
leave there thy gift before the altar,

וְלֵךְ תְּחִלָּה לְהִתְרַצּוֹת לְאָחִיךָ וְאַחַר כָּךְ בּוֹא וְהַקְרֵב אֶת קָרְבָּנֶךָ
velech techillah lehitratzot le'achicha ve'achar kach bo vehakrev et karebanecha
and go thy way, first be reconciled to thy brother, and then come and offer thy gift.

מַהֵר לְהִתְפַּיֵּס עִם אִישׁ רִיבְךָ בְּעוֹדְךָ בַּדֶּרֶךְ אִתּוֹ
maher lehitpayes im ish rivecha be'odecha badderech itto
Agree with thine adversary quickly, while thou art with him in the way;

פֶּן יִמְסֹר אוֹתְךָ לַשּׁוֹפֵט וְהַשּׁוֹפֵט יִמְסֹר אוֹתְךָ לַשּׁוֹטֵר וְתֻשְׁלַךְ לְבֵית הַסֹּהַר
pen yimsor otcha lashofet vehashofet yimsor otcha lashoter vetushlach leveit hassohar
lest haply the adversary deliver thee to the judge, and the judge deliver thee to the officer, and thou be cast into prison.

אָמֵן אוֹמֵר אֲנִי לְךָ, לֹא תֵצֵא מִשָּׁם עַד אֲשֶׁר תְּשַׁלֵּם אֶת הַפְּרוּטָה הָאַחֲרוֹנָה
amen omer ani lecha, lo tetzei misham ad asher teshallem et happerutah ha'acharonah
Verily I say unto thee, Thou shalt by no means come out thence, till thou have paid the last farthing.

'שְׁמַעְתֶּם כִּי נֶאֱמַר 'לֹא תִּנְאָף
shema'tem ki ne'emar: lo tin'af
Ye have heard that it was said, Thou shalt not commit adultery:

וַאֲנִי אוֹמֵר לָכֶם
va'ani omer lachem
but I say unto you,

שֶׁכָּל הַמַּבִּיט בְּאִשָּׁה מִתּוֹךְ תַּאֲוָה אֵלֶיהָ כְּבָר נָאַף אוֹתָהּ בְּלִבּוֹ
shekkol hammabbit be'ishah mittoch ta'avah eleiha kvar na'af otah belibbo
that every one that looketh on a woman to lust after her hath committed adultery with her already in his heart.

אִם עֵינְךָ הַיְמָנִית תַּכְשִׁיל אוֹתְךָ, נַקֵּר אוֹתָהּ וְהַשְׁלֵךְ אוֹתָהּ מִמֶּךָּ
im einecha haymanit tachshil otecha, nakker otah vehashlech otah mimmcha
And if thy right eye causeth thee to stumble, pluck it out, and cast it from thee:

כִּי מוּטָב לְךָ שֶׁיֹּאבַד אֶחָד מֵאֵבָרֶיךָ מִשֶּׁיֻּשְׁלַךְ כָּל גּוּפְךָ לְגֵיהִנּוֹם
ki mutav lecha sheyovad echad me'evareicha misheyushlach kol gufcha legeihinnom
for it is profitable for thee that one of thy members should perish, and not thy whole body be cast into hell.

אָמֵן. אוֹמֵר אֲנִי לָכֶם,
amen. Omer ani lachem,
For verily I say unto you,

עַד אֲשֶׁר יַעַבְרוּ הַשָּׁמַיִם וְהָאָרֶץ אַף יוֹד אַחַת אוֹ תָג אֶחָד לֹא יַעַבְרוּ מִן הַתּוֹרָה בְּטֶרֶם יִתְקַיֵּם הַכֹּל
ad asher ya'avru hashamayim veha'aretz af yod achat o tag echad lo ya'avru min hattorah beterem yitkayem hakkol
Till heaven and earth pass away, one jot or one tittle shall in no wise pass away from the law, till all things be accomplished.

לָכֵן כָּל הַמֵּפֵר אַחַת מִן הַמִּצְוֹת הַקְּטַנּוֹת הָאֵלֶּה
lachen kol hammefer achat min hammitzvot hakketannot ha'elleh
Whosoever therefore shall break one of these least commandments,

וּמְלַמֵּד כָּךְ אֶת הַבְּרִיּוֹת, קָטֹן יִקָּרֵא בְּמַלְכוּת הַשָּׁמַיִם
umelammed kach et habberiyot, katon yikkarei bemalchut hashamayim
and shall teach men so, shall be called least in the kingdom of heaven:

אֲבָל כָּל הָעוֹשֶׂה וּמְלַמֵּד, הוּא גָדוֹל יִקָּרֵא בְּמַלְכוּת הַשָּׁמַיִם
aval kol ha'oseh umelammed, hu gadol yikkarei bemalchut hashamayim
but whosoever shall do and teach them, he shall be called great in the kingdom of heaven.

אוֹמֵר אֲנִי לָכֶם, אִם לֹא תִּהְיֶה צִדְקַתְכֶם מְרֻבָּה מִצִּדְקַת הַסּוֹפְרִים וְהַפְּרוּשִׁים
omer ani lachem, im lo tihyeh tzidkatchem merubbah mitzidkat hassoferim vehapperushim
For I say unto you, that except your righteousness shall exceed the righteousness of the scribes and Pharisees,

לֹא תִּכָּנְסוּ לְמַלְכוּת הַשָּׁמַיִם
lo tikkansu lemalchut hashamayim
ye shall in no wise enter into the kingdom of heaven.

שְׁמַעְתֶּם כִּי נֶאֱמַר לָרִאשׁוֹנִים לֹא תִּרְצָח
shema'tem ki ne'emar larishonim: lo tirtzach
Ye have heard that it was said to them of old time, Thou shalt not kill;

וְכָל רוֹצֵחַ יְחֻיַּב לַדִּין
v'chol rotzeach yechyav ledin
and whosoever shall kill shall be in danger of the judgment:

וַאֲנִי אוֹמֵר לָכֶם: כָּל הַכּוֹעֵס עַל אָחִיו יְחֻיַּב לַדִּין
va'ani omer lachem: kol hakko'es al achiv yechyav ledin
but I say unto you, that every one who is angry with his brother shall be in danger of the judgment;

הָאוֹמֵר לְאָחִיו 'רֵיק' יְחֻיַּב לְמִשְׁפַּט הַסַּנְהֶדְרִין
ha'omer le'achiv reik yechyav lemishpat hassanhedrin
and whosoever shall say to his brother, Raca, shall be in danger of the council;

וְהָאוֹמֵר 'אֱוִיל' יְחֻיַּב לְאֵשׁ גֵּיהִנֹּם
veha'omer evil yechyav le'esh geihinnom
and whosoever shall say, Thou fool, shall be in danger of the hell of fire.

אַשְׁרֵי בָּרֵי לֵבָב, כִּי הֵם יִרְאוּ אֶת אֱלֹהִים
ashrei barei levav, ki hem yir'u et elohim
Blessed are the pure in heart: for they shall see God.

אַשְׁרֵי רוֹדְפֵי שָׁלוֹם, כִּי בְּנֵי אֱלֹהִים יִקָּרֵאוּ
ashrei rodefei shalom, ki benei elohim yikkare'u
Blessed are the peacemakers: for they shall be called sons of God.

אַשְׁרֵי הַנִּרְדָּפִים בִּגְלַל הַצֶּדֶק, כִּי לָהֶם מַלְכוּת הַשָּׁמַיִם
ashrei hannirdafim biglal hatzedek, ki lahem malchut hashamayim
Blessed are they that have been persecuted for righteousness' sake: for theirs is the kingdom of heaven.

אַשְׁרֵיכֶם אִם יְחָרְפוּ וְיִרְדְּפוּ אֶתְכֶם וְיַעֲלִילוּ עֲלֵיכֶם בִּגְלָלִי
ashreichem im yecharefu veyirdefu etchem veya'alilu aleichem biglali
Blessed are ye when men shall reproach you, and persecute you, and say all manner of evil against you falsely, for my sake.

שִׂמְחוּ וְגִילוּ, כִּי שְׂכַרְכֶם רַב בַּשָּׁמַיִם;
simchu vegilu, ki secharchem rav bashamayim;
Rejoice, and be exceeding glad: for great is your reward in heaven:

הֲרֵי כָּךְ רָדְפוּ אֶת הַנְּבִיאִים שֶׁהָיוּ לִפְנֵיכֶם
harei kach radefu et hannevi'im shehayu lifneichem
for so persecuted they the prophets that were before you.

אַתֶּם מֶלַח הָאָרֶץ, וְאִם תֹּאבַד לַמֶּלַח מְלִיחוּתוֹ, כֵּיצַד תֻּחְזַר לוֹ?
attem melach ha'aretz, ve'im tovad lammelach melichuto, keitzad tuchzar lo?
Ye are the salt of the earth: but if the salt have lost its savor, wherewith shall it be salted?

הֵן לֹא יִצְלַח עוֹד לְשׁוּם דָּבָר כִּי אִם לְהַשְׁלִיכוֹ הַחוּצָה לִהְיוֹת מִרְמָס לְרַגְלֵי הַבְּרִיּוֹת
hen lo yitzlach od leshum davar ki im lehashlicho hachutzah lihyot mirmas leraglei habberiyot
it is thenceforth good for nothing, but to be cast out and trodden under foot of men.

אַתֶּם אוֹר הָעוֹלָם. עִיר שׁוֹכֶנֶת עַל הַר אֵינָהּ יְכוֹלָה לְהִסָּתֵר
attem or ha'olam. ir shochenet al har einah yecholah lehissater
Ye are the light of the world. A city set on a hill cannot be hid.

גַּם אֵין מַדְלִיקִים מְנוֹרָה וְשָׂמִים אוֹתָהּ תַּחַת כְּלִי, אֶלָּא עַל כַּן שָׂמִים אוֹתָהּ וְאָז תָּאִיר לְכָל בָּאֵי הַבַּיִת
gam ein madlikim menorah vesamim otah tachat keli, ella al kan samim otah ve'az ta'ir lechol ba'ei habbayit
Neither do men light a lamp, and put it under the bushel, but on the stand; and it shineth unto all that are in the house.

כָּךְ יָאֵר נָא אוֹרְכֶם לִפְנֵי בְּנֵי אָדָם, לְמַעַן יִרְאוּ אֶת מַעֲשֵׂיכֶם הַטּוֹבִים וִיכַבְּדוּ אֶת אֲבִיכֶם שֶׁבַּשָּׁמַיִם
kach ya'er na orechem lifnei benei adam, lema'an yir'u et ma'aseichem hattovim vichabbedu et avichem shebbashamayim
Even so let your light shine before men; that they may see your good works, and glorify your Father who is in heaven.

אַל תַּחְשְׁבוּ שֶׁבָּאתִי לְבַטֵּל אֶת הַתּוֹרָה אוֹ אֶת הַנְּבִיאִים; לֹא בָּאתִי לְבַטֵּל כִּי אִם לְקַיֵּם
'al tachshevu shebbati levattel et hattorah o et hannevi'im; lo bati levattel ki im lekayem
Think not that I came to destroy the law or the prophets: I came not to destroy, but to fulfil.

שִׁמְעוֹ יָצָא בְּכָל סוּרְיָה וְהֵבִיאוּ אֵלָיו אֵת כָּל הַחוֹלִים הַסּוֹבְלִים מִמַּחֲלוֹת
shim'o yatza bechol sureyah vehevi'u elav et kol hacholim hassovelim mimmachalot
And the report of him went forth into all Syria: and they brought unto him all that were sick,

וּמַכְאוֹבִים לְמִינֵיהֶם, וְגַם אֲנָשִׁים אֲחוּזֵי שֵׁדִים, מֻכֵּי יָרֵחַ וּמְשֻׁתָּקִים, וְהוּא רִפֵּא אוֹתָם
umach'ovim lemineihem, vegam anashim achuzei shedim, mukkei yareach umeshuttakim, vehu rippei otam
holden with divers diseases and torments, possessed with demons, and epileptic, and palsied; and he healed them.

הֲמוֹנִים הֲמוֹנִים הָלְכוּ אַחֲרָיו
hamonim hamonim halechu acharav
And there followed him great multitudes

מֵהַגָּלִיל וּמִדְּקַפּוֹלִיס, מִירוּשָׁלַיִם וִיהוּדָה וּמֵעֵבֶר הַיַּרְדֵּן
mehaggalil umiddekappolis, miyerushalayim viyehudah ume'ever hayarden
from Galilee and Decapolis and Jerusalem and Judæa and from beyond the Jordan.

ה

כִּרְאוֹתוֹ אֶת הֲמוֹן הָעָם עָלָה בְּמַעֲלֵה הָהָר וַיֵּשֶׁב, וְתַלְמִידָיו נִגְּשׁוּ אֵלָיו
kir'oto et hamon ha'am alah bema'aleh hahar veyashav, vetalmidav niggeshu elav
And seeing the multitudes, he went up into the mountain: and when he had sat down, his disciples came unto him:

פָּתַח פִּיו וְלִמֵּד אוֹתָם בְּאָמְרוֹ
patach piv velimmed otam be'amero
and he opened his mouth and taught them, saying,

אַשְׁרֵי עֲנִיֵּי הָרוּחַ, כִּי לָהֶם מַלְכוּת הַשָּׁמַיִם
ashrei aniyei haruach, ki lahem malchut hashamayim
Blessed are the poor in spirit: for theirs is the kingdom of heaven.

אַשְׁרֵי הָאֲבֵלִים, כִּי הֵם יְנֻחָמוּ
ashrei ha'avelim, ki hem yenuchamu
Blessed are they that mourn: for they shall be comforted.

אַשְׁרֵי הָעֲנָוִים, כִּי הֵם יִירְשׁוּ אֶת הָאָרֶץ
ashrei ha'anavim, ki hem yireshu et ha'aretz
Blessed are the meek: for they shall inherit the earth.

אַשְׁרֵי הָרְעֵבִים וְהַצְּמֵאִים לְצֶדֶק, כִּי הֵם יִשְׂבָּעוּ
ashrei hare'evim vehatzeme'im letzedek, ki hem yisba'u
Blessed are they that hunger and thirst after righteousness: for they shall be filled.

אַשְׁרֵי הָרַחֲמָנִים, כִּי הֵם יְרֻחָמוּ
ashrei harachamanim, ki hem yeruchamu
Blessed are the merciful: for they shall obtain mercy.

הָעָם הַהֹלְכִים בַּחֹשֶׁךְ רָאוּ אוֹר גָּדוֹל
ha'am haholechim bachoshech ra'u or gadol
The people that sat in darkness Saw a great light,

יֹשְׁבֵי בְּאֶרֶץ צַלְמָוֶת אוֹר נָגַהּ עֲלֵיהֶם
yoshevei be'eretz tzalmavet or nagah aleihem
And to them that sat in the region and shadow of death, To them did light spring up.

מִן הָעֵת הַהִיא הֵחֵל יֵשׁוּעַ לְהַכְרִיז וְלוֹמַר: חִזְרוּ בִּתְשׁוּבָה, כִּי קָרְבָה מַלְכוּת שָׁמַיִם
min ha'et hahi hechel yeshua lehachriz velomar: chizru bitshuvah, ki karevah malchut shamayim
From that time began Jesus to preach, and to say, Repent ye; for the kingdom of heaven is at hand.

כְּשֶׁהָלַךְ לְיַד יָם הַגָּלִיל רָאָה שְׁנֵי אַחִים, אֶת שִׁמְעוֹן הַנִּקְרָא כֵּיפָא
keshehalach leyad yam haggalil ra'ah shenei achim, et shim'on hannikra keifa
And walking by the sea of Galilee, he saw two brethren, Simon who is called Peter,

וְאֶת אַנְדְּרֵי אָחִיו, מַשְׁלִיכִים רֶשֶׁת לְתוֹךְ הַיָּם, כִּי הָיוּ דַּיָּגִים
ve'et anderei achiv, mashlichim reshet letoch hayam, ki hayu dayagim
and Andrew his brother, casting a net into the sea; for they were fishers.

אָמַר לָהֶם: בּוֹאוּ אַחֲרַי וְאֶעֱשֶׂה אֶתְכֶם דַּיָּגֵי אָדָם
amar lahem: bo'u acharai ve'e'eseh etchem dayagei adam
And he saith unto them, Come ye after me, and I will make you fishers of men.

מִיָּד עָזְבוּ אֶת הָרְשָׁתוֹת וְהָלְכוּ אַחֲרָיו
miyad azevu et hareshatot vehalechu acharav
And they straightway left the nets, and followed him.

בְּלֶכְתּוֹ הָלְאָה רָאָה שְׁנֵי אַחִים אֲחֵרִים, אֶת יַעֲקֹב בֶּן זַבְדַּי
belechto hale'ah ra'ah shenei achim acherim, et ya'akov ben zavdai
And going on from thence he saw two other brethren, James the son of Zebedee,

וְאֶת יוֹחָנָן אָחִיו, בַּסִּירָה עִם זַבְדַּי אֲבִיהֶם וְהֵם מְתַקְּנִים אֶת רִשְׁתוֹתֵיהֶם. קָרָא לָהֶם
ve'et yochanan achiv, bassirah im zavdai avihem vehem metakkenim et rishtoteihem. kara lahem
and John his brother, in the boat with Zebedee their father, mending their nets; and he called them.

וּמִיָּד עָזְבוּ אֶת הַסִּירָה וְאֶת אֲבִיהֶם וְהָלְכוּ אַחֲרָיו
umiyad azevu et hassirah ve'et avihem vehalechu acharav
And they straightway left the boat and their father, and followed him.

הוּא סָבַב בְּכָל הַגָּלִיל כְּשֶׁהוּא מְלַמֵּד בְּבָתֵּי הַכְּנֶסֶת וּמַכְרִיז אֶת בְּשׂוֹרַת הַמַּלְכוּת
hu savav bechol haggalil keshehu melammed bevattei hakkeneset umachriz et besorat hammalchut
And Jesus went about in all Galilee, teaching in their synagogues, and preaching the gospel of the kingdom,

וּמְרַפֵּא כָּל מַחֲלָה וְכָל מַדְוֶה בָּעָם
umerappei kol machalah vechol madveh ba'am
and healing all manner of disease and all manner of sickness among the people.

עַל־כַּפַּיִם יִשָּׂאוּנְךָ, פֶּן־תִּגֹּף בָּאֶבֶן רַגְלֶךָ
al-kappayim yisho'unecha, pen-tiggof ba'even raglecha
and, On their hands they shall bear thee up, Lest haply thou dash thy foot against a stone.

אָמַר לוֹ יֵשׁוּעַ: עוֹד כָּתוּב, לֹא תְנַסֶּה אֶת־יהוה אֱלֹהֶיךָ
amar lo yeshua od katuv, lo tenasseh et-hashem eloheicha
Jesus said unto him, Again it is written, Thou shalt not make trial of the Lord thy God.

לָקַח אוֹתוֹ הַשָּׂטָן לְהַר גָּבוֹהַ מְאֹד
lakach oto hassatan lehar gavoha me'od
Again, the devil taketh him unto an exceeding high mountain,

וְהֶרְאָה לוֹ אֶת כָּל מַמְלְכוֹת תֵּבֵל וּכְבוֹדָן
veher'ah lo et kol mamlechot tevel uchevodan
and showeth him all the kingdoms of the world, and the glory of them;

אָמַר אֵלָיו: אֶת כָּל אֵלֶּה אֶתֵּן לְךָ אִם תִּפֹּל עַל פָּנֶיךָ וְתִשְׁתַּחֲוֶה לִי
amar elav: et kol elleh etten lecha im tippol al paneicha vetishtachaveh li
and he said unto him, All these things will I give thee, if thou wilt fall down and worship me.

הֵשִׁיב לוֹ יֵשׁוּעַ: הִסְתַּלֵּק, הַשָּׂטָן
heshiv lo yeshua: histallek, hassatan
Then saith Jesus unto him, Get thee hence, Satan: for it is written,

הֵן כָּתוּב, לַיהוה אֱלֹהֶיךָ תִּשְׁתַּחֲוֶה וְאוֹתוֹ לְבַדּוֹ תַּעֲבֹד
hen katuv, lashem eloheicha tishtachaveh ve'oto levaddo ta'avod
Thou shalt worship the Lord thy God, and him only shalt thou serve.

לְאַחַר מִכֵּן עָזַב אוֹתוֹ הַשָּׂטָן וּמַלְאָכִים נִגְּשׁוּ לְשָׁרְתוֹ
le'achar mikken azav oto hassatan umal'achim niggeshu lesharero
Then the devil leaveth him; and behold, angels came and ministered unto him.

כַּאֲשֶׁר שָׁמַע יֵשׁוּעַ כִּי הִסְגִּירוּ אֶת יוֹחָנָן יָצָא אֶל הַגָּלִיל
ka'asher shama yeshua ki hisgiru et yochanan yatza el haggalil
Now when he heard that John was delivered up, he withdrew into Galilee;

הוּא עָזַב אֶת נְצֶרֶת וּבָא לָגוּר בִּכְפַר נַחוּם לְיַד הַיָּם, בְּחֶבֶל זְבוּלוּן וְנַפְתָּלִי
hu azav et natzeret uva lagur bichfar nachum leyad hayam, bechevel zevulun venaftali
and leaving Nazareth, he came and dwelt in Capernaum, which is by the sea, in the borders of Zebulun and Naphtali:

לְמַעַן יִתְקַיֵּם הַנֶּאֱמַר בְּפִי יְשַׁעְיָהוּ הַנָּבִיא
lema'an yitkayem hanne'emar befi yesha'yahu hannavi
that it might be fulfilled which was spoken through Isaiah the prophet, saying,

אַרְצָה זְבֻלוּן וְאַרְצָה נַפְתָּלִי, דֶּרֶךְ הַיָּם, עֵבֶר הַיַּרְדֵּן, גְּלִיל הַגּוֹיִם
artzah zevulun ve'artzah naftali, derech hayam, ever hayarden, gelil haggoyim
The land of Zebulun and the land of Naphtali, Toward the sea, beyond the Jordan, Galilee of the Gentiles,

יֵשׁוּעַ נִטְבַּל וְעָלָה מִיַּד מִן הַמַּיִם
yeshua nitbal ve'alah miyad min hammayim
And Jesus, when he was baptized, went up straightway from the water:

אוֹתָהּ עֵת נִפְתְּחוּ הַשָּׁמַיִם וְהוּא רָאָה אֶת רוּחַ אֱלֹהִים יוֹרֶדֶת כְּיוֹנָה וּבָאָה עָלָיו
Otah et niftechu hashamayim vehu ra'ah et ruach elohim yoredet keyonah uva'ah alav
and lo, the heavens were opened unto him, and he saw the Spirit of God descending as a dove, and coming upon him;

וְהִנֵּה קוֹל מִן הַשָּׁמַיִם אוֹמֵר: זֶה בְּנִי אֲהוּבִי אֲשֶׁר בּוֹ חָפַצְתִּי
vehinneh kol min hashamayim omer: zeh beni ahuvi asher bo chafatzti
and lo, a voice out of the heavens, saying, This is my beloved Son, in whom I am well pleased.

ד

אָז הוֹבִילָה הָרוּחַ אֶת יֵשׁוּעַ אֶל הַמִּדְבָּר לְהִתְנַסּוֹת עַל־יְדֵי הַשָּׂטָן
az hovilah haruach et yeshua el hammidbar lehitnassot al-yedei hassatan
Then was Jesus led up of the Spirit into the wilderness to be tempted of the devil.

וּלְאַחַר שֶׁצָּם אַרְבָּעִים יוֹם וְאַרְבָּעִים לַיְלָה הָיָה רָעֵב
ule'achar shetzam arba'im yom ve'arba'im laylah hayah ra'ev
And when he had fasted forty days and forty nights, he afterward hungered.

נִגַּשׁ אֵלָיו הַמְנַסֶּה וְאָמַר: אִם בֶּן־הָאֱלֹהִים אַתָּה, צַוֵּה שֶׁהָאֲבָנִים הָאֵלֶּה יִהְיוּ לְלֶחֶם
niggash elav hamnasseh ve'amar: Im ben-ha'elohim attah, tzavveh sheha'avanim ha'elleh yihyu lelechem
And the tempter came and said unto him, If thou art the Son of God, command that these stones become bread.

הֵשִׁיב יֵשׁוּעַ וְאָמַר
heshiv yeshua ve'amar
But he answered and said,

כָּתוּב, לֹא עַל־הַלֶּחֶם לְבַדּוֹ יִחְיֶה הָאָדָם, כִּי עַל־כָּל־מוֹצָא פִי־יהוה
katuv, lo al-hallechem levaddo yichyeh ha'adam, ki al-kol-motza fi-hashem
It is written, Man shall not live by bread alone, but by every word that proceedeth out of the mouth of God.

לָקַח אוֹתוֹ הַשָּׂטָן אֶל עִיר הַקֹּדֶשׁ וְהֶעֱמִידוֹ עַל פִּנַּת גַּג בֵּית הַמִּקְדָּשׁ
lakach oto hassatan el ir hakkodesh vehe'emido al pinnat gag beit hammikdash
Then the devil taketh him into the holy city; and he set him on the pinnacle of the temple,

אָמַר לוֹ: אִם בֶּן־הָאֱלֹהִים אַתָּה, הַשְׁלֵךְ עַצְמְךָ לְמַטָּה
amar lo: im ben-ha'elohim attah, hashlech atzmecha lemattah
and saith unto him, If thou art the Son of God, cast thyself down:

שֶׁהֲרֵי כָּתוּב, כִּי מַלְאָכָיו יְצַוֶּה־לָּךְ
sheharei katuv, ki mal'achav yetzavveh-lach
for it is written, He shall give his angels charge concerning thee:

לָכֵן עֲשׂוּ פְּרִי רָאוּי לִתְשׁוּבָה
lachen asu peri ra'ui litshuvah
Bring forth therefore fruit worthy of repentance:

וְאַל תַּחְשְׁבוּ בִּלְבַבְכֶם לֵאמֹר, אַבְרָהָם הוּא אָבִינוּ
ve'al tachshevu bilvavchem lemor, avraham hu avinu
and think not to say within yourselves, We have Abraham to our father:

כִּי אֲנִי אוֹמֵר לָכֶם שֶׁמִן הָאֲבָנִים הָאֵלֶּה יָכוֹל אֱלֹהִים לְהָקִים בָּנִים לְאַבְרָהָם
ki ani omer lachem shemin ha'avanim ha'elleh yachol elohim lehakim banim le'avraham
for I say unto you, that God is able of these stones to raise up children unto Abraham.

וּכְבָר מֻנַּח הַגַּרְזֶן עַל שֹׁרֶשׁ הָעֵצִים
uchevar munnach haggarzen al shoresh ha'etzim
And even now the axe lieth at the root of the trees:

עַל כֵּן כָּל עֵץ אֲשֶׁר אֵינֶנּוּ עוֹשֶׂה פְּרִי טוֹב יִגָּדַע וְיֻשְׁלַךְ לְתוֹךְ הָאֵשׁ
Al ken kol etz asher einennu oseh peri tov yiggada veyushlach letoch ha'esh
every tree therefore that bringeth not forth good fruit is hewn down, and cast into the fire.

אֲנִי אָמְנָם מַטְבִּיל אֶתְכֶם בְּמַיִם לִתְשׁוּבָה, אַךְ הַבָּא אַחֲרַי חָזָק מִמֶּנִּי
ani omnam matbil etchem bemayim litshuvah, ach habba acharai chazak mimmenni
I indeed baptize you in water unto repentance: but he that cometh after me is mightier than I,

וְאֵינֶנִּי רָאוּי לָשֵׂאת אֶת נְעָלָיו. הוּא יַטְבִּיל אֶתְכֶם בְּרוּחַ הַקֹּדֶשׁ וּבָאֵשׁ
ve'einenni ra'ui laset et ne'alav. hu yatbil etchem beruach hakkodesh uve'esh
whose shoes I am not worthy to bear: he shall baptize you in the Holy Spirit and in fire:

בְּיָדוֹ קִלְשׁוֹן הַמִּזְרֶה לְנַקּוֹת אֶת גָּרְנוֹ וְהוּא
beyado kilshon hammizreh lenakkot et gareno vehu
whose fan is in his hand, and he will thoroughly cleanse his threshing-floor;

יֶאֱסֹף אֶת דְּגָנוֹ אֶל הָאָסָם, אַךְ אֶת הַמּוֹץ יִשְׂרֹף בָּאֵשׁ בִּלְתִּי נִכְבֵּית
ye'esof et degano el ha'asam, ach et hammotz yisrof be'esh bilti nichbeit
and he will gather his wheat into the garner, but the chaff he will burn up with unquenchable fire.

אָז הִגִּיעַ יֵשׁוּעַ מִן הַגָּלִיל לַיַּרְדֵּן וּבָא אֶל יוֹחָנָן לְהִטָּבֵל אֶצְלוֹ
az higgia yeshua min haggalil layarden uva el yochanan lehittavel etzlo
Then cometh Jesus from Galilee to the Jordan unto John, to be baptized of him.

אֶלָּא שֶׁיּוֹחָנָן נִסָּה לַהֲנִיאוֹ מִכָּךְ בְּאָמְרוֹ: אֲנִי צָרִיךְ לְהִטָּבֵל אֶצְלְךָ, וְאַתָּה בָּא אֵלַי
ella sheyochanan nissah lahani'o mikkach be'amro: ani tzarich lehittavel etzlecha, ve'attah ba elai
But John would have hindered him, saying, I have need to be baptized of thee, and comest thou to me?

הֵשִׁיב לוֹ יֵשׁוּעַ וְאָמַר: הַנַּח כָּעֵת, כִּי מִן הָרָאוּי שֶׁנְּקַיֵּם אֶת הַצֶּדֶק כֻּלּוֹ. וְיוֹחָנָן הִנִּיחַ לוֹ
heshiv lo yeshua ve'amar: hannach ka'et, ki min hara'ui shennekayem et hatzedek kullo veyochanan hinniach lo
But Jesus answering said unto him, Suffer it now: for thus it becometh us to fulfil all righteousness. Then he suffereth him.

כִּי נָצְרִי יִקָּרֵא לוֹ
ki natzeri yikkarei lo
that he should be called a Nazarene.

ג

בַּיָּמִים הָהֵם הוֹפִיעַ יוֹחָנָן הַמַּטְבִּיל כְּשֶׁהוּא קוֹרֵא בְּמִדְבַּר יְהוּדָה לֵאמֹר
bayamim hahem hofia yochanan hammatbil keshehu korei bemidbar yehudah lemor
And in those days cometh John the Baptist, preaching in the wilderness of Judæa, saying,

שׁוּבוּ בִּתְשׁוּבָה, כִּי קָרְבָה מַלְכוּת שָׁמַיִם
shuvu bitshuvah, ki karevah malchut shamayim
Repent ye; for the kingdom of heaven is at hand.

הוּא הָיָה זֶה שֶׁנֶּאֱמַר עָלָיו בְּפִי יְשַׁעְיָהוּ הַנָּבִיא
hu hayah zeh shenne'emar alav befi yesha'yahu hannavi
For this is he that was spoken of through Isaiah the prophet, saying,

קוֹל קוֹרֵא בַּמִּדְבָּר פַּנּוּ דֶּרֶךְ יהוה, יַשְּׁרוּ מְסִלּוֹתָיו
kol korei bammidbar pannu derech hashem, yashru mesillotav
The voice of one crying in the wilderness, Make ye ready the way of the Lord, Make his paths straight.

אוֹתוֹ יוֹחָנָן לְבוּשׁוֹ הָיָה מִשְּׂעַר גְּמַלִּים וַחֲגוֹרַת עוֹר עַל מָתְנָיו
oto yochanan levusho hayah misho'ar gemallim vachagorat or al motnav,
Now John himself had his raiment of camel's hair, and a leathern girdle about his loins;

וּמַאֲכָלוֹ חֲגָבִים וּדְבַשׁ הַיַּעַר
uma'achalo chagavim udvash haya'ar
and his food was locusts and wild honey.

אָז יָצְאוּ אֵלָיו יְרוּשָׁלַיִם וְכָל יְהוּדָה וְכָל כִּכַּר הַיַּרְדֵּן
az yatze'u elav yerushalayim vechol yehudah vechol kikkar hayarden
Then went out unto him Jerusalem, and all Judæa, and all the region round about the Jordan;

וְהָטְבְּלוּ עַל־יָדָיו בַּיַּרְדֵּן כְּשֶׁהֵם מִתְוַדִּים עַל חַטֹּאתֵיהֶם
vehutbelu al-yadav bayarden keshehem mitvaddim al chattoteihem
and they were baptized of him in the river Jordan, confessing their sins.

כְּשֶׁרָאָה רַבִּים מִן הַפְּרוּשִׁים וְהַצְּדוֹקִים בָּאִים לְהִטָּבֵל אָמַר לָהֶם
keshera'ah rabbim min happerushim vehatzedokim ba'im lehittavel amar lahem
But when he saw many of the Pharisees and Sadducees coming to his baptism, he said unto them,

יַלְדֵי צִפְעוֹנִים, מִי הוֹרָה אֶתְכֶם לְהִמָּלֵט מִן הֶחָרוֹן הַבָּא
yaldei tzif'onim, mi horah etchem lehimmalet min hecharon habba
Ye offspring of vipers, who warned you to flee from the wrath to come?

וְשָׁלַח לַהֲרֹג אֶת כָּל הַיְלָדִים שֶׁבְּבֵית לֶחֶם וּבְכָל סְבִיבוֹתֶיהָ
veshalach laharog et kol hayladim shebbeveit lechem uvechol sevivoteiha
and sent forth, and slew all the male children that were in Bethlehem, and in all the borders thereof,

מִבְּנֵי שְׁנָתַיִם וָמַטָּה, לְפִי הָעֵת אֲשֶׁר קָבַע מִפִּי הַחֲכָמִים
mibbnei shenatayim vamattah, lefi ha'et asher kava mippi hachachamim
from two years old and under, according to the time which he had exactly learned of the Wise-men.

אָז נִתְקַיֵּם הַנֶּאֱמַר בְּפִי יִרְמְיָהוּ הַנָּבִיא
az nitkayem hanne'emar befi yirmeyahu hannavi
Then was fulfilled that which was spoken through Jeremiah the prophet, saying,

קוֹל בְּרָמָה נִשְׁמָע, נְהִי בְּכִי תַמְרוּרִים, רָחֵל מְבַכָּה עַל־בָּנֶיהָ
kol beramah nishma', nehi bechi tamrurim, rachel mevakkah al-baneiha
A voice was heard in Ramah, Weeping and great mourning, Rachel weeping for her children;

מֵאֲנָה לְהִנָּחֵם כִּי אֵינָם
me'anah lehinnachem ki einam
And she would not be comforted, because they are not.

אַחֲרֵי מוֹת הוֹרְדוֹס נִרְאָה מַלְאַךְ יהוה אֶל יוֹסֵף בַּחֲלוֹם בְּאֶרֶץ מִצְרַיִם
acharei mot horedos nir'ah mal'ach hashem el yosef bachalom be'eretz mitzrayim
But when Herod was dead, behold, an angel of the Lord appeareth in a dream to Joseph in Egypt, saying,

וְאָמַר: קוּם, קַח אֶת הַיֶּלֶד וְאֶת אִמּוֹ וְלֵךְ לְאֶרֶץ יִשְׂרָאֵל
ve'amar: kum, kach et hayeled ve'et immo velech le'eretz yisra'el
Arise and take the young child and his mother, and go into the land of Israel:

כִּי מֵתוּ הַמְבַקְשִׁים אֶת נֶפֶשׁ הַיֶּלֶד
ki metu hamvakshim et nefesh hayeled
for they are dead that sought the young child's life.

הוּא קָם וְלָקַח אֶת הַיֶּלֶד וְאֶת אִמּוֹ וּבָא לְאֶרֶץ יִשְׂרָאֵל
hu kam velakach et hayeled ve'et immo uva le'eretz yisra'el
And he arose and took the young child and his mother, and came into the land of Israel.

אֲבָל בְּשָׁמְעוֹ כִּי אַרְכְלָאוֹס מוֹלֵךְ בִּיהוּדָה בִּמְקוֹם הוֹרְדוֹס אָבִיו, פָּחַד לָלֶכֶת לְשָׁם
aval beshom'o ki archela'os molech biyehudah bimkom horedos aviv, pachad lalechet lesham
But when he heard that Archelaus was reigning over Judæa in the room of his father Herod, he was afraid to go thither;

לְאַחַר שֶׁהֻזְהַר בַּחֲלוֹם יָצָא אֶל סְבִיבוֹת הַגָּלִיל
Le'achar shehuzhar bachalom yatza el sevivot haggalil
and being warned of God in a dream, he withdrew into the parts of Galilee,

הוּא בָּא וְיָשַׁב בְּעִיר הַנִּקְרֵאת נָצְרַת, לְמַעַן יִתְקַיֵּם הַנֶּאֱמַר עַל־פִּי הַנְּבִיאִים
hu ba veyashav be'ir hannikret natzeret, lema'an yitkayem hanne'emar al-pi hannevi'im
and came and dwelt in a city called Nazareth; that it might be fulfilled which was spoken through the prophets,

הֵם נִכְנְסוּ לַבַּיִת וְרָאוּ אֶת הַיֶּלֶד עִם מִרְיָם אִמּוֹ
hem nichnesu labbayit vera'u et hayeled im miryam immo
And they came into the house and saw the young child with Mary his mother;

נָפְלוּ עַל פְּנֵיהֶם וְהִשְׁתַּחֲווּ לוֹ
nafelu al peneihem vehishtachavu lo
and they fell down and worshipped him;

וּפָתְחוּ אֶת צְרוֹרוֹתֵיהֶם וְהִגִּישׁוּ לוֹ מַתָּנוֹת: זָהָב וּלְבוֹנָה וָמוֹר
ufatchu et tzeroroteihem vehiggishu lo mattanot: zahav ulevonah vamor
and opening their treasures they offered unto him gifts, gold and frankincense and myrrh.

לְאַחַר שֶׁהֻזְהֲרוּ בַּחֲלוֹם שֶׁלֹּא לַחֲזֹר אֶל הוֹרְדוֹס
le'achar shehuzharu bachalom shello lachazor el horedos
And being warned of God in a dream that they should not return to Herod,

יָצְאוּ לְאַרְצָם בְּדֶרֶךְ אַחֶרֶת
yatze'u le'artzam bederech acheret
they departed into their own country another way.

הֵם הָלְכוּ מִשָּׁם וּמַלְאָךְ יהוה נִרְאָה אֶל יוֹסֵף בַּחֲלוֹם וְאָמַר
hem halchu misham umal'ach hashem nir'ah el yosef bachalom ve'amar
Now when they were departed, behold, an angel of the Lord appeareth to Joseph in a dream, saying,

קוּם, קַח אֶת הַיֶּלֶד וְאֶת אִמּוֹ וּבְרַח לְמִצְרַיִם וֶהֱיֵה שָׁם עַד אֲשֶׁר אֹמַר לְךָ
Kum, kach et hayeled ve'et immo uverach lemitzrayim veheyeh sham ad asher omar lecha
Arise and take the young child and his mother, and flee into Egypt, and be thou there until I tell thee:

כִּי הוֹרְדוֹס יְחַפֵּשׂ אֶת הַיֶּלֶד כְּדֵי לְהַשְׁמִיד אוֹתוֹ
ki horedos yechappes et hayeled kedei lehashmid oto
for Herod will seek the young child to destroy him.

הוּא קָם וְלָקַח אֶת הַיֶּלֶד וְאֶת אִמּוֹ בַּלַּיְלָה וְיָצָא לְמִצְרַיִם
hu kam velakach et hayeled ve'et immo ballaylah veyatza lemitzrayim
And he arose and took the young child and his mother by night, and departed into Egypt;

שָׁם נִשְׁאַר עַד מוֹת הוֹרְדוֹס
sham nish'ar ad mot horedos
and was there until the death of Herod:

לְקַיֵּם אֶת אֲשֶׁר אָמַר יהוה בְּיַד הַנָּבִיא: מִמִּצְרַיִם קָרָאתִי לִבְנִי
lekayem et asher amar hashem beyad hannavi: mimmitzrayim karati livni
that it might be fulfilled which was spoken by the Lord through the prophet, saying, Out of Egypt did I call my son.

כַּאֲשֶׁר רָאָה הוֹרְדוֹס כִּי הֵתֵלּוּ בּוֹ הַחֲכָמִים רָגַז עַד מְאֹד
ka'asher ra'ah horedos ki hetellu bo hachachamim ragaz ad me'od
Then Herod, when he saw that he was mocked of the Wise-men, was exceeding wroth,

כַּאֲשֶׁר שָׁמַע זֹאת הוֹרְדוֹס הַמֶּלֶךְ נִדְהַם הוּא וְכָל יְרוּשָׁלַיִם עִמּוֹ
ka'asher shama zot horedos hammelech nidham hu vechol yerushalayim immo
And when Herod the king heard it, he was troubled, and all Jerusalem with him.

הוּא כִּנֵּס אֶת כָּל רָאשֵׁי הַכֹּהֲנִים וְסוֹפְרֵי הָעָם
hu kinnes et kol rashei hakkohanim vesoferei ha'am
And gathering together all the chief priests and scribes of the people,

וְשָׁאַל אוֹתָם אֵיפֹה יִוָּלֵד הַמָּשִׁיחַ
vesha'al otam eifoh yivvaled hammashiach
he inquired of them where the Christ should be born.

אָמְרוּ לוֹ: בְּבֵית לֶחֶם יְהוּדָה, כִּי כֵן נִכְתַּב עַל־יְדֵי הַנָּבִיא
ameru lo: Beveit lechem yehudah, ki chen nichtav al-yedei hannavi
And they said unto him, In Bethlehem of Judæa: for thus it is written through the prophet,

וְאַתָּה בֵּית לֶחֶם אֶרֶץ יְהוּדָה, אֵינְךָ צָעִיר בְּאַלּוּפֵי יְהוּדָה
ve'attah beit lechem eretz yehudah, eincha tza'ir be'allufei yehudah
And thou Bethlehem, land of Judah, Art in no wise least among the princes of Judah:

כִּי מִמְּךָ יֵצֵא מוֹשֵׁל אֲשֶׁר יִרְעֶה אֶת עַמִּי יִשְׂרָאֵל
ki mimmecha yetzei moshel asher yir'eh et ammi yisra'el
For out of thee shall come forth a governor, Who shall be shepherd of my people Israel.

אָז קָרָא הוֹרְדוֹס בַּחֲשַׁאי לְחַכְמֵי הַמִּזְרָח וּבֵרֵר אֶצְלָם מָתַי הוֹפִיעַ הַכּוֹכָב
az kara horedos bachashai lechachmei hammizrach uverer etzlam matai hofia hakkochav
Then Herod privily called the Wise-men, and learned of them exactly what time the star appeared.

אַחֲרֵי כֵן שָׁלַח אוֹתָם לְבֵית לֶחֶם בְּאָמְרוֹ: לְכוּ חִקְרוּ הֵיטֵב עַל־אוֹדוֹת הַיֶּלֶד
acharei chen shalach otam leveit lechem be'omro: Lechu chikru heitev al-'odot hayeled
And he sent them to Bethlehem, and said, Go and search out exactly concerning the young child;

וְכַאֲשֶׁר תִּמְצְאוּ אוֹתוֹ הוֹדִיעוּ לִי כְּדֵי שֶׁאָבוֹא וְאֶשְׁתַּחֲוֶה לוֹ גַם אֲנִי
vecha'asher timtze'u oto hodi'u li kedei she'avo ve'eshtachaveh lo gam ani
and when ye have found him, bring me word, that I also may come and worship him.

הֵם שָׁמְעוּ אֶת דִּבְרֵי הַמֶּלֶךְ וְהָלְכוּ, וְהִנֵּה הַכּוֹכָב שֶׁרָאוּ בַּמִּזְרָח הִתְקַדֵּם לִפְנֵיהֶם
hem shame'u et divrei hammelech vehalechu, vehinneh hakkochav shera'u bammizrach hitkaddem lifneihem
And they, having heard the king, went their way; and lo, the star, which they saw in the east, went before them,

עַד אֲשֶׁר בָּא וְנֶעֱמַד מֵעַל לַמָּקוֹם שֶׁהָיָה שָׁם הַיֶּלֶד
ad asher ba vene'emad me'al lammakom shehayah sham hayeled
till it came and stood over where the young child was.

כִּרְאוֹתָם אֶת הַכּוֹכָב שָׂמְחוּ שִׂמְחָה גְדוֹלָה עַד מְאֹד
kir'otam et hakkochav samechu simchah gedolah ad me'od
And when they saw the star, they rejoiced with exceeding great joy.

בְּעוֹד שֶׁהָיָה מְהַרְהֵר בָּזֶה נִרְאָה אֵלָיו מַלְאַךְ יהוה בַּחֲלוֹם וְאָמַר
be'od shehayah meharher bazeh nir'ah elav mal'ach hashem bachalom ve'amar
But when he thought on these things, behold, an angel of the Lord appeared unto him in a dream, saying,

יוֹסֵף בֶּן דָּוִד, אַל תַּחְשֹׁשׁ לָקַחַת אֵלֶיךָ אֶת מִרְיָם אִשְׁתְּךָ, כִּי אֲשֶׁר הוֹרָה בָּהּ מֵרוּחַ הַקֹּדֶשׁ הוּא
yosef ben david, al tachshosh lakachat eleicha et miryam ishtecha, ki asher horah bah meruach hakkodesh hu
Joseph, thou son of David, fear not to take unto thee Mary thy wife: for that which is conceived in her is of the Holy Spirit.

הִיא יוֹלֶדֶת בֵּן וְאַתָּה תִּקְרָא שְׁמוֹ יֵשׁוּעַ, כִּי הוּא יוֹשִׁיעַ אֶת עַמּוֹ מֵחַטֹּאתֵיהֶם
hi yoledet ben ve'attah tikra shemo yeshua', ki hu yoshia et ammo mechattoteihem
And she shall bring forth a son; and thou shalt call his name JESUS; for it is he that shall save his people from their sins.

כָּל זֶה אֵרַע לְמַעַן יִתְקַיֵּם מַה שֶּׁדִּבֶּר אֲדֹנָי בְּפִי הַנָּבִיא
kol zeh era lema'an yitkayem mah sheddibber adonai befi hannavi
Now all this is come to pass, that it might be fulfilled which was spoken by the Lord through the prophet, saying,

הִנֵּה הָעַלְמָה הָרָה וְיֹלֶדֶת בֵּן
hinneh ha'almah harah veyoledet ben
Behold, the virgin shall be with child, and shall bring forth a son,

וְקָרָאת שְׁמוֹ עִמָּנוּ אֵל
vekarat shemo immanu el
And they shall call his name Immanuel; which is, being interpreted, God with us.

לְאַחַר מִכֵּן הֵקִיץ יוֹסֵף מִשְּׁנָתוֹ וְעָשָׂה כְּפִי שֶׁצִּוָּהוּ מַלְאַךְ יהוה. הוּא לָקַח אֵלָיו אֶת אִשְׁתּוֹ
le'achar mikken hekitz yosef mishenato ve'asah kefi shetzivvahu mal'ach hashem. Hu lakach elav et ishto
And Joseph arose from his sleep, and did as the angel of the Lord commanded him, and took unto him his wife;

מִבְּלִי שֶׁיָּדַע אוֹתָהּ עַד אֲשֶׁר יָלְדָה בֵּן, וְקָרָא אֶת שְׁמוֹ יֵשׁוּעַ
mibbeli sheyada otah ad asher yaledah ben, vekara et shemo yeshua
and knew her not till she had brought forth a son: and he called his name JESUS.

ב

בְּעֵת שֶׁנּוֹלַד יֵשׁוּעַ בְּבֵית לֶחֶם יְהוּדָה, בִּימֵי הוֹרְדוֹס הַמֶּלֶךְ
be'et shennolad yeshua beveit lechem yehudah, biymei horedos hammelech
Now when Jesus was born in Bethlehem of Judæa in the days of Herod the king, behold,

בָּאוּ לִירוּשָׁלַיִם חֲכָמִים מִן הַמִּזְרָח שָׁאֲלוּ
ba'u liyerushalayim chachamim min hammizrach, sha'alu
Wise-men from the east came to Jerusalem, saying,

הֵיכָן מֶלֶךְ הַיְּהוּדִים אֲשֶׁר נוֹלַד? כִּי רָאִינוּ אֶת כּוֹכָבוֹ בַּמִּזְרָח וּבָאנוּ לְהִשְׁתַּחֲווֹת לוֹ
Heichan melech hayehudim asher nolad? ki ra'inu et kochavo bammizrach uvanu lehishtachavot lo
Where is he that is born King of the Jews? for we saw his star in the east, and are come to worship him.

לְאַחַר שֶׁהֻגְלוּ בָּבֶלָה הוֹלִיד יְכָנְיָהוּ אֶת שְׁאַלְתִּיאֵל וּשְׁאַלְתִּיאֵל הוֹלִיד אֶת זְרֻבָּבֶל
le'achar shehuglu bavelah holid yechaneyahu et she'alti'el ushe'alti'el holid et zerubbavel
And after the carrying away to Babylon, Jechoniah begat Shealtiel; and Shealtiel begat Zerubbabel;

זְרֻבָּבֶל הוֹלִיד אֶת אֲבִיהוּד, אֲבִיהוּד הוֹלִיד אֶת אֶלְיָקִים וְאֶלְיָקִים הוֹלִיד אֶת עַזּוּר
zerubbavel holid et avihud, avihud holid et elyakim ve'elyakim holid et azzur
and Zerubbabel begat Abiud; and Abiud begat Eliakim; and Eliakim begat Azor;

עַזּוּר הוֹלִיד אֶת צָדוֹק, צָדוֹק הוֹלִיד אֶת יָכִין וְיָכִין הוֹלִיד אֶת אֱלִיהוּד
azzur holid et tzadok, tzadok holid et yachin veyachin holid et elihud
and Azor begat Sadoc; and Sadoc begat Achim; and Achim begat Eliud;

אֱלִיהוּד הוֹלִיד אֶת אֶלְעָזָר, אֶלְעָזָר הוֹלִיד אֶת מַתָּן וּמַתָּן הוֹלִיד אֶת יַעֲקֹב
elihud holid et el'azar, el'azar holid et mattan umattan holid et ya'akov
and Eliud begat Eleazar; and Eleazar begat Matthan; and Matthan begat Jacob;

יַעֲקֹב הוֹלִיד אֶת יוֹסֵף בַּעַל מִרְיָם אֲשֶׁר מִמֶּנָּה נוֹלַד יֵשׁוּעַ הַנִּקְרָא מָשִׁיחַ
ya'akov holid et yosef ba'al miryam asher mimmennah nolad yeshua hannikra mashiach
and Jacob begat Joseph the husband of Mary, of whom was born Jesus, who is called Christ.

וּבְכֵן כָּל הַדּוֹרוֹת מֵאַבְרָהָם עַד דָּוִד אַרְבָּעָה-עָשָׂר דּוֹרוֹת
uvchen kol haddorot me'avraham ad david arba'ah-'asar dorot
So all the generations from Abraham unto David are fourteen generations;

וּמִדָּוִד עַד גָּלוּת בָּבֶל אַרְבָּעָה-עָשָׂר דּוֹרוֹת
umiddavid ad galut bavel arba'ah-'asar dorot
and from David unto the carrying away to Babylon fourteen generations;

וּמִגָּלוּת בָּבֶל עַד הַמָּשִׁיחַ אַרְבָּעָה-עָשָׂר דּוֹרוֹת
umiggalut bavel ad hammashiach arba'ah-'asar dorot
and from the carrying away to Babylon unto the Christ fourteen generations.

כָּךְ הָיְתָה הֻלֶּדֶת יֵשׁוּעַ הַמָּשִׁיחַ: מִרְיָם אִמּוֹ הָיְתָה מְאֹרֶסֶת לְיוֹסֵף
kach hayta hulledet yeshua hammashiach. Miryam immo hayetah me'oreset leyosef
Now the birth of Jesus Christ was on this wise: When his mother Mary had been betrothed to Joseph,

וּבְטֶרֶם הִתְאַחֲדוּ נִמְצְאָה הָרָה לְרוּחַ הַקֹּדֶשׁ
uveterem hit'achadu nimtze'ah harah leruach hakkodesh
before they came together she was found with child of the Holy Spirit.

יוֹסֵף בַּעְלָהּ, שֶׁהָיָה צַדִּיק וְלֹא רָצָה לְהַצִּיג אוֹתָהּ לְחֶרְפָּה
yosef ba'alah, shehayah tzaddik velo ratzah lehatzig otah lecherpah
And Joseph her husband, being a righteous man, and not willing to make her a public example,

הֶחְלִיט לְשַׁלֵּחַ אוֹתָהּ בַּסֵּתֶר
hechlit leshalleach otah basseter
was minded to put her away privily.

*Remember: Hebrew is Read from <u>Right to Left</u>
מַתַּי א

סֵפֶר הַיֻחֲסִין שֶׁל יֵשׁוּעַ הַמָּשִׁיחַ בֶּן־דָּוִד בֶּן־אַבְרָהָם
sefer hayuchasin shel yeshua hammashiach ben-david ben-'avraham
The book of the generation of Jesus Christ, the son of David, the son of Abraham.

אַבְרָהָם הוֹלִיד אֶת יִצְחָק, יִצְחָק הוֹלִיד אֶת יַעֲקֹב וְיַעֲקֹב הוֹלִיד אֶת יְהוּדָה וְאֶת אֶחָיו
avraham holid et yitzchak, yitzchak holid et ya'akov veya'akov holid et yehudah ve'et echav
Abraham begat Isaac; and Isaac begat Jacob; and Jacob begat Judah and his brethren;

יְהוּדָה הוֹלִיד אֶת פֶּרֶץ וְאֶת זֶרַח מִתָּמָר, פֶּרֶץ הוֹלִיד אֶת חֶצְרוֹן וְחֶצְרוֹן הוֹלִיד אֶת רָם
yehudah holid et peretz ve'et zerach mittamar, peretz holid et chetzron vechetzron holid et ram
and Judah begat Perez and Zerah of Tamar; and Perez begat Hezron; and Hezron begat Ram;

רָם הוֹלִיד אֶת עַמִּינָדָב, עַמִּינָדָב הוֹלִיד אֶת נַחְשׁוֹן וְנַחְשׁוֹן הוֹלִיד אֶת שַׂלְמוֹן
ram holid et amminadav, amminadav holid et nachshon venachshon holid et salmon
and Ram begat Amminadab; and Amminadab begat Nahshon; and Nahshon begat Salmon;

שַׂלְמוֹן הוֹלִיד אֶת בֹּעַז מֵרָחָב, בֹּעַז הוֹלִיד אֶת עוֹבֵד מֵרוּת וְעוֹבֵד הוֹלִיד אֶת יִשַׁי
salmon holid et bo'az merachav, bo'az holid et oved merut ve'oved holid et yishai
and Salmon begat Boaz of Rahab; and Boaz begat Obed of Ruth; and Obed begat Jesse;

יִשַׁי הוֹלִיד אֶת דָּוִד הַמֶּלֶךְ, דָּוִד הוֹלִיד אֶת שְׁלֹמֹה מִזּוֹ שֶׁהָיְתָה אֵשֶׁת אוּרִיָּה
yishai holid et david hammelech, david holid et shelomoh mizzo shehayetah eshet uriyah
and Jesse begat David the king. And David begat Solomon of her that had been the wife of Uriah;

שְׁלֹמֹה הוֹלִיד אֶת רְחַבְעָם, רְחַבְעָם הוֹלִיד אֶת אֲבִיָּה וַאֲבִיָּה הוֹלִיד אֶת אָסָא
shelomoh holid et rechav'am, rechav'am holid et aviyah va'aviyah holid et asa
and Solomon begat Rehoboam; and Rehoboam begat Abijah; and Abijah begat Asa;

אָסָא הוֹלִיד אֶת יְהוֹשָׁפָט, יְהוֹשָׁפָט הוֹלִיד אֶת יוֹרָם וְיוֹרָם הוֹלִיד אֶת עֻזִּיָּהוּ
asa holid et yehoshafat, yehoshafat holid et yoram veyoram holid et uzziyahu
and Asa begat Jehoshaphat; and Jehoshaphat begat Joram; and Joram begat Uzziah;

עֻזִּיָּהוּ הוֹלִיד אֶת יוֹתָם, יוֹתָם הוֹלִיד אֶת אָחָז וְאָחָז הוֹלִיד אֶת חִזְקִיָּהוּ
uzziyahu holid et yotam, yotam holid et achaz ve'achaz holid et chizkiyahu
and Uzziah begat Jotham; and Jotham begat Ahaz; and Ahaz begat Hezekiah;

חִזְקִיָּהוּ הוֹלִיד אֶת מְנַשֶּׁה, מְנַשֶּׁה הוֹלִיד אֶת אָמוֹן וְאָמוֹן הוֹלִיד אֶת יֹאשִׁיָּהוּ
chizkiyahu holid et menasheh, menasheh holid et amon ve'amon holid et yoshiyahu
and Hezekiah begat Manasseh; and Manasseh begat Amon; and Amon begat Josiah;

יֹאשִׁיָּהוּ הוֹלִיד אֶת יְכָנְיָהוּ וְאֶת אֶחָיו בִּימֵי גָּלוּת בָּבֶל
yoshiyahu holid et yechaneyahu ve'et echav biymei galut bavel
and Josiah begat Jechoniah and his brethren, at the time of the carrying away to Babylon.

FOR

HEBREW SONGS WITH ENGLISH SUBTITLES
(IN 3 LINE FORMAT)

VISIT:

hebrewsongswithenglishsubtitles.com

FOR

HEBREW BIBLE MP3 CDS

BUY THEM AT:

tinyurl.com/audiobiblehebrew

א	A			א	1
ב	V			ב	2
ב	B			ג	3
ג	G			ד	4
ד	D	אַ	ah	ה	5
ה	H	אֲ	ah	ו	6
ו	V	אָ	ah	ז	7
ז	Z	אָה	ah	ח	8
ח	KH	אֵ	ei	ט	9
ט	T	אֶ	e	י	10
י	Y	אֱ	e	יא	11
כ	KH	אִי	ei	יב	12
כּ	K	אִ	ee	יג	13
ל	L	אִי	ee	יד	14
מ	M	אֹ	oh	טו	15
ם	M	אָ	oh	טז	16
נ	N	אֳ	oh	יז	17
ן	N	אוֹ	oh	יח	18
ס	S	אֻ	oo	יט	19
ע	A	אוּ	oo	כ	20
פ	F	אְ	e		
פּ	P				
צ	TS				
ק	K				
ר	R				
ש	SH				
שׂ	S				
ת	T				

מַתִּי
Mattai
Matthew

Made in the USA
San Bernardino, CA
08 July 2020